Incredi*bull* Stella

Center Point
Large Print

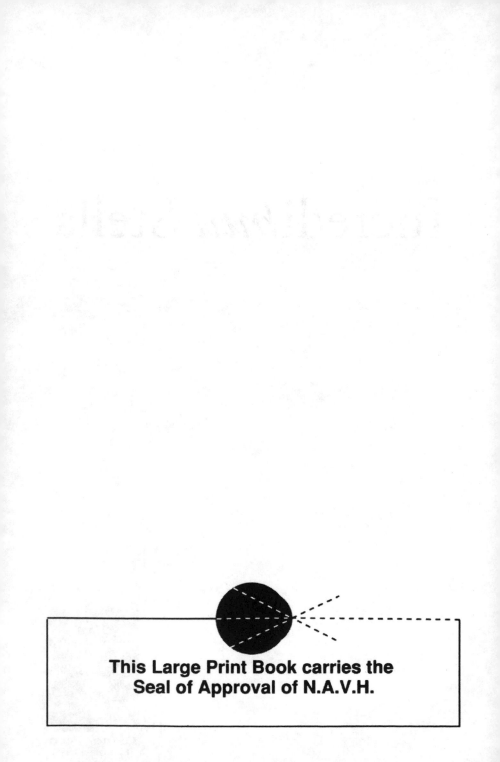

**This Large Print Book carries the
Seal of Approval of N.A.V.H.**

Incredi*bull* Stella

How the Love of a Pit Bull Rescued a Family

Marika Meeks and Elizabeth Ridley

CENTER POINT LARGE PRINT
THORNDIKE, MAINE

This Center Point Large Print edition
is published in the year 2019 by arrangement with
Kensington Publishing Corp.

The text of this Large Print edition is unabridged.
In other aspects, this book may vary
from the original edition.
Printed in the United States of America
on permanent paper.
Set in 16-point Times New Roman type.

ISBN: 978-1-64358-354-9

The Library of Congress has cataloged this record
under Library of Congress Control Number: 2019944725

This book is dedicated to my family
for giving me the reason to continue the fight.

To Stella and all the dogs out there that have
so much to offer, if only given the chance.

And to my husband, Brian,
who is the love of my life and best friend
and, most importantly, my guardian angel.

Somewhere between what she survived,
and who she was becoming, was exactly where
she was meant to be. She was starting to love
the journey. And find the comfort in the quiet
corners of her wildest dreams.

—J. Raymond

AUTHORS' NOTE

Incredi*bull* Stella: How the Love of a Pit Bull Rescued a Family is the true story of how author Marika Meeks and her family adopted Stella in 2016 and how she changed their lives. Some of the names have been changed to protect individuals' privacy, and some characters in the book are composites based on several people.

This book relates personal decisions Marika made about the cancer treatments available to her. It is not intended to offer advice for other cancer patients. The authors encourage everyone facing serious medical issues to do extensive research, talk with medical professionals, and make their own decisions about their treatment plans.

CONTENTS

STELLA'S TOP TEN RULES FOR LIFE

1. Love first, ask questions later.
2. When in doubt, wag.
3. Apologize for chewing up stuff.
4. Sniff before you lick.
5. Love your foster siblings—we are all littermates.
6. A fancy collar goes with everything.
7. An ESA vest is the best accessory.
8. Humor your humans.
9. Your "person" is worth waiting for.
10. A family is forever.

Incredi*bull* Stella

Marika, Stella, and Town of Paradise Valley Council-member Anna Thomasson at the 15th Annual HERO Awards *(photo courtesy Brian Meeks)*.

PROLOGUE

Stella Steals the Spotlight

The 15th Annual HERO Awards,
sponsored by the Arizona Pet Project
Scottsdale, Arizona, Saturday, March 10, 2018

I close my eyes, draw a deep breath, and pull the little black cocktail dress over my head. And when I say "little" black dress, I mean just that—little! A size I wouldn't have dared try on even a couple of weeks ago, but as I stretch the fabric down over my chest and hips and feel it settle snugly but comfortably against my skin, I dare to peek at myself in the mirror.

"It fits! Look, Stella, Mama's dress fits!" I announce proudly to the seventy pounds of pure pit bull love curled up on the bed behind me, head resting contentedly atop her paws. She glances at me sleepily, yawns, then closes her eyes, resuming her nap with a sigh and a satisfied "humpff."

"Well, maybe you aren't excited," I tell her, "but I sure am." I turn around, checking myself from every angle. Stopping just above my knees, the lightweight, sleeveless dress is slit thigh-high on the left side with a trim of silver studs around the hem and arms. A sophisticated, sexy evening look that'll surely turn some heads.

What a day I've chosen to unveil my new look—Stella and I, along with the rest of our family, are on our way to the Pet HERO Awards sponsored by The Arizona Pet Project, where Stella, aka IncrediBullStella, is being honored with the Loyal Companion Award. But "Loyal Companion" doesn't even begin to describe what she means to me. Stella is my best friend, my confidante, my partner in crime. She's also my emotional support animal who gives me strength, keeps me safe, and helps me focus when panic, anxiety, and PTSD threaten to overwhelm me.

Not only that, Stella mended my shattered family, giving us hope, joy, and laughter at a time when we felt lost and utterly broken.

I study myself more closely in the mirror and see a woman, age forty-six, who looks tan, fit, and ready to knock 'em dead! My nails are painted; my long, chestnut-brown hair is blown straight and smooth; I'm wearing a pair of brand-new high heels (Stella chewed up my only other pair yesterday—she may be a hero, but I never said she was perfect!); and I'm sporting my first-ever spray-on tan, giving my skin a warm, healthy glow.

I know I look good, but this has nothing to do with vanity; this is about gratitude, the deepest gratitude for having been given a second chance at life. You see, after battling Stage 3 breast cancer and its aftereffects for more than five years, 2018 represented a new beginning for me, a year in which I vowed to get in the best shape of my life, mentally and physically, and finally kick cancer's ass, once and for all.

And all the hard work paid off! As I turn again, my arms flex and I see new muscles sprout between my shoulder and elbow. I'm so excited, I leave Stella to her nap and run to find my husband, Brian, who's working at his computer just off our kitchen.

"Brian—look! Feel my arm!" I extend my upper arm toward him, getting right up in his face.

"What?" he asks, not glancing away from his screen.

"Go on—feel my muscles!"

Brian's a pretty laid-back guy, a few years older than me, with placid blue eyes and a calm, Midwestern demeanor. In other words, he doesn't get real excited about stuff like this.

"Your muscles?" he asks evenly as he continues typing.

"Yes. All the exercise is paying off. Check it out."

Now he indulges me, laughing a little as he turns, gives my bicep a firm squeeze, and nods his approval before returning to his keyboard. He may not be the most openly emotive guy, but he loves me something fierce, and I never doubt the depth of his feelings. He is my rock, and I couldn't have survived cancer without him at my side, just like I couldn't have survived cancer's aftereffects without my darling Stella.

Once I've finished getting myself ready for our big night out, it's Stella's turn, our not-quite-three-year-old pit bull whom we adopted as a seven-month-old puppy in Indiana in 2016, after she and her sister had been abandoned and left to die by the side of the road. I'm a survivor, but Stella's a survivor, too. We have that in common.

Stella's day began early, with a thirty-minute workout on the treadmill, courtesy of "RunBuddy

Mobile," an air-conditioned, climate-controlled mobile dog gym inside a van that parks in our driveway for Stella's workout sessions. Hopefully she worked off some nervous energy before tonight's big event. After her exercise session, I gave her a nice bath and a good brushing until her coat shone. Tonight, I want everyone to see what a gorgeous dog she is. Let's face it—pit bulls get a lot of bad press, and not everyone appreciates the beauty of these special creatures. That's why raising pit bull breed awareness and acceptance is one of the things about which Stella and I are most passionate.

The final step is dressing her in her bright red T-shirt with her catchphrase, *IncrediBullStella*, emblazoned on the back in large white letters. I stick her front paws through the "sleeves," pop her head through the neck opening, and pull the shirt down to her waist, or at least to where her waist would be, if dogs had waists. She's a good sport, staying more or less still long enough for me to smooth down the shirt so she's all nice and pretty and properly dressed for her big debut.

I know tonight's gonna be crazy, so I take these few quiet moments to sit with Stella, stroking her softly, rubbing her belly, and whispering in her ear. "You're my hero," I tell her. "Tonight, we'll share our story with the world. But for the moment, you're all mine."

She looks at me, gazing straight into my eyes,

and I swear she understands. Stella is such a sensitive, intelligent dog, with typical pit bull features: a large, blocky head; a solid, stocky, muscular build; a flat, brown-and-pink nose; and a short, smooth coat. Her eyes are a deep-set pale amber and her fur is mostly white with swatches of light caramel tan, especially in an adorable patch over her left eye.

"Thank you, Stelly, for giving me a new lease on life." I wrap my arms around her strong shoulders and kiss her on the forehead. "I didn't even know how lost I was before I found you."

Our first view, later that afternoon, as we drive up to the Omni Scottsdale Resort & Spa at Montelucia in Paradise Valley, is absolutely breathtaking. Situated at the base of Camelback Mountain, the resort resembles an Andalusian village, featuring glistening turquoise pools, luxurious spas, towering fountains, and arched walkways bursting with brightly colored flowers. The resort feels like an oasis, a lush jewel hidden in the middle of the harsh Sonoran Desert, surrounded by palm trees and saguaro cactus, nestled between low, rough hills of burnt sienna, brown, olive, ochre, and deep mahogany, beneath a high, bright sky streaked with salmon pink, fuchsia, tangerine, and gold. It's just dazzling, like something from a film.

"Oh, Brian, it's stunning." I clutch his arm for

a moment as I sit back and drink in the scene, feeling like a movie star about to make her grand entrance. But then my nerves start tingling and the all-too-familiar adrenaline kicks in, sending my heart rate soaring and twisting my stomach into knots. *I don't want to do this. I feel sick—I want to go home.*

I've never been comfortable doing public stuff, and I've struggled with self-esteem all my life. I grew up a sickly child, the youngest daughter of brilliant, overachieving parents, and I often felt left behind or left out, not good enough, not pretty enough, not smart enough. *Marika, get over yourself,* I suddenly think. *Tonight's not about you; it's about Stella. You're doing this for her.*

What makes tonight even more special is that in addition to Brian and Stella, also joining me are my two gorgeous daughters, twenty-one-year-old Carly and nineteen-year-old Caitie, both blond, lean, and willowy in their own little black dresses. Caitie in particular has an incredible bond with Stella—the stress and anxiety of my illness and treatment drove Caitie to the brink of suicide, and it was Stella who first helped mend those wounds and then taught me how to reconnect with my deeply hurting teenage daughter.

We cross the courtyard and enter through the front doors. The interior of the resort is as gorgeous as the exterior, featuring hand-painted floor tiles, whitewashed walls, and dark wood with rich-hued accents. We're greeted by a big sign with Stella's picture on it, and beneath her photo, the words *Loyal Companion.* As we make our way toward the ballroom to pose for photos, Stella is pretty excited. There are so many people here and so much going on, so many new and unfamiliar sights, sounds, and smells assaulting her senses all at once, but she's in her glory, happily taking it all in.

I also have my secret weapon, stowed away safely inside my purse—a plastic sandwich bag full of pieces of cooked chicken, Stella's favorite food in the whole, wide world. There's nothing she won't do for chicken, so I'm confident I can keep her in line by giving or withholding treats, depending on her behavior.

We enter the Alhambra Ballroom, an elegant space with glittering chandeliers, waitstaff in suits, and dozens of round tables set with white tablecloths and fine china, and are directed to the stage in front to pose for photos. I don't have time to introduce myself and Stella to the evening's other hero dogs (and cat!) and their owners as I'm trying to get Stella settled into place. She's so wiggly and excited right now, her butt is fishtailing and her tail wagging a hundred miles an hour.

"It's okay to be excited." The man beside me

crouches down to talk to Stella. "Today's a pretty big day, isn't it?"

This guy looks very familiar, but I can't place his face. Wait a minute—it's Jackson Galaxy, best-selling author and host of the Animal Planet series *My Cat from Hell*! He's the honorary chair of tonight's event. For a moment I'm tongue-tied, starstruck, but I manage to find my voice and introduce myself and Stella before I turn into a blubbering mess.

Jackson looks like a cool, sexy hipster with his shaved head, olive skin, warm brown eyes, dark-frame glasses, and neatly trimmed facial hair. The sleeves of his dark shirt and jacket are rolled up, revealing dense, intricate tattoos scrolling up his arms.

Jackson immediately puts us at ease with his soft, gentle voice and calming presence. He may be famous as a "Cat Daddy," but his ability to connect with dogs is on full display as Stella responds to his kind encouragement, posing like a pro as the cameras all around us start clicking and flashing like crazy.

Once the photos are finished, we go back out to mingle as the well-dressed attendees start to arrive. There's a special photo area with a fancy backdrop set aside for the public, and so many people ask to take pictures with Stella. At first, I'm not sure how she'll respond to so many strangers vying for her attention all at once, but she loves every minute of it. She's always been a bit of a camera hound, and this girl knows how to work it, turning this way and that, showing off her best angles like a true canine supermodel.

The 15th Annual Pet HERO Awards sponsored by The Arizona Pet Project is devoted to celebrating heroes, both animal and human, and also to fund-raising for programs, such as spay and neuter initiatives, designed to keep animals in people's homes and out of shelters throughout Maricopa County.

The animals receiving awards tonight have all demonstrated extraordinary love, courage, devotion, and a remarkable will to survive. In addition to "Loyal Companion" Stella, there's "Animal Survivor" BB Bear, who, at only two months old, was severely beaten and abused, suffering a traumatic brain injury so bad the vets didn't think he'd make it. But this little dog not only survived, he became a social media phenomenon during his recovery. Today he's happy and healthy, a beautiful boy with snow-white fur, jet-black eyes, and big, pointy ears, living a normal life with his loving mom, Lisa.

Then there's Nana, the "Service to the Community" award recipient, a large, black-and-white sheepdog with mesmerizing blue eyes who was only two days old when she was found stranded in the desert. Today, she's a therapy dog helping wherever she's needed, whether it's calming anxious passengers at Phoenix's Sky Harbor International Airport or bringing fun to stressed-out students at Arizona State University.

Next is Cuffie, the "Animal Hero" award winner, an extraordinary black-and-white house cat who saved the life of his owner, a little boy named Davis. Davis has diabetes and was heading toward a diabetic coma late one night while he slept. Cuffie sensed Davis's condition and alerted Davis's dad by sitting on his head and trying to get his attention. Dad checked Davis's meter and saw that Davis's blood sugar was dangerously low. If not for Cuffie, Davis might not have lived through the night.

And then there's the awardee who's here only in spirit, the "Over the Rainbow Bridge" recipient, Fozzie, a gorgeous golden retriever. Fozzie was a trailblazer, the nation's first full-time crisis response K-9 who served with the Scottsdale Police Department. Fozzie's handler is here tonight to accept the award on Fozzie's behalf, along with a new member of the police's K-9 Unit.

I'm touched and humbled for Stella to stand alongside these extraordinary creatures. "You're in great company tonight, Stella," I tell her as I bend down and slip her another treat. She looks up at me, tongue wagging and with a smile in her shiny amber eyes.

Also being honored tonight are the "Human

Heroes," the Van Es family—Johnjay Van Es, his wife, Blake, and their three sons, Jake, Kemp, and Dutch. Johnjay is the host of the nationally syndicated Kiss FM's *Johnjay & Rich* morning show. In 2015, he created his own dog rescue foundation, #LovePup, out of his own home, and today the Van Eses have rescued more than five hundred dogs, using the power of social media to place these homeless pups with loving families.

Receiving this award tonight reminds me of the maxim, to whom much is given, much is expected, and how this applies to Stella. She was a nothing dog, a throwaway, abandoned and left to die by the side of the road. She was saved for a reason, and her mission is so much bigger than what she's done so far. *Your journey is only just beginning, Stella,* I realize. *There's so much more for us to do, and we can't afford to waste a moment. Cancer taught me that.*

We make our way into the ballroom to find our table among the more than four hundred and fifty guests. I've brought a little fabric bed for Stella and I place it down on the floor beside my chair so she knows where she's supposed to stay. She circles a few times, then plops down on the bed, resting her chin atop her paws.

The evening's MC, handsome local CBS 5 TV meteorologist Ian Schwartz, takes the stage and people applaud. Stella isn't sure what to make of all the noise and commotion. Her eyes widen and she gets up, turning her head anxiously, sniffing the air. I quickly reassure her and slip her a little piece of chicken each time there's applause. She quickly figures out that applause equals treats, and pretty soon when people start clapping, she looks up at me as if to say, "Okay, Mom, they're clapping now—where's my chicken?"

After the introductory remarks, dinner is served—a starter of truffle cauliflower bisque with turmeric roasted cauliflower followed by slow-roasted chicken with caramelized yam puree or a black-eyed pea cassoulet. The food looks and smells delicious, but I barely have time to take a bite as one person after another comes over to meet Stella. I can't bear to turn anyone away; Stella's key messages—about pit bull breed awareness, the importance of spaying and neutering, the health benefits to humans of pet ownership, and promoting shelter adoption—are just too important, and this venue is the perfect opportunity to spread these messages far and wide.

Dessert is being served as we're ushered up to the stage for Stella's award presentation. The lights go down and the busy chatter and low hum of voices softens as the large screen behind mc springs to life. After a brief animated intro, Stella's video begins. "This is it," I whisper, bending to stroke Stella's head and slip her some chicken before turning my attention back to the screen.

The video opens with stock images of a cold, sterile hospital room and medical monitoring equipment. I shudder. That was my life with cancer, when my horizons stretched no farther than the machines working to keep me alive. Who could have imagined then that I would end up here today? I start to tear up but instead swallow hard, refusing to cry.

The video continues with photos of me during treatment. It's hard to see my face looking so pale and drawn, my brown eyes so dark and hollow, and remember how empty and hopeless I felt as I lay in my hospital bed not knowing if I would live or die.

Cancer. The very word strikes fear, the video's voice-over begins. *When you're on the receiving end of a diagnosis, it's terrifying. When Marika Meeks was diagnosed with Stage 3 breast cancer, she was brought to her knees. She was paralyzed from anxiety and convinced she wouldn't survive. She turned inward, even shutting out her beloved family, including her husband, Brian, and two daughters, Caitie and Carly . . .*

Now, the screen lights up with happier photos, me with Brian, both of us smiling; Carly and Caitie laughing as dazzling sunlight filters through their hair; the four of us, arms entwined and joking around. And now, cut to scenes of

Stella hamming it up, licking her nose, zonked out on the couch, gazing lovingly into the camera with her serious, soulful amber eyes.

Stella's contagious energy, smiling face, and unconditional love became the beacon of hope that pulled the family back together, the narration continues. *And best of all, they learned to not only survive but to live fully. Marika, who at the time of her diagnosis was given a sixty-one percent chance of surviving five years, just celebrated her five-year anniversary with a clean bill of health . . .*

Now the video cuts to me, in closeup. I'm sitting on the floor in our living room at home, speaking directly to the camera. Stella is curled up on the couch behind me, resting her chin on my shoulder. It's hard to describe how bizarre it is to see your own face blown up many times its size and projected on a screen in front of a room full of hundreds of people, mostly strangers, but I fight off feelings of self-consciousness because I know our important message needs to be heard.

"You know, we're not guaranteed tomorrow or even the next minute," I say on-screen, "so are you really living while you're alive? And you know what? I thought I was going to die. I thought I was going to *die*. But I didn't."

The video ends with a clip of me, Brian, Carly, and Caitie walking Stella around our cozy Scottsdale neighborhood surrounded by cactus and brush and sprawling, flat-roofed homes built into the distant hills. The camera expertly captures how happy and relaxed we are when we're all together. *This really is a who-rescued-who story,* the voice on the video intones. *Stella, you may be a rescue, but you're also a rescuer. Thanks to you, you reignited love and hope and for that, you are our hero.*

The screen goes dark as the lights in the ballroom rise and the room erupts with rapturous applause. I worry Stella might get scared by all the hubbub, but she handles it like a pro, drinking in the attention and looking to me for another treat. Does this dog know she's special? I think she does.

Ian Schwartz walks over, kneels, and places a medal on a red ribbon around Stella's neck, officially naming her the evening's "Loyal Companion" award recipient. Stella models it proudly as everyone claps and cheers, and I slip her another small treat for being such a good girl.

The rest of the evening passes in a blur, a busy, beautiful blur as I let Stella choose who she wants to visit. I just follow behind her, holding tight to her leash as she works the Alhambra Ballroom like a veteran politician or a seasoned PR pro. She's a pit bull with a purpose as she bobs and weaves between tables, butt wiggling and tail wagging like crazy, greeting her new friends or gently maneuvering her head between diners' chairs, waiting patiently until someone notices her. And notice her they do!

"Stella! What a pretty girl you are," they remark, or, "Hello, gorgeous! Who's a good doggie then?" as they pat her head, rub her ears, or lean down and plant big, smacking kisses right between her eyes. A few people even slip her leftover food from their plates and feed her by hand, once they glance around to make sure the waitstaff isn't watching.

It's impossible for me to believe, in this moment, that anyone could consider pit bulls to be dangerous. The only real danger is their absolute ability to steal your heart! Stella is in heaven being the center of attention, and by the time we're ready to call it a night, her face, from forehead to snout, is covered with a bright jumble of red, pink, and coral lipstick kisses.

"Oh, Stella." I sigh, lick my fingertips, and try to rub off the kisses, but my efforts only manage to smear the lipstick and make it worse. "That's it, Stelly, another bath for you first thing tomorrow morning," I declare. "You can't go around town looking like a painted lady. What will people think?" Her ears perk up and she gives me that quizzical look—she knows the word *bath* well enough!

It's not until we're in the car driving home, with the cool spring air and its touch of desert dampness wafting through the windows and the dark blacktop road unfurling before us through the valley between the mountains, that I have a chance to reflect on this amazing day. The tears come easily now, in the quiet cocoon of the back seat, where I sit with my arms wrapped around a tired-but-happy Stella, her head resting in my lap as I rub her pink-and-white belly and stroke her short, smooth fur.

I am so lucky to be here, I think. *And so grateful to have those I love most—Brian, Carly, Caitie, and Stella—at my side. And I'm not just fortunate to be here, enjoying this extraordinary evening, I'm lucky to be alive at all. Thanks to Stella, instead of being so self-absorbed in my cancer and terrified of the future, I'm actually living my best life ever. I never even realized how lost I was until I found Stella; until we found each other. Isn't it extraordinary, how love can so completely turn two lives around?*

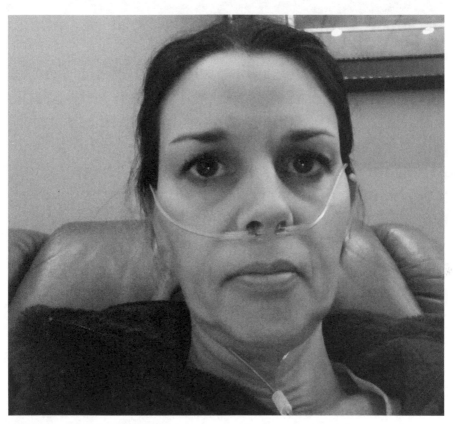

Marika feeling terrible toward the end of her radiation treatment.

CHAPTER ONE
The Call That
Changes Everything

Summer 2012–January 2013

It's a question I constantly ask myself—if I had never gotten cancer, would I ever have gotten Stella? I can't say that I adopted her as a direct response to being diagnosed with a potentially deadly disease, and yet, when I look back, the connection between the two is so clear. Cancer set me on the path that led directly to Stella. Cancer didn't kill me (although it certainly tried), but it changed me on a cellular level, it broke me, it brought me to my knees. It exposed my mind and heart to pain and fear and worry the likes of which I could not previously have imagined.

But cancer opened me in other, less sinister ways, too. It opened me up to humble hope and grace and possibility. It made me vulnerable to great love—and that's the sweet spot where Stella slipped in, she with her wet nose and her big paws, and where she resides to this day, safely stowed in the hidden chamber of my heart that's reserved for those I love most—my husband, my children, and this one amazing dog.

Even so, the journey to Stella began where and when I least expected it. It was early in the summer of 2012 and I was soaping up in the shower one morning when my hand passed across my chest. *Wait. Was that . . . ? Oh no.* I had that sick, sinking feeling that must be familiar to so many women. I stopped, took a deep breath, and felt my breast again. Yes, there *was* something there, a lump just beneath the nipple, about the size and shape of a firm lima bean; small, but definitely there.

Oh shit. As I watched the warm, soapy water

flow between my toes and swirl down the drain, my head was swirling, too. I felt my breast a third time, hoping I'd been wrong. *No. This is really happening.* Still, I tried not to panic. I was forty years old, in excellent health, and with no family history of breast cancer. Not only that, I'd had my first mammogram at age thirty-eight, which came back clear, and then a second mammogram just a few months ago, which also came back showing no evidence of cancer. I had been a sickly child, so as an adult I had always been very proactive about my health, which was why I insisted on yearly mammograms beginning at age thirty-eight, even without a family history of breast cancer.

"It's probably nothing," I told myself as I turned off the shower and reached for a towel. "But I'll get it checked, just to be sure."

I called my doctor and got an appointment first thing the next morning. I felt nervous when I arrived at the clinic but I tried to stay optimistic. I knew that, statistically, only a small percentage of lumps turn out to be cancer, and this was probably just a benign cyst or something similar.

I was examined by a PA, and she, too, was able to feel the lump during the manual breast exam. "Well, it's not cancer," she said, and rattled off a number of reasons why it wasn't cancer, based on the location of the lump and other factors.

Frankly, I was so relieved, I barely heard the rest of what came after, "it's not cancer."

"It's probably hormonal, or just typical breast tissue changes," she continued. "We'll check it again when you have your regular mammogram in six months, but in the meantime, don't worry. You're fine." (I've since learned that standard protocol, when a forty-year-old woman presents with a palpable mass in her breast, is to immediately order a biopsy. For whatever reason, that didn't happen in my case.)

Even though I hadn't been terribly worried about the lump, it was still a huge relief to have a professional assure me it wasn't cancer. *Now I can get back to living my life,* I thought. And what a fun and busy life it was! At the time, I was living in Fort Wayne, Indiana, with Brian, my second husband. Carly and Caitie, my daughters from my first marriage, were sixteen and thirteen and in high school and junior high.

As a single woman, before marrying Brian, I had purchased and opened the first Jimmy John's restaurant franchise in Fort Wayne and now Brian, who had joined the business, and I were in the process of securing a third Jimmy John's location with plans to expand. I'd had a lonely, isolating childhood and a rough first marriage, so I could honestly say that by age forty, after having overcome so much, I was living my best life so far. Things were finally falling into place for me, personally and professionally, and I could not have been happier.

I was still living this "best life" a few months later when, in October, out of the blue, I suddenly felt an overwhelming urge to get all my personal affairs in order. Looking back now, I think I was unknowingly preparing for my death, but that idea wasn't remotely on my radar at the time. It was just like a voice inside my head, nudging me on, saying, "You must do this. Marika, do it now, while you still can."

I couldn't understand where this strange desire was coming from. Even after getting the all-clear from the PA, I continued to keep an eye on the lump in my breast, checking it in the shower or before I went to bed. I was hoping, of course, that it would go away on its own, but even when that didn't happen, I didn't panic. It didn't seem to be getting any bigger or smaller; it was just "there," and most of the time, I did my best to ignore it. I certainly didn't associate it in any way with this sudden, overwhelming urge to put all my affairs in order.

But once I heard this inner voice pressing me to get my life organized, I became like a madwoman on a mission. I made sure both Brian's and my wills and insurance documents were up to date, that Brian's name was on all our business and personal accounts, and that he knew how to do the Jimmy John's payroll and other tasks that I normally handled. Brian's background was in commercial real estate, not restaurants. We'd been married less than two years at this point and he hadn't been working with me long, so there was a lot for him to learn about all the paperwork and the day-to-day running of the business.

Brian, for his part, never seemed suspicious or worried that I was suddenly scrambling to get all our affairs in order. After all, he was relatively new to this, and it made sense to get him fully on board with the myriad details. I never shared with him that something deep inside me, some powerful force, was urging me to do everything possible to make sure he and the girls would be okay if I suddenly wasn't around anymore.

Maybe I thought if I told Brian how I felt, he'd think I was crazy. *Maybe I am crazy,* I told myself. None of this was making sense, but my instincts, my intuition, had already saved me more than once in my life, so if something was telling me to see to all my personal paperwork, you can be sure that's exactly what I was going to do.

During this frantic period of getting my affairs in order, I got out of the shower one morning, lifted my arm to put on deodorant, looked at my left breast and armpit and thought, "Something is wrong." Visually, everything appeared normal—the skin wasn't bulging, puckered, bruised, discolored, or anything like that, nothing that would have been an obvious warning sign. It was just a sensation, a feeling deep in the pit of my stomach that all was not well.

I felt for the lump again and it was still there, still roughly the same size and in the same position as before, like a little lima bean beneath the nipple. *The PA said it was nothing,* I thought, *and I want to believe her. I really do. I couldn't really have cancer, could I?*

It was during this same time period that I began to experience debilitating attacks of anxiety. I'd been dealing with anxiety and PTSD (Post-Traumatic Stress Disorder) for much of my life, but this was something totally unlike anything I'd experienced before and, unlike with previous anxiety attacks, there were no clear or obvious triggers for the attacks, which seemed to hit me out of the blue. Every single day, while I was driving to work at Jimmy John's, I would feel an overwhelming sense of dread and a sick feeling deep in the pit of my stomach. These attacks made me so frustrated and angry. *Marika, get a grip,* I'd tell myself. *You make sandwiches for a living. What the heck is wrong with you?*

I was spiraling into such a dark, lonely, desolate place, and I didn't know how to reach out to anyone for help because I couldn't even explain what I was feeling or why. People always saw me as this calm, confident, levelheaded businesswoman who had it all together. How

41

could I allow them to see the truth? I was terrified of being a disappointment and letting everyone down.

All my affairs were pretty much in order, but I was still suffering regular anxiety attacks when January 2013 rolled around a few months later and it was time for my yearly mammogram, just a few days before my forty-first birthday. By this time, the lump felt slightly bigger, and I was a little more anxious now about it, but not panicking. I trusted the mammogram to give me an impartial assessment of what was really going on.

Mammograms are a painful and uncomfortable experience for most women, but I've always found them particularly so. As a naturally small-chested woman, it's difficult to get enough of my breast tissue clamped between the plates to take the picture. During the scan, I tried to stay positive, focusing on getting good news. *At least I'll have an answer,* I told myself. *And I won't have to think about this again. Or at least not until next year, anyway.*

A few days later, the results of the mammogram arrived via a letter in the mail. My heart was pounding and my hands shaking as I walked back from the mailbox, tearing open the envelope as I walked. I stopped midstride, pulled out the report, took a deep, deep breath, and started to read, the paper quivering in my nervous hands.

Yes! It's good news!! The report showed that there had been no change in my status since my previous mammogram a year earlier. On a scale of 1 to 5 with 1 meaning no cancer and 5 being positive for cancer, I was still at a 1. "No evidence of cancer" was the report's final verdict.

My whole body flooded with relief. I hadn't really believed I had cancer, and now I had proof, in black-and-white, that I was cancer-free. The PA had told me the lump wasn't cancer, and here was a machine designed specifically to evaluate these things, also confirming that I didn't have cancer. I was thrilled and went back inside with a huge smile on my face. *Thank God that's over,* I thought. But even after that, there was just a tiny, niggling little seed of doubt, somewhere in the back of my mind, that wasn't entirely convinced. "I so want this report to be enough, to be my answer," I realized. "But is it? Is it really?"

It was just a few days later, a cold-but-cozy Sunday night in late January after a typical weekend shopping, running errands, catching up on paperwork, and watching movies when Brian and I were about to call it a night. He was already under the covers, reading a book. I crawled into bed beside him and stretched across to kiss him good night. As I leaned over, I suddenly felt as if I had been struck by lightning; my hair stood straight up on my arms and neck and I was filled with the deepest, darkest, most horrible sense of dread I've ever felt in my life. Then a huge whoosh of panic sent me reeling, like a bolt of adrenaline that lit me up from head to toe.

"What's wrong?" Brian asked, concerned, seeing my face go pale.

"I'm not sure." My voice cracked. "Something just doesn't feel right." I lay back in bed, shaken to my core, and tried to rewind my thoughts and actions as Brian turned off the bedside light. What had I been doing when this feeling hit me? As I replayed the past few minutes, I realized that when I had reached across my body to kiss Brian, my right arm had grazed my left breast, just over the lump, and it was at that moment of contact that utter terror engulfed me. I knew right then that, regardless of what the doctors and mammogram said, something was very, very wrong.

"Brian," I said, my voice thin and shaky, rattling in the dark of our bedroom, "about this lump in my breast. I'm phoning tomorrow morning and demanding a biopsy."

"Okay. That sounds like a good idea," he said, reaching over to comfort me and hold me close. *I'm probably just being silly,* I tried to tell myself as I relaxed into the warmth of his embrace and felt him kiss my forehead. *This is probably nothing. I'm sure I'm going to be fine.*

I phoned the first thing Monday morning and scheduled the biopsy for that very same day. It was another anxious few days waiting for the results, but Brian and I had a lot on our minds to distract us as we were negotiating with the owner of the Jimmy John's that we wanted to buy and make our third location.

That Friday, we spent all morning in negotiations, trying to nail down the final points of contention. It had been such a long, stressful day when we finally got home around three p.m. "I need a drink," I joked, but we both realized that wasn't such a bad idea after all, so we made plans to go to our favorite local steakhouse to have a cocktail, eat dinner, and relax.

I was sitting at our kitchen counter, waiting for Brian to change clothes, when I got a call on my cell phone from Alicia, the manager of one of our Jimmy John's. "Marika, I hate to bother you," she began, sounding troubled, "but there's a woman who keeps calling here asking for your cell phone number. She says she's your doctor. She's called here three times, trying to get a hold of you. Of course I didn't give her your number, but I think you should call her back. It sounds important."

What? My head was spinning, and I wasn't sure if I was even hearing her correctly. "Did she leave a number?" My voice sounded strange and distant, almost robotic.

"She did." Alicia gave me the number, which I quickly scribbled down on a notepad and ended the call. I was more confused than worried or upset as I punched in the numbers from the notepad and listened to it ring. Dr. Patel answered right away.

"Dr. Patel? It's Marika Meeks. I understand you've been trying to reach me?"

"Marika," she replied. "Thanks for phoning me back." She paused awkwardly, and I could hear her take a deep breath and clear her throat. "I'm so sorry to have to tell you this, but the biopsy results came back, and it shows that you have cancer."

I was stunned, unable to catch my breath. "What?" I managed to whisper. She told me again that I had cancer and then unleashed a torrent of words that meant nothing to me at the time: *cell type, margins, moderately differentiated.*

I don't even remember ending the call, I was in a state of such overwhelming shock and disbelief. I do remember walking to our bedroom, standing in the doorway, shaking and sobbing as I told Brian, "The doctor called. I have cancer." He immediately rushed over and hugged me, doing his best to comfort me as he dealt with his own shock and confusion.

Unfortunately, Carly was home at the time along with two of her friends, and when they heard the commotion, they quickly came downstairs to see what was wrong. In no universe was this the right or best way to tell my daughter that I had cancer, but that's what I had to do, right then and there, in front of her friends. She was understandably devastated. (Caitie wasn't home at the time, having already left for church camp that weekend, so I was able to tell her later, after I'd had more time to consider how best to break the terrible news.)

I felt like I was on auto-pilot, spinning through another dimension as I phoned my parents and my sister Martine, and then emailed my other sister, Michelle, who was living in England at the time, and asked her to call me back when she could.

"Now what?" Brian asked softly after I finished my calls and pocketed my phone.

"Well." I sighed. "I don't know about you, but I could really use that drink about now."

He looked at me, shocked and confused.

"We were planning to go to dinner before Dr. Patel called. I think we should still go," I explained. "We gotta eat, right?" He seemed surprised but agreed, even though neither of us had much of an appetite. Brian is a "fixer"; it's his nature to want to fix whatever's wrong, and I could see the hurt and pain on his face, not knowing what to say or do that could help me now, now that my whole world, *our* whole world, had been turned upside down.

As we pulled out of the garage on the way to the restaurant, I couldn't help but notice the other vehicle in our driveway, a new Dodge Durango, Citadel Edition, dark metallic brown, that we had just leased for Brian. The lease was for three years, and I thought to myself, *That SUV might be with my family longer than I am.*

I now knew that I had breast cancer, but I had no idea what type of breast cancer, what stage, or how advanced it was. I would need more tests to determine those things, and none of that would come until next week at the earliest. My head was still spinning with question after question. *Has the cancer spread beyond my breast? What's my prognosis? Do I have weeks to live? Months? Years? Will I need surgery, hormone therapy, radiation, chemotherapy? Will I be one of the lucky ones who is cured?*

I could only pray that we had caught my cancer early, and yet I knew that there'd been a lump in my breast for at least six months now. *And who knows how long it was there before I was able to feel it. How long has this sickness been growing inside me without my knowledge?*

We arrived at the steakhouse, sat down at the bar, and ordered drinks. I was going through the motions but felt empty and hollow, as if all the life had drained out of my body. While Brian and I sat staring into space, neither of us having a clue what to say, my sister Michelle phoned me back from England. I stepped outside so I could hear her better, and I broke down again as I told her the news, and we cried together, sharing our sorrow across four thousand miles.

After ending the call, I sat for a moment, freezing on a concrete bench just outside the steakhouse, holding myself and rubbing my arms for warmth. I watched the busy stream of life flowing all around me, so many happy, smiling people, laughing and talking as they entered the restaurant, celebrating the end of another long week. But nothing meant anything to me anymore; I was observing life as an outsider now, rather than living it. This is what cancer really steals from you—not just the life you were living, but all your hopes and dreams for the future as well. Suddenly paralyzed with fear, anxiety, and utter despair, even the simplest pleasures are beyond your reach.

For me, the grieving process really began in those hopeless moments. I thought about everything cancer might take from me: *Will my girls grow up without a mom? Or will I be able to watch them graduate from high school and college, meet their boyfriends and future husbands, hold back tears as they walk down the aisle? Will I live to be a gray-haired granny, balancing my daughters' babies on my hip? Brian is here for me, but who will be there for him in his old age, holding his hand when he's ill, if I'm no longer alive?* Suddenly, my very existence on this earth seemed to hang in the balance. *I won't know anything more until Monday at the earliest,* I realized. *This will be the longest weekend of my life.*

Marika as a baby in England, 1972 (photo courtesy Peter Harrison).

CHAPTER TWO

The Toughest Decision

Early 2013

No one could honestly say that he or she felt "ready" or well-positioned to have cancer, but I felt particularly unprepared for such a devastating diagnosis. Maybe I was born an introvert, a naturally shy person who often felt awkward, insecure, and who shunned the limelight, but the events and circumstances of my early life also conspired to leave me tentative, uncertain, and seriously short of self-esteem.

I was born in Bury St. Edmund's, England, in 1972, the youngest of three daughters, and my family emigrated to the United States when I was five so my dad could pursue better career opportunities in his work as a defense contractor. Moving halfway around the world was a huge culture shock for me, a proper little English lass accustomed to Mini Coopers, fish-and-chips, Sunday roast dinners, and weekend trips to the seaside with high tea, sticks of rock candy, and dodge 'em bumper cars.

I was like Dorothy waking up in Oz, except my Oz was flat, landlocked Fort Wayne, Indiana, an old Rust Belt town surrounded by cornfields and peopled by big, burly, freckled farm kids who did Little League and 4-H and chores after school. My fellow first-graders at Lafayette Elementary mercilessly mocked my accent, asking me to pronounce "aunt," "lorry," "dustbin," and other British words they found hilarious. My response was silence—it was better to say nothing at all than risk humiliation, and this became a core belief of my life that followed me into adulthood. *If you don't put yourself out there, you don't risk getting hurt.*

Not only did I have a weird accent, I'd been born with what's called a branchial cleft, a hole in my neck that didn't close up in utero, as is normal. Sometimes drainage from my throat would ooze out of the hole just above my collarbone. When the passage got blocked, my dad had to wrap his hands around my neck and gently squeeze to try to clear it, and yes, this was exactly as gross as it sounds. I wore my shirts buttoned up as far as they would go, even in summer, and I worried constantly about leaking into my clothing. So I was afraid to speak, and I was afraid to ooze. Most days I wished the ground would just open up and swallow me whole.

I was a sickly child, and my already delicate health grew worse starting from the age of about seven or eight. I was always ill, especially ear, nose, and throat infections, followed later by chronic mono, Epstein-Barr, strep throat, and chronic fatigue. I was hospitalized multiple times and missed three years of school, from grades seven through nine, and had to be homeschooled by a tutor to keep up. Doctors prescribed drug after drug, mostly antibiotics, but nothing seemed to help.

By the time I reached high school, my health was stable enough that I could get back to class, but I still felt tired and achy all the time, and the pains in my legs made it hard to sleep at night. Doctors ran test after test, but there was never a definitive diagnosis, even though some mornings I didn't even have the energy to climb out of the car when Mom dropped me off at school. I just wanted to drag myself home and crawl back into bed, pull the covers over my head, and sleep the rest of the day away. My only refuge from illness, loneliness, and insecurity came from my many animals, whom I loved fiercely, and from whom I received the unconditional love I so coveted.

We never had dogs, interestingly, but that was the only animal I didn't grow up with. We had cats, snakes, ferrets, a flying squirrel, a possum, and, at one point, thirty-seven rabbits. (We just had two to start with, but you know what those bunnies get up to . . .) I also took in litters of baby rabbits that had been orphaned, and I bottle-fed them until they were big enough to release back into the wild. We had so many animals that the vet would come to our house to treat them, rather than us going to him. I can still picture myself setting up a triage center on my mom's kitchen counter and administering IV fluids one by one to a bunch of especially vulnerable bunnies that all had upper respiratory infections.

It wasn't until I was twenty-one and had my tonsils removed that my health finally improved. I was still groggy when, after the surgery, the doctor came into my room carrying what looked like some weird mushroom soup. I blinked several times and realized it was actually my tonsils, floating in a jar of cloudy fluid. "No amount of antibiotics could ever address this much strep throat, Marika," he said, lifting the jar to the light so we could both see it better.

"Your tonsils were so badly scarred, and the scars were so deep." It seemed the damage was related to my branchial cleft not being properly treated when I was younger. *Hopefully the worst is over,* I thought. *And now I can get on with my life without always being so ill and sickly.*

And get on with my life I did, in good health for the next twenty years, until the cancer diagnosis in 2013. I was like a zombie after receiving the news; walking and talking and behaving like a normal person on the outside, while inside I was an empty vessel, hollowed out, with just a thin layer of skin. I couldn't focus; I couldn't connect. I had no conscious sensation other than fear. Everything around me felt strange and surreal. At one point, I was at the store picking up groceries when I suddenly felt overwhelmed, like I couldn't go on. I started to cry, sobbing right there in the aisle, tears streaming down my face as other shoppers maneuvered their carts around me, whispering hostile "excuse me's" under their breath.

Come on, Marika. Get a grip. Shift yourself out of this. What would it take to get you out of this headspace? Just do it. Shift your mind right now. I happened to be in the aisle full of greeting cards. *Okay, look at the cards. What do they say? Happy birthday? I don't even know if I will live to celebrate another birthday. Happy anniversary?*

I don't know if I'll be here with Brian to mark year three. Congratulations on the new arrival, with a cute cartoon of a stork ferrying a bundle in its beak. My children aren't babies anymore, but they are still too young to lose their mom.

I turned away from the cards; they were too depressing, stark reminders of all the milestones I might miss. *Okay, Marika, imagine that you've just won ten million dollars in the lottery—wouldn't that be amazing? No. Not if I'm not here to enjoy it. I'd rather not have cancer than win ten million dollars.* This thought was so shocking. We truly don't appreciate what we have until we face the very real possibility of losing it.

After getting the cancer diagnosis, Brian and I took some time to decide on our next steps. With cancer, of course, time is of the essence, but then again, I'd already had the tumor for at least six months, so we figured we could take a few weeks to meet with different doctors and explore our options before rushing into what would be a life-altering decision. My doctor recommended, and we agreed, to start by having a lumpectomy to remove the tumor. The results of the surgery would dictate the course of action after that.

The night before the lumpectomy, Brian and I were at Kroger doing some last-minute shopping to stock up on food so we wouldn't have to go out again once I was home from the hospital. My cell phone rang and I looked down at the number.

Oh God—It's my surgeon. My hand was shaking as I answered. "Hello?"

"Marika, this is Dr. Stein." She sounded really pissed off, like I'd just ruined her entire day. "I'm at my office. Why am I just getting your scan results now?"

"What?" My voice cracked. "I have no idea. I had my MRI last week, along with all my lab tests." I'd done everything I'd been told to do, or at least I thought I had.

"Well, that may be, but the report just landed on my desk today," she snapped. *And that's my fault how, exactly?* I quickly handed the phone to Brian—Several weeks into my cancer journey, I found I could no longer process information during medical-related calls. The rational part of my brain cut out and terror took over. Brian, calm, steady as a rock, could handle this better than I could.

"Yes, Dr. Stein, this is Brian Meeks." He pressed the phone to his ear. "What exactly is the problem?" I scanned his face for a reaction as he listened carefully. "Uh-huh. Yes. I see," he said evenly. A true stoic, he tried not to give anything away, but I caught his pale blue eyes narrow and his jaw tighten.

He finished the call, handed me back the phone, and gently took my elbow, guiding me away from the checkout line with its colorful rows

57

of candy bars, chewing gum, and trashy tabloid magazines.

"No." I pulled away and stood firm. "Just tell me. Right now. What is it?"

He drew a deep breath. "It's the MRI. It shows that the tumor is larger than they thought."

Oh no. No no no. Please, God, no. Brian folded me into a firm embrace before I collapsed. "It's okay, shhhhh, it's okay," he whispered in my ear.

"No, it isn't." I brushed away the hot tears that had risen to my eyes. Ever since I'd been diagnosed, I'd felt like I was falling through an old, abandoned, multistory building, and each time I thought I'd hit bottom, that floor gave way and I descended even farther, plummeting another level toward the ground, falling, falling, falling, stopping, then falling again. *The tumor's larger than they thought.* The words echoed through my mind and settled like a stone in the pit of my stomach. *Please, God. How much worse can this get?*

My most powerful and lingering memory of my surgery the next day is being wheeled on the gurney away from Brian and my older sister, Martine, both there to support me, and down the hall to the surgical suite, which was stark-white and freezing cold. I was surrounded by people and yet I'd never felt more isolated or alone— the doctors and nurses and techs were talking, laughing, giggling, joking around and planning their weekends as if I wasn't even there. It was like I stopped being a human being once they strapped me onto that gurney and instead became an object or a project, a problem to be solved or a number to be checked off a list.

My whole life, my body, my world, is collapsing around me, and no one even cares. I suddenly wondered how many people were in the hospital at that moment. Hundreds, maybe thousands, if I counted doctors, nurses, patients, visitors. And out of all those thousands of people, there were only two—Brian and Martine—who loved me, and they couldn't help me now. *I just want my life to mean something to somebody, you know? I just want someone to care.*

Suddenly, tears began rolling down the sides of my face, trickling into my ears. No one noticed, or if they did, they never thought to brush them away. What would it have meant in that moment, if someone had looked me in the eye, or squeezed my hand? If someone had just smiled and told me not to worry, and that it would be okay?

The anesthetist bustled in, a tall, slim guy with slick, sharply parted, sandy blond hair and a gruff, grumpy manner. My arms werc stretched out on either side of me. I already had an IV line inserted in my right arm and he began administering the anesthetic. "This might burn a little bit," he said nonchalantly, not even making eye contact.

Within moments, I felt the most intense, searing, burning pain I've ever felt. I bolted upright, coming straight off the table and screaming in pain as I clutched my right arm in agony. The anesthetist and two nurses grabbed my arms and forced me back down, holding me in place as the drugs took hold. My last moments of consciousness were sheer terror before everything went black.

The surgery to remove the tumor was supposed to take one hour. It took three. During the procedure, dye was injected into my lymph nodes in order to show whether the cancer had spread and if so, how far. But the surgeon could see as soon as she opened me up that the cancer had spread. She removed fourteen nodes from my left side, and seven of those fourteen were cancerous.

When the surgeon got to my tumor, she found it was actually two tumors, not one, and they were very close to the chest wall and therefore difficult to remove. Once the tumors were out, the incision was closed, but the surgeon had to wait for the pathology report to find out if the margins were clear, meaning that all the cancer had been removed.

The report came back. The margins weren't clear. She had to re-open the incision and remove more tissue in order to get clear margins.

Meanwhile, Brian and Martine were in the waiting room, frantic with worry, wondering why the surgery was taking so much longer than expected and why no one was providing them with any updates or news . . .

After the surgery and pathology report, my cancer was diagnosed as Stage 3, estrogen-positive, with lymph nodes fully involved. We were all devastated—Brian, Caitie, Carly, my parents, sisters, and me. The radiologist told me that now that they knew where the tumor had been located in my breast, they could see it on all four of my previous mammograms. Not only that, they estimated that it had been growing inside me for as long as seven or eight years.

Oh my God, I thought. *Seven or eight years? That means I've had cancer since I was in my early thirties.* I felt myself falling yet again, plummeting through yet another floor of that old, abandoned building that went on forever and ever with no bottom, no end.

After the lumpectomy, we met with the oncologist. The standard of care they prescribed included chemotherapy, radiation, and ten years of hormone therapy. If I followed this course of treatment, I was told that I had a "sixty-one percent" chance of surviving five years. *Sixty-one percent? Put myself through all that hell and still only have a little better than a fifty-fifty chance of living to see my forty-sixth birthday? I might as well flip a coin . . .* Not to mention that when I looked at the possible side effects of these three treatments, all ran the risk of causing more cancer.

I still hadn't decided on my next steps of treatment when we had a follow-up appointment with the surgeon who had done the lumpectomy. At the end of the appointment, as the surgeon was heading toward the door, she said casually, "We've got you scheduled for your next surgery in three weeks."

I looked at Brian and he looked at me, both of us dumbfounded. I was so shocked, it took me a moment to find my voice. "Next surgery? What are you talking about?" I asked. "No one's said anything to us about another surgery."

"You're having a port implanted so they can administer the chemotherapy drugs," she said matter-of-factly. I had no idea what she was talking about, so, looking a bit annoyed, she went out and quickly returned with an anatomical model of a human chest and torso that she sat down on the exam table in front of us.

"It's a simple surgical procedure." She pointed to the model's shoulder with a ballpoint pen. "They'll be inserting a line here and then they'll weave it through your ribs," the pen zigzagged helpfully between the ribs to demonstrate, "so they can administer the chemo as close to your heart as possible."

I blanched. "Close to my heart?"

She nodded. "They administer the chemo close to the heart because the blood flow is at its more active and tumultuous at that point, where it exits the heart. Circulating the drugs through the body quickly helps you to better tolerate the toxic nature of the chemo."

I felt light-headed and dizzy, like I might faint. Toxic nature? Tumultuous blood flow? I hadn't even consented to the chemo yet, but that didn't seem to matter. At no point had a doctor or anyone else asked me how I felt or what I wanted to do. They were moving forward with their plan, and I seemed inconsequential. Cancer was terrifying, but almost as frightening was the thought of not even being consulted or informed about what would be happening to my body.

The more I thought about my treatment options and the more Brian and I discussed it, the more scared and confused I became. I started getting a strong, overpowering message from my intuition. It told me, "If you do chemo, you will make it through the treatment and go into remission. Then you will have a recurrence and die during the second round of chemo." *Oh my God!* This inner voice was something I couldn't ignore.

It might be easy for some people to discount intuition, but it had saved my life more than once. After all, it was my intuition that made me demand the biopsy after both a doctor and a mammogram assured me I did not have cancer. If I'd followed their advice instead of my own intuition, it's doubtful I'd be alive today.

After much thought and intense soul-searching, I declined chemotherapy in favor of a non-traditional treatment plan. This was the most difficult decision of my life, and one I struggled with constantly, always worrying and wondering if I had made the right choice. Frankly, I was terrified. Brian always supported my decision, but so many other people, friends, family, even people we barely knew, were convinced not only that I was making a terrible mistake but that it was their responsibility to put me right, and they set about to actively undermine my choice. Some people assumed that by turning down chemo I was choosing to "just let the disease run its course," implying that I had given up and was not even trying to be cured.

Some people even phoned Brian and said things like, "I knew a woman with breast cancer who did what Marika is doing and eighteen months later, she was dead." I think some people thought, if they couldn't change *my* mind, they could pressure Brian to make me change my mind. Dealing with the cancer itself was so stressful for us, and then dealing with so much negative feedback from people trying to talk us into doing what they thought was best that we basically just shut down and withdrew, for our own sanity and to focus on my health without so much outside distraction.

I think it's important to emphasize here that I'm not advocating for other cancer patients to make the same choice I did. I would never say to someone, "This is what worked for me; you should try it, too." I have nothing against chemotherapy as a cancer treatment and believe that for some people, it is the right choice. If Brian or someone else in my family was diagnosed with cancer, was offered chemotherapy as a treatment option and wanted to pursue it, I would support that decision wholeheartedly.

From my perspective, the most important thing should be to honor and support the wishes of the person who is ill, even if you don't agree with his or her decision. By all means, share your feelings and concerns with that person, but don't try to force your choices on someone else, or shame them or shut them out if they choose a path you don't approve of. When someone is sick with cancer, they need all the love and support, all the care and concern you can muster. Love without judgment—that's the greatest gift you can give. Trust that that person has made an informed choice and is doing what is right for them.

At first, my parents, like Brian, supported my decision to forgo the chemo, but then they changed their minds and began pushing me to take traditional treatment. I knew they were acting out of love; they feared for my life and believed I would die if I didn't do chemo. But once I had made my choice, it just added so much stress, fear, and confusion to not have them supporting my decision.

Things got so strained between us that at one point I found myself writing in an email to my parents, "I love you and I appreciate everything you do for me, but I'm the CEO of my life and Brian is my project manager. I get to choose my treatment plan, and this is what we've chosen. I have to do what I believe is right for me, and what's right for my family." It was so painful to have to write those words, but sometimes you just have to take a step back, even from the people you love most, in order to put your own health and well-being first.

It was still only a few weeks after my diagnosis in January 2013 and I'd had the lumpectomy but hadn't started my nontraditional treatment yet as I was still exploring my options. I also hadn't spoken to my parents for a while, but I suddenly had this powerful, overwhelming urge to see them again. I knew this was another nudge from my intuition that I couldn't afford to ignore.

Their home base was Fort Wayne but they had become seasonal "snow birds" and were leaving the next day to spend the rest of the winter in

Florida. *I need to see them before they go,* that voice inside me insisted. *I have to see them, talk to them, tell them that I love them.* I couldn't bring myself to express the rest of what weighed heavily on my heart: that I needed to see them again in case this was my last chance, in case this ended up being the last time ever that we were together as a family. Scenes from that visit in early 2013 remain so vivid in my mind.

* * * * *

Brian and I are in the living room with Mom; Dad's stepped out for a moment. Brian is engrossed in the March Madness basketball playoffs on TV. Mom is in her chair knitting and I'm on the sofa beside her with a small table between us. The mood is so strained, so awkward, as neither of us knows what to say or where to begin. The only sounds are the click-click-click of her knitting needles and the loud drone of the TV, alternating between cheering and moaning, depending on the score. This isn't right, I think. I didn't come here just to sit in silence, counting the minutes until we can go home. I need to find a way to bridge this gap. Especially if this *is* the last time ever . . .

Slowly, carefully, I reach across the table and take Mom's hand. She puts aside her knitting and holds her hand in mine. It feels so good to absorb that warmth, that softness, that I haven't felt for so long.

Still holding her hand, I rise from the sofa, walk to her chair so I'm facing her, then kneel down and place my head in her lap. "Mom," I whisper, and begin to sob. "This is so hard. I'm so scared."

"I know, honey. I know." Her shoulders sag and she drapes herself over me, holding my shoulders as we sob together.

Suddenly, I'm no longer a forty-one-year-old wife and mother with cancer, I'm a little girl again, so lost and hopeless, wanting to run into the arms of Mommy and Daddy and have them make it better.

"Peter," Mom calls out, and Dad comes back into the room. He must be shocked to see me kneeling on the floor with my head in Mom's lap, but he comes to us and puts his arms around me from behind, rocking me back and forth, the strength of his embrace a contrast to Mom's softness.

I realize, in that moment, that as terrible as it is to have cancer, it would be so much worse to have a child with cancer, to have your daughter come to you literally on her knees crying for help, desperate for you to fix it and knowing there's nothing you can do to make it better. Suddenly, I'm glad it's me who's sick and not Caitie or Carly; I couldn't bear that. I couldn't, but my parents have to.

I let my tears flow freely, feeling safe and

secure enough in the circle of their love to finally release the emotions I've held in for so long.

"It's okay," Mom whispers, stroking my hair.

Dad clears his throat. "Honey, just do the chemo," he says softly as he rubs my back. "You've got to do it."

"I can't," I reply, lifting my head from Mom's lap.

"Please, just do the chemo," he says again, his voice more insistent.

I understand that they are pushing me because they love me so much and they truly believe chemotherapy offers my best chance for survival. But I can't do it just to make them happy. My mind is made up—I have to follow my own intuition.

"I can't do the chemo. If I do, it will kill me."

"But Marika, think of your girls," Mom pleads, tears coursing down her cheeks.

Suddenly, my sorrow evaporates, replaced by fury. "You think that I'm *not* thinking of them?" I jump to my feet. "They are all I'm thinking about, the girls and Brian. This is not a selfish decision. I'm doing what I believe will save my life."

And just like that, the spell is broken, and that moment of closeness is gone forever. It's like I grow up in that moment, and I go from being a child, wanting to please my parents, to an adult, making the scariest and most important decision of my life and then standing by that decision, even against their wishes.

* * * * *

I didn't talk to my parents again until the day before what was supposed to be my second appointment with my oncologist, which I canceled. Mom phoned as I was upstairs in the loft, sitting at my desk, and Brian and Caitie were downstairs watching TV.

After some very stilted small talk, Mom said, "You have your oncologist appointment tomorrow, don't you?"

I sighed, dreading this conversation. "It was supposed to be tomorrow, but I canceled it."

"Oh, Marika, please reconsider," she begged. "Just go to the appointment."

That's it. I've had enough. I pushed back my chair, stood up, and yelled, "I have to do what I have to do for me—you can be there for me or not." I was terrified and overwhelmed enough; this was more than I could cope with. "I'm in the middle of the scariest, most stressful time of my life, and I don't have the luxury of doubt," I explained. "If you can't support me in this, then you can't be part of my life right now."

I hung up the phone and looked down from the loft to the den below. Brian and Caitie were looking up at me, open-mouthed and in shock. "Who were you talking to?" Caitie asked.

"That was Grandma," I replied, and Caitie's surprise turned to all-out astonishment.

I realized with a start that for the first time in my life, I felt like I was actively going against my parents' wishes. I had been such a quiet, inhibited, insecure child, and it was still so unlike me to defy them in any way. Did my life have to be on the line before I could stand up to them? I wondered. I'd spent my life in the shadows. Did it take cancer to finally give me this strength and help me find my voice?

Marika with her best friend, Betsy Olson *(photo courtesy Randy Olson)*.

CHAPTER THREE

A Chance Meeting with Sweetie Pie

Spring 2013–Autumn 2015

Being diagnosed with cancer was a living nightmare that haunted not only my days but my nights as well. Sometimes, I would toss and turn for hours in my bed, punching my pillow, scissor-kicking the sheets, and fighting off the dark thoughts as I had visions of my own death. I could see, clear as day, my parents, Brian, Carly, and Caitie in a barren desert churchyard marked with simple white crosses, standing in a circle around my grave, weeping as my coffin was lowered into the ground. Blessed sleep, when it finally came, if it came, in those bleak early morning hours, offered no relief, as the dreams of my demise were even more vivid, more surreal than what my conscious brain had sent me while awake.

During the worst of my cancer battle, I often woke up mid–panic attack, shaking, sweating, my heart pounding, my throat clamped shut, unable to breathe. *It's just a dream,* I'd think, trying to calm myself; *it's okay, you're awake now,* but then the awful reality whispered into my ear: *It wasn't a dream, Marika, you do have cancer after all.*

And here's the thing about cancer: The bad dreams don't go away just because you're cured. The disease may be gone, but the nightmares linger, still stalking you in your sleep, reminding you that you could get sick again at any time. I still have bad dreams, but it's so different now, because now I wake up to Stella at my side. As soon as she crawls in for a cuddle and I feel her wet nose, her wriggly body, and her big feet pawing all over me, I know I'm going to be okay. Stella keeps me steady, grounded, focused on the here and now. I wrap my arms around her rib cage, press her to my chest, and just relax, enjoying her warmth and her presence, her goofy grin, as we breathe together, getting ready to face the day. This is true bliss.

• • •

Back in the spring of 2013, long before Stella, I was still in the midst of my battle, fighting for my life. Having declined chemotherapy, in March I flew to New York and began a highly aggressive alternative treatment protocol that involved taking 189 pills every day, along with following a highly restricted diet (no sugar, oil, butter, meat, or beans), along with raw juicing, and numerous cleanses. The goal of the program was to break down my immune system and then rebuild it from scratch. The regimen was brutal, but I was determined to stick with it, even after Brian and I returned home to Indiana and I tried to resume some semblance of a normal life, working with Brian to manage our three Jimmy John's locations and being a mom to Carly and Caitie.

The treatment protocol I began in New York kept the cancer at bay for the rest of 2013 and 2014, but by early 2015, I had found another lump in my breast and I was terrified and desperate. My anxiety was at an all-time high and I could barely function. It felt like my life was slipping away from me and I didn't have long to live.

For spring break, we drove to the Florida panhandle and as we slept in our hotel room one night, I heard a voice inside me saying over and over, "You're going to die; you're going to die." I woke up crying and panicking, afraid to tell Brian, afraid to tell anyone, and feeling I had nowhere to turn.

When we got home from Florida, I started a three-day water fast. By the third day with no solid food, I was delirious. I was taking a shower when my intuition told me, "You've got to do something!"

"I'm already doing everything I can," I cried out.

"Then you've got to do something else," came the reply. Following that moment of clarity, I began researching more options and found a clinic in Mexico that offered a new alternative cancer treatment. The catch was, it would cost fifty thousand dollars. *This is my last resort,* I thought. *If I don't do this, I will die.*

I called my parents and told them about the clinic in Mexico, but didn't tell them I believed it was my last resort. I think I was basically calling them to say good-bye. After I'd hung up with them, Mom called me back and asked me if I'd heard of a clinic in Scottsdale, Arizona, that offered a holistic approach to treating cancer. I promised her I would check it out, and so I did. I was skeptical at first—I had been through so much with doctors and the medical community, but once I read the patient testimonials online and spoke to the clinic director by phone, I felt more optimistic. *They're interesting,* I thought. *I should at least give them a try.*

Days later, I flew out to Scottsdale for my first meeting with Dr. Santiago and his team, a meeting that lasted four hours. It was important to me that I stay involved, informed, and empowered in my own treatment plan, rather than being just a passive "patient" at the mercy of doctors and nurses, as I'd so often felt with conventional medical care. I was so impressed with Dr. Santiago and his team that by the end of that initial meeting, I decided to forgo Mexico and instead stay in Arizona and enter their program.

Even so, this decision was far from easy, because I knew it would involve being away from my family, for several months or possibly even longer. I planned to rent a condo in Scottsdale and undergo treatment while Brian and the girls stayed in Indiana so Brian could run the restaurants and the girls could stay in school. There just wasn't any practical way for us to be together during this time. I was heartbroken to leave them, but I truly believed that by sacrificing time with them now, I'd be gaining more time with them in the future. I saw this as my best chance to beat cancer, so I had to go for it, no matter the sacrifice.

My first two weeks in Arizona were the hardest. I was at the clinic for three to four hours a day undergoing intensive treatment. My lymph nodes swelled up and I felt so weak and sick as my body adjusted to the new protocol. I also felt so alone and lonely, returning to an empty condo after a long, grueling day at the clinic, worn out, exhausted, scared, and in pain.

Being separated from my family was taking a terrible toll on me, and also on them. Brian, being Brian, was always so stoic, staying strong and positive at all times. Carly was busy in college, so I think that protected her from the worst of my illness. Caitie, on the other hand, still in high school, was having a hard time coping with me being gone, but the full, horrible extent of the toll it was taking on her wouldn't be revealed until months later, when it was almost too late.

Overall the treatment I received at the Scottsdale clinic seemed to be working, but then in July 2015, the tumor in my breast felt like it was getting bigger. I underwent a PET scan and the results showed some additional spots, localized to the breast and with one on the inside chest wall. At that point, I made the very difficult decision to have a mastectomy, followed by thirty-six consecutive days of radiation.

I had my surgery in Arizona at the end of August 2015. Brian was there for me during the surgery, but he had to return to Indiana before I started my radiation treatments in October, and I was alone and lonely once again, by myself in my rented condo. I so longed for love and companionship. *What about a dog?* I sometimes pondered. *Maybe I wouldn't be so lonely here if I had a dog to keep me company.* But as much as I loved animals, I didn't consider myself a "dog person," and I hadn't expected that to ever change.

I was extremely nervous about the radiation treatments, and my fears weren't exactly allayed when I had to sign the required paperwork a few days before my sessions were set to begin. The standard informed consent sheet included a page and a half spelling out, in great detail, all the terrible things that radiation could do to my body, especially damage to my heart and lungs and other major organs. At the bottom of the document, I had to sign my name attesting that, "I understand that no warranty or guarantee has been made to me as to result or cure, and I am initialing here that nobody at the clinic has told me that the radiation will be successful."

Wow. In other words, I was agreeing to put my body through absolute hell, causing untold, and possibly permanent, internal damage, and I had to certify that I understood that it might be for nothing. My hands were shaking and my throat was tight, but I managed to hold it together long enough to sign, initial, and then hand in the forms.

I made it all the way out to my car before bursting into tears. I sat in the driver's seat and cried and cried, feeling so scared, confused, lost, and alone. *What am I doing?* I asked myself. *Should I have declined the radiation? Every time I think I'm getting better, something worse happens.* I thought I'd hit the bottom floor of that abandoned building a long time ago, but now I felt like I was in free fall yet again.

I indulged in a full-blown, Oprah-approved "ugly cry" all the way to Whole Foods, but when I pulled into the parking lot and stopped the car, I thought, *WTF? Marika, get a grip. You're still in charge. You didn't choose cancer, but you can damn well choose what you do next.*

I decided right there and then that if I was going to have radiation, then I was going to go all-out badass and ride a mountain bike to my treatments, raising a metaphoric middle finger and shouting a loud "FU" to all this cancer crap. I'd been fighting this disease for more than two and a half years; it was time to kick cancer to the curb once and for all.

I returned to my condo feeling stronger and more defiant than I had in months, and immediately began searching online for a used mountain bike, nothing fancy, just something decent and not too expensive. On the "Next Door" community website I found one that looked promising: a man's used mountain bike, green, not too old, a hybrid that could be ridden both on- and off-road.

I arranged to take the bike for a test ride and took my new friend Betsy with me. Betsy, a local real estate agent, and her husband, Randy, had become my closest friends in Arizona after Dr. Santiago introduced us. Betsy, a fortysomething bubbly blonde with big blue eyes, is a native Minnesotan who settled in Arizona. Her warmth and kindness cheered me up during some of my darkest days, and I was so glad I had in her someone I could turn to for help and support when Brian and the girls were so far away.

Betsy and I drove out to the affluent suburb of McCormick Ranch and found the lovely modern home that matched the address I'd been given over the phone. We rang the doorbell and were greeted by Jerry and Pat, a friendly, older retired couple who were selling the bike.

Yapping at their heels was a little tan-colored Chihuahua that darted back and forth between their feet, nearly getting trampled. I knelt down and let the dog sniff me, then gently stroked its head. "Well, hello there," I cooed, scratching its ear. "Aren't you a friendly guy?"

Suddenly, I heard the scampering of four more paws-with-claws on the tile floor as a boisterous puppy wheeled around the corner into the foyer and nearly bowled me over, wagging her tail and jumping up to lick my face. "And who do we have here?" I laughed, rubbing her ears and forehead as she consumed me with kisses.

"Oh, that's Sweetie Pie," Pat explained. "We're fostering her until she goes to a new home." Sweetie Pie was so cute—a medium-size mixed breed, short-haired, mostly tan with a black coat along her back, black eyes, a black nose, and adorable white accents resembling a bib under her chin and white socks on her paws. She looked like she might be part German shepherd, with a couple other breeds thrown in. I guessed she was just a few months old and would probably grow into a good-size girl once she got older.

Her tail was wagging a mile a minute as I stroked her back and shoulders and she licked me happily, addressing me in that high-pitched, energetic puppy bark. I knelt down to get closer to her, and she catapulted her body against me and stayed there with her paws around my hips and resting her head against my chest, becoming perfectly still, like she was hugging me. *Wow. What was that?* In that moment, I felt something I'd never felt before—it was like she had reached inside my chest, clasped my heart, raised it up, and bathed it in love. The connection was intense and immediate. *This dog and I are meant to be.*

I wrapped my arms around her as she burrowed into my sternum. The warmth of her, the weight, the pressure of her head, the softness of her fur, that milky puppy smell, touched me so deeply that I didn't want to let her go. *What the heck?* I wondered. *Why do I feel this way? She's just a dog. And I'm not even a "dog person." At least, I don't think I'm a dog person.*

"So would you like to take the bike for a test ride?" Pat cleared her throat, breaking Sweetie Pie's spell. "Jerry's got it waiting in the garage if you'd like to take it out."

"Yes, of course," I replied quickly, standing up and brushing off my shorts. I gave Sweetie Pie a final rub around the ears and resisted the urge to kiss her forehead. She wasn't my dog, after all, and I had just met her.

She scampered in an enthusiastic circle around my legs before lying down. I took out my phone and snapped a quick photo of her, stretched out on the colorful, Native American–themed rug on the tile floor in the foyer. She was so cute, I just had to have a picture of her.

Betsy stayed behind with Jerry, Pat, Sweetie Pie, and the Chihuahua while I hopped on the mountain bike and rode through the neighborhood, past the gorgeous, swanky Scottsdale Resort, the McCormick Ranch Golf Club, the man-made lakes and tennis courts. To be honest, I barely noticed the lush, beautifully manicured scenery or even the rugged bike beneath me as I pedaled furiously, clutching the handlebars. My mind and heart had been left behind with Sweetie Pie, and I still felt that strange warmth throbbing in my chest, in the precise spot where her head had lain.

I need this dog, I thought. *I know it's crazy, but I trust my intuition, and my intuition tells me this dog and I are meant to be. Something led me to this place, to these people, and to this bike. It's all led me to meeting Sweetie Pie.*

In my head, I ran through the details of adopting a dog without prior planning. I was living alone in a small condo and scheduled to start radiation in a few days, but I was convinced I could make it work. *She'll need food and toys, of course. I'll buy her a crate, and if I take her out every morning before I go to the clinic, and then again when I get home . . .*

Of course, there was the issue of what I would say to Brian if I returned to Fort Wayne after completing radiation with a dog in tow. Brian had made it clear when we got engaged that he did not want us to have dogs. *Well, I'll figure it out,* I told myself. *If I love Sweetie Pie, Brian will fall in love with her, too.*

By the time I got back to Pat and Jerry's, sweaty and slightly breathless, I had worked it all out in my mind, how I could adopt Sweetie Pie. *This is just meant to be! I'm going to be a dog mama!* I was so excited, I couldn't wait to tell them.

"What do you think of the bike?" Jerry asked as I pulled into the garage, stopped the bike, and dismounted.

"Oh, right. The bike." I wiped my forehead with the back of my arm. In my excitement about

Sweetie Pie, I had almost forgotten my original reason for being there. "The bike's perfect. I'll take it." I paused. "I'm wondering about Sweetie Pie. You mentioned you're fostering her. Will she be up for adoption?"

"Technically, yes," Pat replied. "But we've been looking for another dog for a while and we've decided to keep her." A smile lit up her suntanned features. "She's such a lovely animal."

"Oh. I see." I managed to maintain a neutral expression, but inside, my heart felt crushed. I knew it was crazy, but it felt as if something beautiful and precious had been whisked away from me, suddenly leaving me empty and bereft.

I paid for the bike and we stowed it in the back of Betsy's pickup truck, then climbed into the front seat. I couldn't bear to say good-bye to Sweetie Pie; my heart hurt too much, but as I turned and looked out the window, I saw Pat silhouetted in the doorway, holding Sweetie Pie in her arms.

Betsy was about to start the truck, but then she stopped and turned to look at me, her big blue eyes round and thoughtful. "You really wanted to take that little dog home with you, didn't you?" She'd become so good at reading me in the little time we'd known each other.

"Yes," I admitted, releasing the tears I'd worked so hard to hide in front of Pat and Jerry. "I feel so crushed, and I don't even know why.

It's not like she was ever mine, you know? I just had a feeling she was special."

As we drove back to my condo, my mind was still churning. *Maybe it's a sign,* I thought. *Maybe Sweetie Pie wasn't meant to be mine, but maybe I'm supposed to adopt a dog. I'm so sick and scared and lonely out here, and my family is so far away. I've got an empty space inside me that a dog could fill. But, given my past history with dogs, do I dare try again? Can I even hope that it might be different this time?*

I hadn't grown up around dogs, and my few previous experiences owning dogs had been harsh, sad, and disappointing. My first dog was Annie, a black Lab/Shar–Pei mix I came across as a ten-week-old puppy in a vet's office in 1992. I was twenty and had been unhappily married for a year to my first husband, Don. I was at the vet with our cats, Wilma and Betty, when I noticed an adorable little black puppy cowering in a crate in an exam room in back, looking abandoned and utterly despondent.

"What's her story?" I asked the vet tech. It turned out Annie had been at the park playing with her family when she jumped off a picnic table and broke the elbow of her front leg. Her owners couldn't afford the surgery to fix it, so she was scheduled to be euthanized that very afternoon.

"Oh no! The poor little girl." I knelt in front

of her crate and slipped my fingers through the wire bars. The pup couldn't stand because of her broken elbow, so she dragged herself closer to me, then sniffed my hand, nudged me with her coal-black nose, and gave me a little lick. She was solid black with soft, dark eyes and didn't yet have the deep, distinctive wrinkles that make the Shar-Pei breed unique, but her skin was a little baggy, like she was wearing a loose overcoat, a size or two too big.

"If I agree to pay for her surgery, could I adopt her?" I asked impulsively. I had no idea what I was doing; Don and I had never talked about getting a dog, and I knew he'd blow up about spending money on surgery for a dog that wasn't even really ours. And yet, that powerful voice inside me told me I couldn't let this little dog die.

So I paid for the surgery and arranged to adopt Annie. I was so excited the night before we were going to bring her home, I could barely sleep. I couldn't wait to have this new little bundle of fun in the house.

The surgeon had to place metal pins in Annie's elbow to stabilize it, and she looked so sad and defeated with her little chin resting on the floor of her cage when we arrived to pick her up the next day. Gazing at her soft face and floppy ears, it hit me: *I'm falling in love.*

I just wanted to cradle her in my arms and hold her close, nuzzling the many folds of her neck and promising she'd be okay. I sat in the back seat of the car beside her crate the whole ride home, talking to her softly and stroking her head.

The vet had warned us, but it wasn't until we got home that I realized how truly difficult it was to care for an injured puppy. While Annie was recovering, she had to be on crate rest, meaning she could only be out of the crate to go potty. The vet stressed to us that the crate was the safest place for her so she wouldn't run around and re-injure her leg. But she hated being cooped up like that, and when we took her out for a bathroom break, she was so hard to control and would try to run away. I was terrified she'd hurt herself, but the more I tried to control her, the more she fought me and the worse it became.

When Don and I took her back to the vet for a follow-up after the surgery, before the appointment, I carried her to the grassy area outside the building to do her business, but when I put her down, she tried to run away. The more I tried to control her, the wilder and more defiant she became, until finally I ended up on the ground, rolling around in the soiled grass, trying to contain her.

Don, who was watching from inside the clinic, came out to help. I went inside to calm down, and when I looked out the window, Don, too, was now rolling around in the grass, trying to wrangle Annie. *What is wrong with her?* I thought sadly. *What is wrong with* us? *Are we such terrible people? Why can't we manage one little puppy?*

I would like to say that things got better once Annie's leg healed and she grew older, but unfortunately, they didn't. She developed an amazing ability to push my buttons. She seemed to instinctively know what I wanted her to do and then would do the exact opposite. I wanted so badly to love her, but I didn't; I couldn't. It was my great sadness that we were never able to connect that way.

Annie was always well cared for, and we did the best we could for her, but she remained a hard dog to handle throughout her life. Everything seemed to trigger her and she would run off at a moment's notice. She'd bolt out the door as soon as we opened it, and we were constantly chasing after her. If it thundered, she'd react by tearing the wood paneling off the wall. Sometimes I'd take her to work with me and she'd go nuts for no reason. Once I put her in a time-out in a quiet office hoping to calm her down, and when I went back to check on her, I found she'd chewed up and swallowed an entire section of drywall.

All in all, it was a hopelessly sad situation. I sometimes wondered if maybe she hadn't actually jumped off a picnic table as a puppy and broken her elbow but that she'd actually been abused by her first owners, and that early abuse caused her lifelong behavior problems. Sadly, we'll never know.

I felt like such a failure with Annie, and she seemed to cement my deepest fear that, as much as I loved animals, I just wasn't meant to be a "dog person." I doubt I ever would have had another dog in my lifetime, but then Chrissy came along. Chrissy was my sister Michelle's dog, and we took her in when Michelle got divorced.

Chrissy was a flat-coat retriever and looked a bit like a golden retriever but with black fur. Michelle and her husband had rescued Chrissy from an abusive environment, and she was a shy dog, anxious and self-conscious, always looking for a place to hide. *Maybe she's the dog that will capture my heart,* I thought hopefully.

Chrissy was so different from Annie, quiet and obedient. Although she was shy, she was well behaved and never gave us much trouble. I wanted to be close with Chrissy, but she was too badly damaged to give or receive love. Any attention made her uncomfortable, and she would just try to hide. It was like she wanted to be invisible. The more I tried to reach her, the more she pulled away. At best, she tolerated my affection, but never returned it. *It's me,* I finally decided. *It's not the dogs' fault this keeps happening. There's gotta be something wrong with me. Maybe the dog-loving part of my heart just doesn't work.*

My third try at dog ownership (or maybe I should call it "third strike," because that's what it felt like when it didn't work out) was Sampson. By now it was the early 2000s. I'd been unhappily married to Don for more than ten years, and Carly (born in 1996) and Caitie (born in 1999) were out of diapers and starting school. I began to think about adding a furry member to our family. I hadn't had the best of luck with dogs, but that didn't mean my girls shouldn't have pets. *I just need to find the right dog to turn things around.*

I began researching different dogs that would fit in well in a family with two boisterous, curious little girls. I decided we should get a female Lab, a quiet, gentle dog about three to four years old. Don agreed, but once we got to the ASPCA, he fell head over heels in love with Sampson, a large male black Lab about a year and a half old, extremely strong, and very energetic. "Well, what do you think?" Don asked me, struggling to hold tight to the leash as Sampson barked and lunged, nearly pulling Don across the floor.

"Oh, Don, he's beautiful, but I just don't think he's the right dog for us," I replied. "That's way more dog than we can handle, and I'm worried how he'll be around the girls. We'd be better off with an older, more relaxed animal. Let's keep looking."

We looked around the shelter some more,

but Don kept returning to Sampson. He didn't even want to consider a different dog. Finally, against my better judgment, I gave in. "Okay, we can take Sampson," I told him. "But on one condition. You have to work with him and train him, and take him for a walk every single day."

"I will," Don promised. "He'll be a great dog for the family."

I tried to keep an open mind, but I knew, almost as soon as we got home, that we'd made another mistake. Sampson was Annie all over again. He was so smart and stubborn and so much hard work, always playing games and trying to outmaneuver me. No matter what I did, this dog always had a countermove. He barked at the neighbors, wrecked the front door, and never wanted to be close or cuddle. To me, caring for Sampson became an obligation and not an act of love. There was no joy in our relationship.

As I walked him around the block for the millionth time one freezing winter night, holding tight to the leash with both hands so he didn't pull me over and drag me, flailing, down the icy streets (despite his promise, after the first day or two, Don never walked Sampson again), I thought bitterly, *I've ended up with the wrong dog again. When will I accept that the universe is telling me I'm just not meant to have a dog?*

Don and I split up in 2008 and in 2010, Brian Meeks, a friend who became so much more, arrived at my front door one evening and asked me to marry him. My response was an enthusiastic "yes!"

"I just have one condition for our marriage," Brian warned. "And it's a deal-breaker for me. I do not want us to have dogs." It wasn't that Brian had anything personal against dogs—he loves animals, too—but his first wife had had dogs that she lavished with love and attention while ignoring him, and he didn't want to go through that again.

"That's one thing you'll never have to worry about," I promised, hugging him tightly. "Given my track record, I have no intention of *ever* getting another dog."

Brian and I got married in 2011, and for our first four years together, I hadn't even thought about us getting a dog. We were so busy with Carly and Caitie, with growing the business, and of course, dealing with cancer, pets were the furthest thing from my mind. But by 2015, Sweetie Pie was making me reconsider our agreement. *There must be a reason why this little dog, who I only held for a few moments, touched me so deeply,* I thought. Although I couldn't have known it at the time, Sweetie Pie was the near-miss that brought me one step closer to Stella. Sweetie Pie softened me, ripened me for love. But there would be one more near-miss before I finally found my forever friend in Stella.

A scared Stella's first car ride home with Caitie, February 13, 2016

CHAPTER FOUR

London, Laverne and Shirley, and Love at First Sight

Fall 2015–February 2016

Meeting Sweetie Pie had a huge impact on me, especially in terms of reawakening the child inside me who loved animals so much she set up a clinic in Mom's kitchen to give a batch of sick bunnies IV medication. I was clearly looking for something to take my life in a new direction. Could it be that my ever-present intuition that I relied on so much was now nudging me to find a four-legged soul mate, a fur-ever friend, to guide me through life post-cancer?

I started researching on PetFinder, learning more about different breeds and the types of dogs that might be available. *If I'm going to do this, I'm going to do this right.* But I was overwhelmed when I saw the sheer number of dogs that were looking for good homes. *How will I ever find the right dog among so many?* I was sad to think about so many unloved and unwanted animals out there, especially knowing that many of them would be put down for no other reason than lack of a loving home to go to. *The majority of the dogs listed are pit bulls, or pit bull mixes,* I realized. *Are these dogs really so difficult and dangerous? Or are they just misunderstood?*

The more I searched, the more I found myself asking, *What am I doing?* I had promised Brian we wouldn't get a dog. *How can I go back on that promise? Not only that, our lives will be so complicated when I go home to Indiana; adding a dog to the mix can't possibly be a good idea. But, on the other hand, if I'm not meant to be a dog mom, why can't I stop imagining myself cuddling a beautiful dog in my arms, kissing its head and stroking its soft fur? A powerful force is working on me, and I can't just ignore it.*

• • •

I began my thirty-six consecutive days of radiation in October 2015, and while I didn't ride my mountain bike to the clinic every day as I had hoped, I biked there often enough both to justify buying the bike and to feel suitably badass. The radiation sessions themselves were mercifully brief, only about fifteen minutes long, but the aftereffects left me feeling sick and exhausted, battling burned, tender skin and terrible bouts of nausea. When my doctor said, "But this type of radiation doesn't cause nausea," I had to find another doctor to prescribe something to help me manage it.

The whole experience was debilitating, demeaning, and demoralizing. The only thing that kept me going was the thought of beating cancer and getting back home to my family. *I'm doing this for them,* I would remind myself in my lowest moments.

It was a struggle to lie perfectly still on that cold metal table in that pitch-black room as the machines around me sparked and whirred to life, zooming right up in my face until they were almost on top of me, claustrophobically covering my body from shoulder to chest. Meanwhile the radiation techs rushed out of the room and closed the heavy metal door behind them to avoid the beams of invisible energy that invaded my body, seeking to kill any lingering cancer cells while also killing healthy cells as collateral damage. As I lay there, I tried not to cry. The tears would come later, alone in my car, where I could cry freely, and no one would see.

Once I finished the thirty-six radiation treatments, Brian and the girls flew out to Arizona in November so we could spend Thanksgiving as a family with Brian's sister in Glendale. My mood should have been high as I celebrated the end of my treatment at last, but I was utterly miserable. The effects of radiotherapy are cumulative, so you don't feel the full impact on your body until some time after you finish your final session. I was wiped out—exhausted and sore, aching all over, and with dry, itchy, burning skin on my chest. Not only that, I'd had a PICC line (peripherally inserted central catheter) placed in a vein in my arm to deliver IV medication during my treatment and the arm had become badly infected, making me really sick for several weeks. At one point, I felt so vile during Thanksgiving that I had to lie down on the floor in the living room while everyone else sat on the sofa, watching football and eating leftovers. *Is this it?* I wondered. *Is this what life after cancer looks like?*

After Thanksgiving, Carly and Caitie flew back to Fort Wayne while Brian and I drove my car back home to Indiana, where I struggled to readjust to my old life. I'd been gone for seven months and I wasn't sure where I fit in anymore. Life, as I had known it, had gone on without me.

When you are diagnosed with cancer, it's like an atomic bomb goes off right in the center of your life, sending out shock waves of total destruction, and even if you somehow manage to survive the initial blast, once the mushroom cloud clears, you're left with the realization that you'll never be the person you were before you heard those fateful words, "You have cancer." Instead, you must somehow carve out a "new normal" that will allow you to at least feel functional again.

Cancer left me struggling with intense feelings of loss, fear, and anxiety that haunted me, night and day. *What am I doing with my life?* I kept asking myself. *I fought so hard for this second chance, and now what am I doing with it? Am I just going to throw it away on nothing, or am I actually going to accomplish something significant?* I was feeling better physically, but I just couldn't get back on track mentally.

I knew I should be grateful I survived cancer when so many other people don't, and I *was* grateful, but I still felt so lost, scared, and alone. What was the point of surviving a potentially deadly disease, if I was merely going through the motions and not really living my life with meaning and intention anymore?

Some survivors describe cancer as a "gift," a

wake-up call that inspires them to slow down, take stock of their lives, and stop sweating the small stuff. For those lucky people, made suddenly, shockingly aware how fragile, fleeting, and precious life is, cancer snaps everything into sharp focus, and daily life becomes vivid and magical, as even the smallest and most insignificant moments are infused with wonder and joy.

But in my case, cancer left me not so much with a new appreciation for life but instead with a pervasive, overwhelming sense of dread. *What if the cancer comes back? What if it's* already *back and I just don't know it? A few rogue cells could be floating around inside me this very moment, plotting their next attack.* Was this just a reprieve and not a pardon? A pause for breath before the cancer returned with a vengeance?

I've never felt completely comfortable with the concept of "cancer-free." How can anyone know for sure that he or she is completely free of cancer? I think we've all known someone who celebrated getting the all-clear and being deemed "cancer-free" after treatment, only to suffer a recurrence months or even years later and then have it end tragically. Part of me didn't want to believe I was "cured" and that my ordeal was truly over. It was like I didn't want to get my hopes up, only to be crushed if bad news came my way again.

I understood it was pointless, not to mention

deeply unhealthy, to wallow in these dark, depressing, negative thoughts. I needed something exciting and challenging to take me out of my funk and give me something to focus on besides my illness. But the trouble was, nothing sparked my interest or ignited my passion. The things I used to love just didn't appeal to me anymore.

Whenever I felt sad or down, which was often, I would catch myself thinking about Sweetie Pie. I still kept her picture on my phone, and sometimes I would bring it up just so I could stare into her deep, dark eyes and gaze at her innocent, soft-puppy-dog expression. I wondered how she was and hoped Pat and Jerry were loving her as much as I would have. *Marika, admit it—you've got some kind of weird puppy crush going on here,* I decided. *You either need to get a dog, or you need to move on.*

Meanwhile, I continued searching dogs on PetFinder. One morning after breakfast I was clicking through photos of available dogs when I came across a puppy named London, a beautiful black Lab, only a few months old, with deep, dark eyes; shiny, jet-black fur; a round, coal-black nose; and adorable floppy ears. *What a beauty,* I thought. I imagined holding her in my arms, feeling her round little body wiggle and squirm, yapping happily and covering my face with pink-tongued kisses. What a joy that would be. I continued scrolling through other dogs, but something kept bringing me back to London.

Feeling somewhat shy, at breakfast I showed London's picture to Brian and Caitie. "What do you think?" I asked, holding out my phone.

"She's okay," Brian said mildly, barely glancing at the screen.

"Cute," Caitie pronounced, briefly looking over as she buttered a piece of toast.

"Oh." I tried not to be disappointed. I knew I couldn't expect them to share my burgeoning interest in dogs.

"Her name's London and she's at the shelter. I'm thinking of going over there to take a look at her," I told Brian. "Wanna come along?"

"No, I don't think so," he replied. "We're leaving tomorrow anyway, so why bother?"

Brian was right. What was the point? Why get my hopes up, only to be crushed again? We were flying out the next morning to attend the national Jimmy John's convention, so adopting a dog right now was out of the question.

I had just decided I wouldn't go to see her either when Brian came back into the kitchen as I was rinsing dishes, cleared his throat, and said, "Marika, if you really want to see the dog, I'll go with you."

Yes! I was so excited as we grabbed our coats, climbed into our SUV, and pulled out of the garage. Even though I was sure there was no way we could bring her home today, maybe there was a teeny, tiny corner of my heart that was thinking, *Well, maybe, if we really bond with her, we could fill out the paperwork and put the adoption on hold until after we get back from our trip.* Something was drawing me to this little dog; I couldn't put my finger on exactly what it was, but I just felt such a deep and powerful connection that I couldn't ignore.

It didn't take us long to get to Fort Wayne Animal Care & Control, a sprawling, single-story, brown-brick complex on Hillegas Road, northwest of downtown Fort Wayne. My heart was thumping as we parked and went inside, following the PET ADOPTIONS sign to the front desk. The complex opened at noon to view the animals and arrange adoptions, and it was only 12:15 when we got there.

The receptionist at the front desk greeted us warmly. "Hello. What can I do for you today?" she asked.

"We're here to see London," I replied. "She's a little black Lab I saw on PetFinder."

The woman turned, typed something on her computer, frowned, then looked up at me apologetically. "I'm really sorry," she said, "but someone just adopted London. She's not here anymore."

"Oh," I managed to squeak out. My heart felt crushed again.

"It's okay." Brian squeezed my arm. "It's not like we were going to take her home."

"I know. I just wanted to meet her, that's all." I felt so foolish and tried to stifle my tears. I felt as bad as I had when I missed the chance to adopt Sweetie Pie, like something beautiful and precious had been ripped away from me forever, leaving in its place a huge, empty void, a hollow spot in the center of my chest.

"Do you want to look around a little bit?" Brian asked.

"Sure." I shrugged. "We made the trip here, so why not?"

Brian and I did a quick walk-through of the shelter and saw so many beautiful dogs, but I barely looked at any of them, I was in such a fog. My heart was broken, and I was frustrated with myself for reacting so emotionally.

As we got in the SUV to go home, I burst into tears. I thought, *What's wrong with me? I knew we weren't going to adopt her today.* I just wanted to meet her and see what she was like. *Marika, get a grip. You gotta pull yourself together.*

After Brian and I returned from the Jimmy John's convention a few days later, I continued looking at dogs on PetFinder. For some reason I was drawn to the pit bulls, even though I knew almost nothing about the breed, other than their reputation as dangerous, unpredictable animals. *That sounds like a terrible match for me,* I thought, and yet, in the photos these dogs looked so strong, so intelligent and loyal. I was convinced there was another side to this misunderstood breed and I wanted to learn more.

Tuesday, February 9, 2016, was the day that my life changed forever, only this time, it was being changed for the better. My online search had led me to the Fort Wayne Pit Bull Coalition. They didn't have a location of their own, but they worked with pit bulls that were in local shelters, getting them into foster care and from there, into permanent homes. I really wanted to meet some of these dogs. According to the website, I could attend a meet and greet, but first I'd have to submit the adoption application and be approved.

I started to fill out the application online. The form was very comprehensive, asking not just for things like my name, birthdate, contact details, and history with animals, but also questions like, "Where will my animal sleep at night? Where will my pet stay when I'm not home during the day? If not employed, how will you provide vet care and general expenses for your new pet?"

I got about halfway through the form but then I stopped. *This isn't right,* I thought. *I'm not ready to adopt a dog, and especially not a pit bull. I haven't even talked it over with Brian and the girls. This is a major decision that would affect not just me but the whole family.* With this realization, I left the form half-completed on the screen and put my laptop into sleep mode while I made dinner.

That evening we were all sitting around the dinner table talking. I very tentatively mentioned the Pit Bull Coalition and that I was interested in meeting some of the dogs; a couple in particular had really caught my eye. "But first I'd need to fill out an adoption application and be approved, and I know we haven't really talked about that yet," I explained.

Brian sighed and said, "Just fill out the application, Marika, for God's sake." He sounded a bit annoyed, but he was probably just tired of hearing me going on about pit bulls and showing him pictures of cute dogs I saw online.

Okay! I made a little bargain with myself in that moment—if, when I go back to my computer, the application form is still open, I'll take that as a sign from the universe that this is meant to be. But if the page logged me out, I won't fill out the form. This might sound silly, but as always, I deferred to my trusty intuition.

I couldn't wait to finish eating and get back to my laptop. After dinner, I tiptoed into the room, pressed a key on the keyboard, and watched the screen surge back to life. *Yes!* The browser tab for the Fort Wayne Pit Bull Coalition was still open and the application had not timed out. *That's my sign!* I quickly filled in the rest of the form and felt a little trill of happiness as I hit the submit button.

That was Tuesday night. The next day, Wednesday, I heard nothing from the coalition. *They wouldn't reject me, would they?* I worried. Had I inadvertently put something on my application that raised a red flag? *Maybe it's not the universe telling me I shouldn't adopt a pit bull, maybe it's the Pit Bull Coalition (even worse!) telling me I'm not a good fit.*

By Thursday, I couldn't take it any longer. I had to know what was going on, so I emailed the coalition to confirm they received my application. They responded quickly, saying not only had they received my application, but I was approved for the meet and greet! "See you at the adoption event this Saturday," was the final line of the email.

This Saturday? I wasn't expecting it to be so soon. I was excited to meet the dogs, but also nervous. *What am I doing? Is this just too much, too quickly? I don't want to fall in love and then be disappointed. I don't want this to be Sweetie Pie and London all over again—my poor heart couldn't take it.*

I spent the rest of Thursday and then Friday on the Pit Bull Coalition website, looking at the dogs that were coming to the meet and greet. The coalition were bringing nine dogs to the event, and three of the younger females in particular caught my eye: Star, Anna, and Laverne. *I'm not going there to adopt one,* I reminded myself. *I'm just going to meet them, and see what pit bulls are really like.*

Saturday morning, February 13, dawned, and I was so nervous! And yet it felt so good to be excited about something, to have something going on that made my blood rush a little faster. I'd been so down since finishing radiation, meeting these dogs was one of the first things that made me focus on something other than my illness and the fear of it returning.

I was still in the bedroom getting ready that morning when Caitie shyly knocked on the door. "Hey, hon, what is it?" I asked.

"Can I come with you guys to the meet and greet?" she asked softly, tucking a strand of long blond hair behind her ear.

I was a little surprised; Caitie hadn't been interested in any of the dogs I had shown her online. She and I had been having a hard time connecting ever since I got back from Arizona, and it always seemed like we were walking on eggshells around each other, each afraid to say the wrong thing or make the wrong move that would shatter our very fragile mother-daughter detente. I was also surprised because Brian and I had helped Caitie find a used car to buy, and we were scheduled to pick it up later that day.

"Sure," I replied, "I'd love for you to come with us. But here's the thing—this is really important to me. We aren't going there to adopt a dog, and I don't want to feel pressured into getting a dog just because we're there. We can't afford to leave with the wrong dog. These things take time."

She said she understood, and like me, she just wanted to meet the dogs and see what they were like. I was so glad she was suddenly taking an interest in this, but I worried how she'd feel if I had to disappoint her once we got there and she fell in love with a dog that wasn't a good fit.

The meet and greet was taking place at Rural King, a large farm and home supply store that carries every item a Midwesterner might ever need, from hunting gear, chain saws, tackle boxes, gun safes, and manure spreaders to toys, cookware, and bedding.

I was so excited to see the dogs that we arrived at ten thirty a.m., even though the event didn't start until eleven. We parked the SUV and as we walked from the parking lot toward the store, I said a little prayer under my breath: *If it's meant to be, help me come home with the right dog. Guide me to my perfect match.*

The store was really busy with Saturday morning shoppers as we made our way down the aisles to the area where the Pit Bull Coalition had set up shop. I was hoping to see the three dogs I had picked out online—Star, Anna, and Laverne, but when I asked about Star, I was told, "Oh, Star's not here. Someone adopted her last night." *Oh.* I felt my heart go into that now-all-too-familiar free fall, careening toward my feet. *I'm too late again. Why does this keep happening? Well, at least there are two others . . .*

Next, I took a look at Anna and I knew right away she was not "the one." She was a beautiful dog, but she was so sad and so little. She'd just given birth to a litter of puppies, even though she was much too young to breed, barely more than a puppy herself. I knew instinctively her story would not be a happy one, and adopting her would only lead to heartbreak.

So with regret I moved on to Laverne, the third dog I hoped to meet. Laverne was a pit bull mix puppy, a female about seven months old. Laverne was adorable, mostly white with some gray spots. As cute as she was, she seemed to be a very nervous, excitable dog, jumping all over the place and barking like crazy. I knelt and stroked her head, hoping she would calm down, but she was a very hyper and needy girl, and I knew in my heart, if I got a dog, it would have to be one that was calm and relaxed.

I was so disappointed, but I told myself, *You just wanted to meet some of the dogs, and now you have. If your perfect dog is out there somewhere, you will find each other. You just gotta believe.*

Even though none of the three dogs proved to be a match, I wasn't ready to go home yet. Brian, Caitie, and I had just started browsing the aisles when out of the corner of my eye, I saw a fortysomething guy and his teenage kids come in with a pit bull puppy on a leash. *Hmmm, that dog's really cute,* I thought. *I wonder what his or her story is?*

I approached the guy and as soon as I got close enough, the dog rolled over, threw back her head, kicked her legs, and begged me to rub her belly. She was so happy, she just radiated joy. Even in this busy, loud, chaotic environment, she was so relaxed and so chill.

"Who do we have here?" I asked the man, who introduced himself as Gary.

Gary explained the dog's name was Shirley and she was Laverne's littermate. They had been abandoned a few weeks ago, dumped by the side of the road along a frozen field and left to die in the harsh Indiana winter. Fortunately, some kind person found the two pups in the nick of time and took them to Fort Wayne Animal Care & Control.

"From there, the Fort Wayne Pit Bull Coalition arranged for them to be fostered, which is how we got Shirley," Gary said. "We've only had her for a couple of days, but she's been great. I've got six kids and three other dogs, and nothing seems to bother her. She's about seven months old now. She's going to be a fantastic dog for someone."

I knelt down close to Shirley's face, noticing her sweet, golden-amber eyes and warm, smiling expression. She was a gorgeous girl, mostly white with caramel-tan markings, especially in an adorable patch over her left eye. "Yes, you are such a pretty girl." I rubbed her belly, which sent her straight to canine nirvana. She tossed her head back, limbs akimbo, and pedaled her legs like crazy, big paws kicking the air.

It broke my heart to think how cruelly she and her sister had been treated. And who knew if she'd been abused before that? And yet she seemed to have suffered no long-term effects. *She's special.* I just knew it instinctively. *This dog has a special soul.*

"Hey Mark, look at this one," a woman called from behind me. She knelt beside me and rubbed Shirley's belly, elbowing me aside. The woman's husband came closer and bent down to look at the dog. "Wow! She's really cute. And she seems so friendly."

I was annoyed at these people muscling in on "my" dog. *Go away. I was here first,* I thought. I didn't want this couple to steal Shirley away before I even had a chance to get to know her. Something told me she might be "the one," but I knew I had to act quickly or risk losing her, just like I'd lost Sweetie Pie and London.

"Do you mind if I take Shirley on a little walk around the store?" I asked Gary. "Just to see how she reacts to different things." In truth, I wanted to get her away from the annoying couple and have some time with her alone.

"Sure, no problem." Gary handed me her leash. Shirley popped right up off the floor and fell into perfect step beside me as I walked her up and down the aisles of rakes and hoes and wheelbarrows. She was so alert and curious, sniffing everything on the shelves, then turning back to look at me for encouragement. Kids came up and wanted to pet her, and she so patiently accepted and returned their affection. The store was crowded with shoppers and shopping carts and booming with voices and announcements over the loudspeaker, and yet nothing seemed to faze Shirley.

She's still just a puppy, I thought. *And yet she's so calm and has a wonderful disposition. She had such a rough start in life, but she's so sweet, so gentle and calm. What am I going to do? I have to make up my mind.*

If I didn't take her today, someone else surely would. *A dog like this won't be in foster care for long. Who am I fooling? She's everything I've been looking for. She is the one. I just know it. It's time to take that leap of faith.* I couldn't imagine myself *not* going home with this dog. In my mind, she became mine in that moment, and I saw our future unfold before us.

I'm getting this dog! But there was still one

roadblock, and it was a significant one. I walked Shirley back to where Brian was waiting, near the other dogs. He looked bored, scrolling through something on his phone.

"Well, what do you think of her?" I asked, my heart in my throat. This was such an important decision, I didn't want to pressure him to say yes just to appease me or not hurt my feelings.

He knelt down and stroked her head, then rubbed behind her ears. "She looks like a nice dog." He shrugged. "If that's what you want to do, go ahead and adopt her."

Yes! Yes! Yes! Brian's response might not have sounded like a ringing endorsement to most people, but given his low-key nature, it was good enough for me.

Then Caitie came over, and her big blue-green eyes lit up the moment she saw the dog. "Mom! She's so cute!" she squealed as Shirley jumped up and covered her with kisses. "I love her already!!" Caitie sank to the floor and wrapped her arms around Shirley's shoulders in a moment of true bonding as they loved on each other. I hadn't seen my daughter so happy in months, and that sealed the deal.

I'm going to do it! I'm going to adopt this dog! Shirley and I had connected, no doubt about it, and this was what I had been waiting for. You just know when it's right, and I knew. I was falling again, but this time, I wasn't falling through the floors of an abandoned building—I was falling in love.

Having made the decision, we walked Shirley over to the representative from the Pit Bull Coalition and told her we were ready to adopt Shirley. Caitie and I sat down on the cold linoleum floor, right there in the middle of the busy store, and Shirley plopped right down in our laps, as if she'd been our dog forever. We stroked her belly and rubbed her ears and told her what a good dog she was. Her tail wagged like crazy as she rolled back and forth and slobbered us with kisses, just soaking up all the love.

Does she already know us? I wondered. *Has she been looking for me as long as I've been looking for her? What angels conspired to send her here to us today?*

The representative from the Pit Bull Coalition knelt down in front of us and began reading aloud the contract I needed to sign in order to make the adoption official, but I barely listened. I was so thrilled, gazing down at the beautiful white-and-caramel dog cuddling between me and Caitie—the dog that was coming home to be ours forever. In that moment, there was no cancer, there was no family struggle, there was no fear or anxiety about the future—in that moment, there was only love. Tomorrow was St. Valentine's Day, and this was the sweetest, most beautiful gift I could have gotten.

Shirley was already spayed and had all her shots so the adoption fee was $150, but we paid $200, to help cover costs for other dogs in foster care. We picked out a crate for Shirley, then walked her out to the parking lot. Brian opened the SUV's back door to get her in, but suddenly this happy, relaxed, very chill dog was terrified. *Oh no,* I thought. *Was I totally wrong about her?* Pushing my fears aside, I tried to coax her to jump up into the SUV, but she wasn't having any of it.

"Come on," I said gently as I slipped my arms around her midsection and tried to lift her. Even though she was only about seven months old, she was a solidly built, good-size dog, strong and stocky and already close to sixty pounds. The more I tried to lift her, the more fearful she became, whimpering and shaking, with her butt firmly planted on the ground. I just about threw my back out and still couldn't get her into the SUV.

Seeing me struggle, Brian stepped in to help, scooping her up in his arms and depositing her in the back seat. She was still nervous and scared, so Caitie climbed into the seat beside her and held her close, stroking her gently and whispering in her ear. That seemed to calm the dog a bit, but she was still shaking, her amber eyes round and terrified.

Inside, I was scared and shaking, too, but I tried

not to show it. *Please don't let this be another mistake,* I prayed. *Please don't tell me I got the wrong dog again.* But then I reasoned, *Of course she's nervous. We've taken her away from the people she was just getting comfortable with, away from everything that was familiar. Let's just give her some time.*

As we headed toward PetSmart to pick up food, toys, and other supplies, I couldn't resist snapping a picture on my phone of Shirley in the back seat, being cuddled and comforted by Caitie. The two of them looked adorable, wrapped up in each other's arms. I sent the photo to Betsy back in Arizona. She texted back immediately.

Beautiful! she wrote. *Thinking of adopting her?*

I typed back: *We just did.*

Betsy: *Hooray!*

Now we just needed a new name. To me, this dog didn't look like a "Shirley." Nothing wrong with that name, it just didn't seem to suit her. I texted Betsy to see what she thought.

How about Stella? she wrote back.

Stella! Not only did I like the name, but coincidentally, one of my mom's best friends when I was growing up was named Stella, and I had always really liked her, so the name brought back fond memories.

As Brian drove, I turned around in my seat so I was facing Caitie and our new pit bull pup, her head bowed shyly, forehead wrinkled, and her shoulders still quivering. She had stolen my heart, no doubt about it. I was utterly and absolutely head-over-heels in love. I sighed. "Hello, Stella," I announced. "And welcome to the Meeks family. You're one of us now."

The Meeks family: Stella, Marika, Brian, Caitie, Carly.

CHAPTER FIVE

Stella Settles In

February 2016

I was so nervous when we brought Stella home that first day. *What if she doesn't like us? What if she can't settle in? What if she's more dog than we can handle? And what happens if pit bulls really* are *as dangerous as everyone says?*

I couldn't bear the thought that we might have to give her back if things didn't work out. I was already falling in love with this dog I had just met. *It's going to take a leap of faith, on all our parts, to make this work. Then again, the past three years of my life have been nothing but one big leap of faith . . .*

Brian parked in our driveway and we all got out of the SUV, except Stella, who cowered in the back seat, head down, looking scared. "Come on, girl, we're home now. Come on out," Caitie and I coaxed, but to no avail. Finally, Brian reached inside, scooped her up in his arms, and gently pulled her out.

She was still nervous and shaking as we brought her into the house, but then we gave her free rein and let her run around a bit, rushing from room to room, up and down the stairs, exploring every corner and sniffing everything in sight. Her anxiety gave way to curiosity, and I considered that a good sign.

"I think we need to establish some ground rules," Brian announced as Caitie and I got busy setting up Stella's crate, unpacking her food and toys, and just generally making the house Stella-friendly. "Before she develops any bad habits. We want to start her off on the right foot."

I was surprised but couldn't really disagree. "Sure," I replied. "What do you have in mind?"

"Well, first of all, I don't think she should be allowed up on the couch or on any of the furniture."

Oh. The images in my head of me cuddling

Stella on the couch, on the bed, anyplace I could grab hold of her soft face and wiggly butt, were quickly quashed. But I knew Brian was probably right. As a pit bull, Stella was destined to be a large, powerful dog one day, and we needed to start training her for good behavior right from day one.

"Okay. Anything else?" I asked.

"Not yet," he answered, "but I'll let you know if I think of anything."

"All right." *Is Brian really okay with this? I wondered as he walked away. Did he just say yes to Stella because he saw how much I was drawn to her? Now he's stuck being a dog-dad, whether he likes it or not. Was I not being fair in considering his feelings? Well, maybe she'll win him over. I can only hope he'll fall in love with her, too.*

Once Stella had finished her initial survey of her new home (no complaints—at least none that she voiced!) and been outside to do her business, I sat down on the floor in the living room with my legs crossed and my back against the couch, since we just agreed that she wouldn't be allowed *on* the couch. "Come here, girl. Come here, Stella," I called softly, and she trotted over, plopping herself right down in my lap as if we'd been friends forever.

"Let's get to know each other better, shall we?" She relaxed right away with her chin balanced on

119

my knee and her tail softly slapping the floor in a steady, staccato rhythm. I stroked her head and back and shoulders, feeling her short, stiff-but-soft fur, and then rubbed her little caramel-brown ears and massaged her head.

"You're a beautiful girl," I whispered, tracing the patterns of her coat, the mostly caramel brown of her back and hips, the mostly white of her chest and tummy with a few tan spots, and the adorable fawn-colored patch over her left eye. Her eyes were such a beautiful deep amber, a little sad in expression but also sweet and steady, and I could feel myself falling into them forever. *This dog is ready to trust. She's ready to give and receive love. She just needs someone—us—to show her how.*

I reached behind me and pulled the fringed cotton throw off the couch and wrapped it over my shoulders and around Stella. This way we could cuddle even closer, while fending off the damp February draft that whispered from the doors and windows and tiptoed across the floor. "How do you like that?" I tucked the throw under Stella's belly. "You don't have a lot of fur, so we've got to keep you warm."

When Caitie saw us cuddling like this, she came over and crawled under the blanket beside me, wrapping one end over her shoulder. Stella scooted over, repositioning herself so she was spread between both our laps. For a while, we just sat there, the three of us, lazing together and petting Stella, not saying a word, just enjoying the gentle closeness of the moment.

I have missed this so much I realized as my throat swelled and tears filled my eyes. I swallowed hard. I didn't want to cry and have Caitie think I was upset. *All those months I spent at the clinic in Arizona, when I was so sick and scared and lonely. All I wanted was to feel safe and warm and happy, close to my family again. I just wanted to feel normal. This kind of normal.* Suddenly, cancer seemed to be a million miles away; the disease had no hold over me today. How long had it been since I was able to say that?

"So what's going on this week?" I asked Caitie, trying not to break the spell Stella had cast, but seizing this opportunity to talk to my daughter in this close, casual, stress-free environment. Maybe this could be the first step in rebuilding our relationship.

She shrugged. "Not much. I'm supposed to be studying for a history quiz on Tuesday." She scratched Stella behind the ears. "The Civil War—First Battle of Bull Run."

"Do you think you're ready?"

Now she grinned, pushing up her glasses. "July 21, 1861. The first major battle between Union and Confederate forces."

"And who won?"

"The Confederates."

"Ah."

"It was a pretty decisive victory," she explained. "Neither side was well prepared, and none of the officers were experienced . . ."

I'm not sure how long we sat there on the floor talking with Stella zonked out between us, but it was absolute bliss. We could just talk; nothing felt forced or artificial. It didn't seem like I was grilling her, or pressuring her to open up to me. The conversation didn't get too heavy—we mostly stuck to simple things like school and friends and what she'd been watching on TV. But I was on cloud nine, just being able to sit so close, feeling her shoulder pressed against mine, and listening to her talk about what was going on in her world. So much had changed for both of us since I'd been gone. It was going to take time to find ourselves and our relationship again. *Baby steps,* I thought. *This is step one. And maybe with Stella's help . . .*

Caitie, Stella, and I were still cuddling in front of the couch when Brian walked in, looked at the three of us, and shook his head. "We're supposed to go pick up Caitie's car." He gave a wry smile. "But I'm guessing you two probably don't want to go anywhere now."

Both Caitie and I burst out laughing. "That's the furthest thing from my mind at the moment," I admitted. At first, Stella was startled by our laughing, but then she understood and wagged her tail. *We're going to surround you with love and laughter,* I promised Stella. *That's the gift we can give you for bringing so much happiness into our home.*

I worried how Stella would do that first night with us. I thought, after having so much fun running around the house all day and snuggling, it might be hard to get her into her crate once it was time for bed. But she was a trouper, darting right inside when we opened the door, motioned her in, then closed and locked it behind her, and she didn't cry, whine, bark, or complain all night. *She's such a good dog,* I thought. *She's not even trained yet and still she behaves so well. But does she have another side that we haven't seen yet?* I wondered. *She is a pit bull, after all.*

After Brian and I crawled into bed and turned off the light, I rose up on one elbow and looked at him beside me in the dark. We were still negotiating our "new normal" since I'd returned from Arizona, and I wanted to make sure we were good.

"Brian, how do you really feel about Stella? You can tell me the truth."

"She seems like a really nice dog," he said evenly. "And she's very well behaved for a puppy," he added.

"Right, but are you okay with us adopting her? I know you never wanted us to have a dog. I don't want it to seem like I pushed this on you."

He sighed, and I felt nervous, waiting for him to speak.

"She makes you happy," he said at last. "I can't remember the last time I saw you look so happy, so healthy and relaxed as you did this afternoon. If she makes you happy, that's good enough for me."

I lay back down and closed my eyes, feeling somewhat better. *Brian still doesn't sound thrilled,* I admitted to myself, *but at least he's open to this. Now I'm counting on Stella to work her magic on him, too, like she has on Caitie and me. And I have a dog now! The dog of my dreams. I can't believe I get to be Stella's forever mama!*

For the first time in a long time, I went to sleep that night not thinking about cancer, sickness, or the fear of my disease returning. I went to bed thinking about Stella, and to me, that was a dream come true.

It was still pitch-black outside when the alarm went off at five the next morning. Even though it was a Sunday, Brian was heading out to do his rounds at our Jimmy John's restaurants. After I was first diagnosed with cancer, Brian took over running all four of our locations in the greater Fort Wayne area, and that was a huge undertaking. He spent an hour and a half every morning, seven days a week, driving to each location, making sure the managers and staff were all there, prep work was underway, and the bread was baking. (If the bread, which took three hours to bake, wasn't in the oven by six a.m., we wouldn't be ready to open by ten thirty and we'd be behind schedule all day, struggling to catch up.)

I felt so guilty for not being able to help more with the restaurants, especially since it was me who started the business in the first place, but when I had tried to go back to work after my initial cancer treatment, I'd become so stressed, exhausted, and overwhelmed that Brian had to "fire me" in order to protect my health and my sanity.

I was still half-asleep when, dressed and ready to go, he leaned over the bed to kiss me good-bye. "Hmmmm, see you later," I mumbled, sinking back into the pillow and pulling the winter quilt up to my chin. February mornings in Indiana are decidedly brisk, and I wanted to maintain as much warmth as possible before I, too, would have to get up and start my day.

A little while later, my drowsy reverie was broken by Stella, this big, happy puppy, bounding into the bedroom and catapulting herself up onto the bed, rolling and wiggling, tongue wagging, begging me for cuddles.

"Hello, girl! How's my Stella? Did you have

a good night?" As I rubbed her belly, she rolled over and her thick paws pedaled madly in the air. As would become his custom, Brian had let Stella out of her crate and taken her for a walk before releasing her back inside the house before he left for work.

She knew exactly where to find me, the source of all the cuddles. Once she settled down, I pulled her under the covers with me and just held her close. What a blissful way to start the day! *I never want to get out of bed now,* I thought. *I just want to stay here like this forever.*

Stella became a member of our family amazingly quickly, even if there were a few bumps in the road. She was such a happy, good-natured dog, right from day one. She loved to do "zoomies"— when Brian would open the door to her crate, she'd come bursting out like a shot out of a cannon, run circles around all the furniture, her paws slip-sliding on the tiles until she tumbled over, limbs flying everywhere, before she popped up and started zooming again.

Brian's rule about Stella not being allowed on the couch only lasted about forty-eight hours. On the third day we had her home, I was again sitting and snuggling with her on the floor in front of the couch, which wasn't the most comfortable place to sit, especially when it was cold and drafty, and my legs were falling asleep from being crossed for so long. Brian noticed my discomfort and said, "Do you want to let her sit on the sofa?"

"Only if you think it's okay," I replied. I didn't want us to break all his rules at once, even though I had been secretly hoping he would ask.

"I guess it's okay," he offered with a shrug. Stella and I immediately bounced up, settled our butts on the couch, and curled up again under the blanket. To this day, Stella absolutely loves couches, and that's the first place she'll go in any room.

Every day with Stella offered a new discovery. For example, I was surprised to find out that Stella was scared of being on a leash. The first time I took her out, I realized that even though she was seven months old, she had never been out for a walk before. *What was your life like before we found you?* I wanted to ask her. *How did your people treat you?* Sometimes I wished she could talk to me and describe what she had been through before being dumped in a field to die, but other times I was glad I didn't know the details—they would have broken my heart, without a doubt.

I had to start from scratch to teach Stella how to walk on a leash, and it took her a while to get the hang of it—she kept walking in front of me, blocking my path, or she'd rush ahead and then stop suddenly, or cut me off so I almost tripped over her.

It also took some time and effort to help get Stella over her fear of cars. She'd been so scared of the SUV that first day we brought her home from Rural King, and that fear seemed to linger even after she settled in. To address this, I would let her loose in the garage, open the SUV's back passenger door (the vehicle was not running at the time!), and sit in the back seat holding a treat of some baked chicken.

Fortunately, Stella's love of chicken outweighed her fear of cars, so when I'd offer her the treat, she'd jump into the back seat with me. But only long enough to snatch the treat from my hand, then she'd jump right out again. Each time we did it, I'd make her stay inside the SUV with me a little longer. Eventually, once she was comfortable getting in and out of the vehicle, I started taking her on little drives that got progressively longer as she felt more and more relaxed.

On one of our longer drives, I could feel the first hint of the winter chill lifting across the Midwest. The sun was finally shining again and I had the radio blasting. As I sang along to the Red Hot Chili Peppers' "Dani California," I glanced in the rearview mirror and saw Stella sitting up in the back seat, nose pressed against the window as she watched intently as the world sped by. "Hey, Stella—what are you looking at?" I asked her, and laughed as she turned to give me a quizzical look, as if she was preparing to answer.

If it wasn't for Stella, I wouldn't be out here, driving around, singing my lungs out with the sun warming my face, I suddenly realized. Instead I'd probably be stuck at home, on the couch and still in my pajamas, trapped in that miserable funk I just couldn't get out of, wanting to do things but feeling overwhelmed with no idea how or where to begin.

I desperately wanted to make the most of my post-cancer second chance, but I felt paralyzed and powerless to take even the first step. I had been so, so broken by the experience. And I was feeling so guilty, like such a fraud, for not being the inspirational cancer warrior-survivor people could admire and look up to. I felt like a failure. Just like in my childhood, I felt like I basically just sucked at life. Whoever would have guessed that it would take a nervous pit bull puppy and her fear of cars to get me out of my head, out of the darkness, and back into life?

In those early days with Stella, she often showed us what a sensitive soul she could be. Stella loved to hang out with Caitie in Caitie's bedroom, where they could cuddle, roughhouse, and play games. A few times, Stella became overstimulated and vomited, which isn't unusual for a puppy with a growing tummy. The first time it happened, Caitie came downstairs to tell me, and when I went up to help her clean up, we found Stella utterly distraught, hiding in the corner of the bedroom with her head bowed, as if she'd just done the most horrible, unforgivable thing in the world and was waiting for her punishment.

"Hey, Stella, it's okay," I said softly, slowly approaching her. I didn't want to frighten her or upset her any more than she already was. "Don't worry, girl. I know you didn't mean it. Your tummy's just a bit upset, that's all. Happens to everybody once in a while."

I hoped my voice might soothe her. She looked up with her sad, sorrowful, deep amber eyes just as I reached out to touch her, but before I could make contact, she jumped up, bolted out of the room, and scrambled downstairs, where we later found her in the living room cowering behind the couch, shaking and staring at the wall.

Caitie's face was ashen. "I'm sorry, Mom," she whispered. "I didn't mean to get her all riled up."

I went over, wrapped my arm around Caitie and gave her a big hug, kissing the top of her head. "It's not your fault, hon," I reassured her. "She's still a puppy; she's still learning her limits. She'll be fine." I loved that Caitie and Stella had bonded so quickly, and that my daughter seemed happier, less anxious or depressed than she'd been in recent months. I didn't want anything to stand in the way of their developing relationship.

When I went downstairs after cleaning up the mess, Stella was still behind the couch. I tried to comfort her, but she was inconsolable. I finally decided it would be less stress on her if I just let her have some time and space to herself and didn't push her to engage. It wasn't until after dinner, when Brian and I were sitting on the couch watching TV, that Stella finally reemerged, tentatively, looking extremely remorseful, head still bowed.

"It's okay, Stella, you're not in trouble," I said softly. "You didn't do anything wrong." She looked skeptical, but finally she jumped up on the couch to join us, curling up in the space between our legs, and I petted her gently, long strokes across her back and shoulders until finally, she seemed to relax.

"I wish I could tell you it's okay and have you understand my words," I told her. "But since I can't tell you, I have to show you what it means to be loved and cared for, and what it means to be forgiven. I'm not sure what people did to you in your past, but we aren't those people. I promise, we will never hurt you."

She looked up at me then, and even though her eyes looked sad and uncertain, ever so slowly, her tail began to wag.

As easy as Stella was in those early days, I still had some lingering doubts and questions because she was a pit bull. I knew we were dealing with an unknown entity, so I was super committed to making sure she was trained and got tons of exercise to burn off any excess energy. Still, I wondered and worried if her sweet, gentle personality would eventually change, hardening and toughening as she grew older and stronger.

Once, after a late spring snow, I was in the front yard clearing the front walkway when Stella ran over and attacked the shovel, barking like mad and trying to bite the metal edge. It was actually funny to watch because she was so focused on stopping this evil implement tossing snow off the pavement, but I knew that someday, it might not be so comical. *What happens when she's bigger, and so much stronger than me, and I can't control her anymore?*

And sometimes, too, when we'd play tug-of-war with one of her toys, she'd show a more intense side of her personality, bearing down and determined to tear the toy from my hand. She was already so strong and still only seven months old. *Oh my God, I've got a pit bull,* I'd think, and none of the stuff I was reading online about the breed made me feel any better.

My fears came to a head a few weeks later, when Brian and I had to take Stella to the vet for a possible bladder infection. They had to keep her in for a while so they could draw some urine via a catheter and do a culture. I couldn't believe how much I missed her, just in those few hours she was away from home. The house was so quiet and empty without her presence. *How did I ever get by without her?* I wondered. *It's only been a few weeks, and yet I can't imagine not being Stella's mama. What is the magic power of dogs that allows love to happen so quickly?*

I was so excited when it was time to go pick her up and bring her home, but when we got to the vet clinic, the tech, Josie, led us back to one of the exam rooms with a very serious, solemn look on her face. *Oh no,* I thought. *Please don't tell me Stella is seriously ill. Please let her be okay.*

"Marika, Brian, I need to talk to you," Josie said gently, closing the door behind her.

"All right," I said, trying to keep my voice steady and hide the rising panic surging through my chest. I felt like I was having a flashback, remembering all my horrible doctor and hospital appointments, when it seemed I only ever received dire news. Being scared for Stella took me right back to those moments, triggering feelings of terror, anxiety, and powerlessness. "Is something wrong with Stella?" I asked.

She pursed her lips and sighed deeply. "There's no easy way to say this, but I'm sorry to have to tell you, she's a very, very dangerous dog."

I gasped. "Oh my God! What happened? Did she hurt someone? Is she okay?"

"Nothing's happened—yet," Josie warned ominously. "But she's a pit bull, and they are a dangerous and unpredictable breed. You and your family have no idea what you've gotten yourselves into."

She paused. Brian looked skeptical while I was too stunned to speak. "I'm telling you this for your own good, before something tragic happens. Before someone—you, your family, or someone else, maybe an innocent child—gets hurt or killed. Do you realize that, if Stella attacks someone, there'd be a lawsuit and you could lose your home, your business, all your possessions, everything? I've seen it happen too many times with dogs like this." She sighed, shaking her head.

"They look so cute and innocent when they're puppies, but then things change," she continued. "Have you even talked to your insurance agent about adding Stella to your homeowner's policy? Most won't even provide coverage for these dangerous dogs . . ."

She went on and on for what seemed like twenty minutes, lecturing us about the danger of pit bulls, but I was no longer listening; I was so stressed and upset. I had been worried about adopting a pit bull, and now I was hearing that every bad thing I had read in the media and online was true. *What have I done? My God— what have I done?*

134

When Josie finally stopped talking, she left to go get Stella.

"Oh my God, Brian, what have we done?" I exclaimed. "We adopted a dog that's going to ruin our lives. What are we gonna do now?"

I could see that he was taking the news in stride. "I'm not buying it," he replied. "Stella's not dangerous. I just think Josie is trying to scare us."

"Well, it's working!" I snapped.

Josie came back into the exam room with Stella on a leash by her side. "The culture does show that she has a minor bladder infection," she explained. "The doctor prescribed some antibiotics for you to give her twice a day with food."

I was listening, but the words barely registered. Now, when I looked at Stella, I didn't see my beautiful, smiling Stella, I saw this monster, this ticking time bomb we had apparently adopted, disguised as the cutest, gentlest puppy I had ever met.

"Come here, Stelly, how are you doing?" I asked softly, beckoning her closer. I felt sick to my stomach. Looking at Stella, she appeared to be the same sweet pup as ever, and her tail wagged madly as I stroked her head. I already loved her so much, but now everything seemed to be in jeopardy. *What will we say to Caitie? This will break her heart. She's already bonded with Stella. We all have.*

I was in a daze as we walked Stella out to the parking lot, opened the SUV, and got her to jump in the back. "There you go . . . there's my good girl," I reassured her as I closed the door behind her. She looked at me, her eyes bright, tongue lolling in her doggie-smile, but I could barely meet her loving, trusting gaze. *I'll never be able to look at her the same way now,* I thought.

As I climbed into the passenger seat, Brian started the SUV and pulled out of the parking lot. My heart ached and my head was spinning. *My God, what have we done? What have we done?* I was beyond distraught. *I brought this massive liability into our family home, put everyone and everything I love at risk, and now she'll have to be managed for the rest of her life. This could be the worst mistake I've ever made. I wish we'd never done this. I wish we'd never adopted Stella.*

(photo courtesy Erica + Jon Photography)

Marika, age four, with older sisters Michelle, left, and Martine, right. *(photo courtesy Peter Harrison)*

Marika, age three, in England. *(photo courtesy Peter Harrison)*

Marika, modeling as a teen. *(photo courtesy Peter Harrison)*

Stella and the dad who was "sure he didn't want a dog."

Adoption Day! Stella finds her fur-ever family.
February 13, 2016. *(photo courtesy Robert Snyder)*

Three Sleeping Beauties! Carly, Stella, Caitie.

Carly home from college, with Stella and Marika. *(photo courtesy Brian Meeks)*

Carly and Stella.

(photo courtesy Erica + Jon Photography)

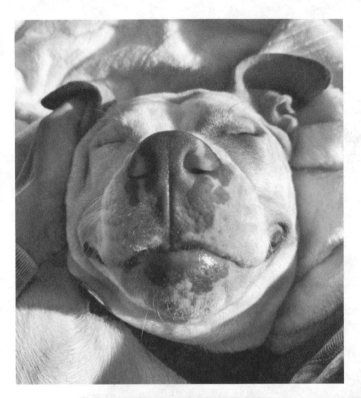

Caitie,
Stella, Carly,
Christmas
2017.

Stella and her foster sister Roxy.

148

(photo courtesy Erica + Jon Photography)

Caitie and Stella.

CHAPTER SIX

Stella Works Her Magic

Spring 2016

The drive home from the vet clinic seemed to take forever, and I barely noticed any of the landmarks or familiar sights we passed along the way. I was distraught as Josie's words rushed through my head in a seemingly never-ending loop: *A very dangerous dog. Liability. Injury. Insurance.* And yet, when I turned and glanced into the back seat, I just saw Stella, my Stella, with her amber eyes and sweet expression, the same beautiful pup I'd fallen in love with.

"Don't worry," Brian tried to console me as we waited at a stoplight. "Josie probably tells that to everybody, whether their dog is dangerous or not. They just want to cover their bases. We'll keep an eye on Stella. She'll be fine."

I appreciated Brian's confidence, and I knew he wouldn't have said it if he didn't mean it—if he truly believed our family was in any danger, he'd be the first to insist on returning Stella to the Pit Bull Coalition, regardless of how deeply Stella had burrowed herself into our home and our hearts.

"You're probably right. I just don't want to have this constant question mark hanging over our heads." I sighed. "I don't want to always be holding my breath, waiting for the other shoe to drop and Stella to show a different side to her personality." I suddenly realized how similar this fear was to the fear I'd been feeling since I'd finished cancer treatment. *Everything's okay at this moment, but for how long? When will this fragile sense of peace come crashing down?* I worried about getting sick again, and now I had to worry about my gentle, loving puppy turning into a monster, hurting us or someone else. *It feels like I just can't catch a break . . .*

Later that night, we were all at home and Caitie and I were relaxing on my bed, watching TV with Stella curled up at our feet. Stella was still a little groggy from the anesthetic she'd received at the vet's, but overall she seemed to be doing okay. *That's my Stella,* I thought. *And she's done nothing wrong. She doesn't deserve to have me look at her differently, just because of what Josie said.*

I glanced over at the clock. "Caitie, it's getting late. It's time for Stella to go to bed," I said sleepily. "Can you take her to her crate?"

"Sure." Caitie sat up, reached toward Stella's collar, and was about to grab hold when Stella's head swiveled toward Caitie and she opened her mouth, baring her teeth. A small gesture, but clear in meaning and intention. Caitie quickly pulled back her hand, a shocked look on her face. I doubt Stella meant any harm; most dogs don't like being grabbed by the collar, and Stella was probably feeling tired and cranky because of the anesthetic, but her reaction terrified me, tapping into my worst fears.

"You! Go to your bed right now!" I ordered Stella. "Right this minute!" She wasn't used to hearing me use that tone of voice, and it must have shocked her because she rose, jumped off

153

the bed, raced downstairs and into her crate, where she lay down with a sad look on her face and her chin resting on her paws.

Now I have to be worried about everything, I thought bitterly. *I'll have to monitor her so closely, regardless of where we are or what she's doing. How will I ever be able to trust this dog again?*

I had a hard time falling asleep that night, I was so consumed with worries about Stella, and then, when I did finally fall asleep in the early morning hours, I was plagued by nightmares.

* * * * *

In this dream, I'm alone, driving along a dark, dusty country highway with just one car in front of me, when a dog springs out of the weeds by the side of the road and darts into the right-hand lane. With a screech of the tires, the car in front jerks to the shoulder, barely missing the dog. I pull over and watch in horror as the scene plays out in slow motion. The dog, momentarily stunned, gathers itself and trots off, unhurt. I gasp, finally finding my breath.

The driver turns back, I assume to help, but the way he swerves, stops, and jumps out of his car, leaving the engine running, shows his intention is far more sinister. He stalks toward me and I quickly throw my car into drive and peel away. Whew—that was a close one, I think. I've only just stopped shaking when I glance in my rearview mirror and see headlights, burning through the haze, in the distance but gaining on me with great speed. It's him. I know it's him . . .

He follows me all the way back home. I pull in the driveway, jump out of the car, rush inside and try to lock the door, but he's on the other side now, grabbing the doorknob, banging hard and trying to shoulder in. We struggle but I know it's too late, I can't hold him back, he's coming inside. I have no choice but to run. The next I know, I've been knocked to the ground near my bed. Stella! She's here, hackles up, growling, warning him off.

Now he's standing over me and I try to fight him off. Stella, in a flash, lunges at him, tearing into his chest. Furious, the man throws his arm at her, knocking her to the ground, and she yelps in pain.

"Leave, Stella! Leave! Just go!" I scream. "Run!" I'm terrified he will hurt her. If I can't save myself, please, God, let me at least save her . . .

* * * * *

The nightmare was cut short as my eyes flew open and I woke with a start, back home in my own bed, with my heart pounding and my head spinning. I grabbed on to the sheets to steady myself and took several deep breaths, trying to calm down. The dream was so real, so present, I struggled to surface from its oppressive

155

weight, clawing my way back to reality. *Why am I still so tormented?* I asked. *When will these nightmares go away?* If I didn't dream about my illness, I dreamed about being attacked, or other terrible events. I thought, now that I was home and healthy, I wouldn't feel so victimized, but I still so often woke to fears and anxieties that threatened to consume me.

Suddenly, my dark thoughts were interrupted by the music of four paws, and all those toenails, scrambling across the kitchen floor, circling a few enthusiastic zoomies, and rushing up the stairs. Brian must have just gotten back from his early morning walk with Stella because moments later, she rushed into the room and jumped on the bed beside me.

"Good morning, Stella. How's my girl today?" She panted happily, tongue and tail wagging, then rolled over to request a belly rub. My nightmare receded to the corner of my mind as Stella consumed all my attention. There's no way I could be scared or anxious, depressed or fearful, when I've got this gorgeous, goofy dog in my face, spreading nothing but affection and love. Once she calmed down, I curled my arms around her and nuzzled her neck, cuddling under the covers. The morning suddenly became a million times brighter.

I hadn't forgotten what Josie said about Stella being dangerous, but another voice inside me argued, *Don't let Josie steal your joy. You know Stella, even if you haven't had her long. You're with her every day now, day and night. This dog you're holding in your arms is not a dangerous animal, and she never will be.* I felt so much better than I had the day before. Still, I was committed to being a responsible dog parent, and I would continue to handle her very carefully. We would do everything we could to make sure this dog, and our family, didn't become another sad statistic.

A few weeks later things were going so well with Stella that we agreed to take in Belle, another foster dog from the Fort Wayne Pit Bull Coalition, just for one night when Belle's foster mom had to leave town suddenly for a family emergency. Stella and Belle did great together, teasing each other, goofing around, and playing fetch.

Stella seemed to have the instinct to be a natural "big sister," and I began to think maybe we could start to give back by fostering other needy dogs. Stella had brought so much joy to our lives already, I felt we should pay it forward. *Could this be my mission?* I wondered. *Could this be what I'm supposed to do with my second chance at life, work to help animals in need, along with the people who love them?*

The next day, Stella, Belle, and I went to drop

Belle off with her foster mom who'd just returned home. With us was Megan, a brown-haired, blue-eyed dynamo, a law school student who also served as the president of the Fort Wayne Pit Bull Coalition. In addition, Megan also happened to be the manager of the veterinary clinic where Josie had handed down the terrible prediction about Stella's future.

I walked Stella while Megan walked Belle as we followed a trail into the trees behind the apartment building where the dogs could get some exercise before we dropped Belle off. I had always gotten along well with Megan, so I took this opportunity to ask her about what Josie had told us regarding pit bulls.

"Megan, I'd love to hear your opinion on something that's been bothering me," I began, choosing my words carefully. "When Brian and I brought Stella into the clinic a few weeks ago with a possible bladder infection, Josie read us the riot act, going on and on about how dangerous and unpredictable pit bulls are, and saying we'd put our whole family and our home at risk by adopting Stella. I left there pretty shaken, I must admit. Do you think she could be right?"

Megan stopped in her tracks and tugged Belle's leash to bring her closer. "Oh, Marika, I'm so sorry she said that. I wish you had told me earlier. We fired Josie—she no longer works at the clinic."

"What? Not because of what—"

"No, no, not because of what she said to you," she answered quickly. "We'd been having problems with her for quite some time. She had a pattern of behavior of telling clients her own agenda, rather than that of the vets. Her assessment of Stella wasn't based on Stella, it was based on stereotypes. From everything I've seen of Stella, you have nothing to worry about."

"Oh my God, I wish I would have known!" My words poured out in a rush. "I just thought Josie was trying to be helpful. I assumed she was speaking to me from her own personal experience of pit bulls. I had no idea."

I felt like a huge weight had just been lifted off my shoulders, followed by a moment of deep regret. *I'm so sorry, Stella. I'm sorry for doubting you.* I crouched down in the damp grass and Stella came trotting back toward me, nudging me and licking my hand. I slipped her the treat I'd been hiding and she gobbled it down, then looked up at me, asking for more. I stared into her bright amber eyes and realized that for the first time since the encounter with Josie, I was seeing the real Stella again, the dog I had fallen in love with and adopted within minutes of meeting her.

I rubbed her head and scratched behind her ears. "This is a learning experience for both of us," I said. "You're learning how to be part of our family, and I'm learning how to overcome my fears and my preconceived notions about pit bulls, putting aside the things I've read in the media and online, and just seeing you for you; loving, accepting, and embracing you for the dog you really are. I promise, I will be a better mom to you from now on."

One of the most extraordinary things that happened after we adopted Stella was the effect it had on Caitie, my bright, beautiful, sensitive baby girl. Caitie took my cancer diagnosis hard, and in the midst of my treatment and recovery, I was so focused on trying to stay alive for my daughter, I lost sight of how to just be present for her, not as a "sick mom," but as an everyday mom. It became harder and harder to reach her, especially since being in Arizona meant I was physically and geographically so far away. Eventually I decided to try a new strategy: rather than working so hard to connect with her, I chose to back off, give her some space, and let her come to me. During this period, Caitie descended into a very dark place, but how dark that place was, I didn't even realize until it was almost too late.

Caitie was born in January 1999 in Fort Wayne, two and a half years after my first husband, Don, and I had our first daughter, Carly. Caitie was a lovely baby, with big, round, blue-green eyes that were so serious and inquisitive, eager to see everything and just draw in the world around her. She was very bright, loved puzzles and crafts, and was reading on her own by age four, later devouring the Harry Potter books as fast as they were published. When it came time for kindergarten, she was already way beyond the other kids, and when she was tested, the school wanted to advance her not just one grade but two. I didn't want that for her, though, because I didn't want her to be so much younger than her classmates, and didn't want to put this sensitive, thoughtful girl under so much pressure.

As Caitie was growing up, she always felt things very deeply and took everything to heart. She had just turned fourteen when I was diagnosed with cancer, a terrible age for a girl to get that kind of news. In the days and weeks after my diagnosis, she became depressed and shut down emotionally. I tried so hard to reach her, but I didn't know what to say or do to help her. It wasn't like when she got hurt as a child, and a kiss and an ice cream cone could make any boo-boo all better. I knew she was scared and confused; I was scared and confused, too. Her grades, always exceptional, began to dip, and she was having trouble in class. We tried to help, offered her support and counseling, but she rebuffed us at every turn.

One conversation in particular really stands out in my mind. I'd become so frustrated with Caitie not communicating with me, not willing to open up and let us help, I finally said, "Look, I'm your mom. I love you. I'm always going to love you, no matter what. But you have to invest in our relationship, too, if this is going to work. If you're willing to work with me, this will go one way; if not, this will go another way. It's up to you how this plays out." She just shrugged, muttered "whatever" under her breath, and gave me that just-barely-making-eye-contact scowl that every parent of a teenager knows all too well.

Secretly I worried that Caitie was destined to be introverted and fearful, like her father. I wasn't sure how much of her personality change was genetic, how much of it was due to normal teenage stuff—hormones, boys, teachers, grades, peer pressure—and how much was a result of me being ill. *Is this just a phase that she's going through, or is this who she's going to be, long term?* I wondered. *Is this the real Caitie I'm seeing now, and not that bubbly little baby I loved so much?*

When I made the difficult decision in spring 2015 to go to Scottsdale for further treatment, I knew it would be tough not just on me but on the whole family. By this time, Carly was in college at Indiana University and Brian needed to stay behind in Fort Wayne to run our Jimmy John's restaurants. Caitie, now sixteen, was not doing well, in school or out. She was so advanced academically that by freshman year of high school she was already taking college-level math, but the courses were hard and the grades weren't weighted, so her GPA took a hit.

I was worried that she was being set up for failure and that this gifted student was even at risk of dropping out of school. Not knowing what else to do, we decided she should live with her dad, Don, while I was in Arizona, rather than staying with Brian. "Your dad will give you the structure you need," I told her. "You'll get into a routine with him, and that will make things easier. He'll help you stay on track."

I hoped that Don would be a normalizing force for Caitie, giving her some stability while I was so far away. It broke my heart to leave her behind, along with Brian, Carly, our home, our business, and everything else, but I was convinced I was going to die if I didn't take the treatment in Arizona. *I can't be a mom from the grave,* I reasoned. *I need to save my own life first, before I can save my family.*

During my seven months in Arizona, I rarely heard from Caitie, and the few times we spoke, our conversations were awkward, strained, and superficial. I decided just to continue giving her some space and not pressure her to engage with me; that seemed to be what she wanted and needed most at that moment. Little did I know, I could not have been more wrong.

It was a beautiful, sunny Sunday morning in October and I was at church in Scottsdale with my new friends Betsy and Randy. I had turned off my cell phone during the service, and when I turned it back on afterward, I saw that I had missed three calls from Don. My heart immediately tumbled to my feet. *Oh no,* I thought. *Don never calls me. Something must really be wrong.*

My hand was shaking as I called him back. He answered on the first ring. "Don—it's Marika. What's wrong?" I tried to control my rising panic as Betsy and Randy looked on, concerned.

"It's Caitie. I found a note—in the kitchen—"

"What kind of note?" My heart was pounding in my throat; I'd never heard Don sound so shaken, and I was terrified.

"It looks like a suicide note." His words poured out in a garbled, nervous rush. "Marika, I don't know where she is."

"What?" I gasped.

"I heard her come home, she did something in the kitchen, she called out 'good-bye,' and then I heard the front door close. She took the car and drove off. When I went to the kitchen, I found a note on the counter. It says, 'I'm not good enough. I can't do this anymore.'"

My mind was reeling as I fought off gruesome images of her car in a ditch, or her wrists slashed, or her body, broken and bloodied on the concrete

164

after a multi-story fall. "Have you tried calling her? Is she picking up?"

"She doesn't have her phone," he replied, distraught. "I took it away as a punishment for her last report card."

Oh my God. My child is suicidal and we have no way to reach her. Not only that, I'm eighteen hundred miles away. This was my worst nightmare come true—I'd take a hundred cancers over something happening to one of my children.

"Find her, Don. Dammit, find her!" I shouted over the phone, and then hung up. *I've got to call Brian,* I thought. *Brian will know what to do.* Brian had been my rock through my worst moments, and now I needed him more than ever.

I quickly explained what was going on to Betsy and Randy, and with trembling fingers I called Brian. He answered on the second ring. "Brian, it's about Caitie." I was so breathless, I could barely push out the words. "She left a suicide note with Don and no one knows where she is. She doesn't have her phone."

"Don't worry," he said. "I will find her. I promise." He sounded so calm and confident. My rock to the rescue once again. "I'll call you as soon as I have any news. Stay strong. I will find her." As we hung up, I knew he wouldn't rest until she was safe—he loved her as much as if she were his own—and for a brief moment, I was able to breathe again.

Betsy and Randy saw the state I was in and jumped in to help. I was on the verge of collapsing when Betsy guided me to a bench and sat me down while Randy went to get some water. "Betsy, what am I going to do?" I struggled to hold back my sobs. "I can't lose Caitie. I just can't." I sent up a million prayers in that moment—*Please, God, please, let my baby be okay. Please let Brian find her safe and sound.*

Betsy sat down beside me, wrapped her arm around my shoulder, and pressed her head to mine, rocking me gently and holding me close. "It's okay," she whispered, "Brian will find her."

Suddenly, my phone rang. I looked down and it was Brian's number. I answered quickly, fumbling so badly I nearly dropped the phone. "Brian! What's wrong?" He couldn't have found Caitie already; we'd only just hung up.

"Mom?" The voice was timid; scared, broken, breathless.

"Caitie? Where are you? Are you all right?" *She's alive; she can speak. Thank you, God. Whatever is wrong, we can handle it as long as my daughter is alive.*

"I'm okay, Mom. I'm with Brian." She started to sob.

I wasn't able to get a lot out of her, but apparently, what had happened was that just as Brian was rushing out the door to go search for her, Caitie pulled into the driveway. After leaving the note at Don's, she had driven around for a while, feeling scared, confused, and hopeless, losing herself to the depression and anxiety she'd been struggling to control. She didn't want to die, but she didn't know what else to do. She was in so much pain and just wanted to escape. Life had become unbearable. She went to Brian because she knew he'd be a rock for her, too; he'd be there to help. As soon as she'd gotten out of the car, Brian had handed her his phone so she could call me and let me know she was okay.

"I love you, Caitie, I love you so much," I repeated over and over, sobbing hard as relief rushed through me. "I need you. I know this is rough, but please just hold on. Let's make a promise to each other—if you hold on just one more day, then I will, too. I'll be home next month; let's both hold on for that. Let's both agree to make it to Thanksgiving. I promise you, things will get better."

She promised me that she would hang on and get through each day until we'd be together again at Thanksgiving. We talked a bit longer, but we were both pretty broken down by that point. For me, it was enough just to hear her voice, and listen to her breathing between words. *My baby girl is alive. We'll be okay.* When Brian came back on the phone, I begged him, "Take care of her. Please. She's so fragile right now."

"Don't worry," he replied. "I'm not letting her out of my sight."

As I hung up the phone, I felt a mixture of incredible relief and intense anger. I wasn't angry at Caitie; I was angry at cancer. This damned disease had almost cost me my life, and now it had almost cost me my daughter. This illness had caused so much havoc and upset in her life, she considered ending it all. *How much more can you take from me? What more can you do to ruin my life?* I raged. I had left my family in Indiana and gone to Arizona in hopes of getting better, and now I wondered if instead I had just made everything worse, for myself and for everyone.

I also realized that my "hands-off" approach to Caitie's troubles and my decision to let her come to me instead of me going to her was not worth the risk. I vowed to call her more often, and to make more of an effort to reach out to her, to let her know how much I loved and cared for her, even when she rebuffed or rejected me. Still, I worried. *Is the gap between us so great now that we'll never be able to bridge it? Have I lost my daughter forever, not to suicide, but to the effects of my cancer, and to being so far away from her when she needed me most?*

Once I was home from Arizona, I kept my commitment to stay more connected with Caitie, more involved in her everyday life, but it was hard. We just didn't seem to know each other anymore, and our conversations, when we did talk, were stilted, awkward, as if each of us was afraid to say what we were really feeling for fear of upsetting the other.

My relationship with Caitie might have continued on that slow, sad path toward total estrangement, but then something changed, and that something was Stella. Suddenly, we had this dog in common. Now, Caitie was coming into my bedroom in the morning when I was cuddling with Stella and crawling into bed between us. Here, we could talk easily, about anything and everything, or nothing at all. I found myself sharing this close, intimate space with my daughter again, treasuring these precious, gentle, quiet moments, and it never felt awkward because we had this goofy dog between us to focus our attention on if the conversation got too intense. Stella was the glue that brought us back together and helped us mend our relationship.

Thank you, Stella, I often thought as the three of us snuggled in bed, warm and safe and soft beneath the covers. *Thank you for helping me be a better mom, and for giving me my daughter back. We've got a lot of healing left to do, but you're helping us get there.*

Brian with foster pup Cena, spring 2016.

CHAPTER SEVEN

Booker and Cena

Spring 2016

Once Megan from the Pit Bull Coalition had assured me that Stella wasn't a dangerous dog, I was able to enjoy Stella again, enjoy Stella just being Stella, a naturally happy and rambunctious pup, without constantly worrying that her personality would suddenly change and she'd become violent and out of control. Still, I knew that no dog was completely predictable in terms of behavior, and the better we trained Stella, the better it would be for her and for us in the long run. I remained cautious and careful with her, spending a lot of time and energy on exercise and training, making sure she understood the rules and limits we set for her.

As much as I loved working on my own with Stella on training and commands, I believed there was more I could do. I showed Brian the website for the Fort Wayne Obedience Training Club. "I want to take Stella here," I told him. "They have an eight-week beginners' obedience course for dogs over six months old, so they can work on mastering the basics like sit, stay, lie down, walking on a leash, coming when called, and so forth. Most of the stuff she already knows, but I think it would be really good for her to get this kind of reinforcement, and I could make sure I'm training her the right way, too."

He nodded. "Sounds like a good idea. I'll come with you, if you want."

Wow! I hadn't expected that he'd offer to join me, but I was so glad he did. He worked so hard, so many long hours running the restaurants, I couldn't believe he'd give up precious time when he could be relaxing at home, watching basketball or reruns of *M*A*S*H*, in order to work with me and Stella. *He's doing this for me,* I thought. *So we can spend more time together.* It was little gestures like this that made me love him even more than I already did, which is saying a lot.

Classes were held Tuesday nights at seven p.m. in the Home Loan building on the Allen County Fairgrounds in Fort Wayne. I was so excited as we drove to our first session with Stella quietly sitting on her haunches in the back seat of the SUV. I didn't want to be one of those overbearing moms, but I couldn't help thinking, *My dog is brilliant! She'll be an A+ student for sure!* I certainly pictured her graduating the top of her class.

As Brian and I walked Stella through the quiet fairgrounds on that cool, early spring evening, I remembered how alive this place was at the end of July when the Allen County Fair was in full swing, with the merry carnival atmosphere of the midway, the noise and the music, the Ferris wheel, the Tilt-a-Whirl, the House of Mirrors, all lit up with flashing neon, and the air rich with the delicious aroma of cotton candy, funnel cakes, and roasted corn on the cob. But now, out of season, the fairgrounds were almost ghostly, dark and dusty with the wind whistling through the empty concrete pavilions.

Brian and I linked arms and I rested my head on his shoulder and sighed. When I was in Arizona, I could only dream about moments like this, something as ordinary as walking the fairgrounds with my husband by my side. *What a long journey back it has been. And now I've got Stella to make everything better.*

The Home Loan building was located on the west side of the fairgrounds next to the 4-H exhibits buildings and across from the livestock and show barns. It was a clean, basic space with few distractions, making it perfect for training dogs.

Once Stella caught sight of her classmates, the other dogs in the group session, she got so excited, she started running back and forth, yelping, crying, and carrying on like crazy. "Oh my God, what have we done?" I asked, and Brian and I both laughed. "Is our dog insane?" *Maybe she's not going to be a straight-A student after all . . .*

Fortunately, Stella adjusted quickly to the high-energy atmosphere of the class and became a model student, just as I expected. The club's training area was divided into two halves. On one side was the beginners' obedience class with Stella and her classmates, while the other side was for agility training with the more advanced dogs. Stella got so excited watching the dogs on the agility side, clearing hurdles, climbing walls, and maneuvering the obstacle course, all at frenetic speed, that she would jump up and bark and then turn around to look at me as if asking,

"Why aren't we on that side, Mom? Why? I want to be over there!"

Stella's training wasn't just limited to the classroom. I worked hard with her every day at home, too, between sessions, refining her behavior and mastering commands. Stella's absolute favorite food in the whole world is cooked chicken, so I learned to incorporate that into her training, making it her incentive and reward. Each time she did a task correctly, she got a little piece of chicken in return.

When Stella graduated from the eight-week obedience class, we let her do a run on the agility course as her graduation gift. She made the most of it, bolting back and forth and doing zoomies, even if she didn't exactly clear every hurdle or follow the course precisely as designed.

The obedience classes were great because they allowed Stella to become socialized to other dogs and other people while also learning new skills and gaining confidence. The classes helped me as well, giving me yet another reason to get out of the house, out of my funk, and back into the world of people and dogs. Don't get me wrong—I still had bad days, and down times, particularly when I thought about everything I had missed when I was sick, especially precious time with my family that I could never get back. And I was still dealing with my fear and anxiety about the cancer returning, along with the guilt that I wasn't doing enough with my second chance, or expressing enough gratitude for surviving my brush with death.

Tell me what I'm supposed to be doing, I asked the universe. *What is my grand plan? What is my passion? Please, just give me a sign and I will follow. I want to give back while I can.*

On my worst days, I didn't even feel like getting out of bed, but then there was Stella, bounding upstairs and into my bed, bombarding me with kisses and cuddles, so happy and excited to face the world. Maybe I didn't feel like going anywhere that day, but she certainly did, and wanting to do what was best for her got me out of bed and moving even when just brushing my teeth felt like a struggle.

The other wonderful result of Stella's obedience classes was that Brian and I were spending more time together as a couple. Since class started at seven p.m., we'd make an evening of it, grabbing dinner and hanging out. We started getting reacquainted as husband and wife, and interacting not as a couple facing cancer, but as a couple with a big, energetic pup learning the skills to be a good dog. *Stella gave me back Caitie,* I thought. *And now she's giving me back Brian as well. What more can this girl do?*

I was so profoundly impacted by the positive changes that Stella brought to my life that I took steps to have her certified as my ESA or Emotional Support Animal, which would allow her to go more places with me and help me handle stressful situations. I had been dealing with anxiety, panic attacks, and PTSD most of my life, even before my cancer diagnosis, and those issues only got worse once I had cancer and then afterward as I struggled to recover.

I had never considered that a dog could help me with this, and I definitely didn't adopt Stella for that reason. But once I began working with her and we spent so much time together, I noticed that her presence alone helped to calm and soothe me, and I was better able to manage my anxiety and fear when she was by my side. She was a good distraction, too—focusing on her and her immediate needs took my attention away from the dark, anxious thoughts that so often raced through my mind like a runaway freight train.

Once I started taking Stella with me to public places as part of her ESA training, I was amazed by how people reacted to her. She became a favorite visitor at our local Kroger grocery store, where the butcher and the crew manning the cheese counter would come out to say hello and save special treats for her.

On one visit to Kroger, I approached three section managers chatting in the produce department to thank them for their hospitality and for making Stella and me feel so welcome in the store.

"We love having her visit," the older balding man in glasses said as he bent down and stroked Stella.

"In fact, her name came up in a staff meeting just last week," his younger colleague added eagerly.

"Really?" I asked, surprised. "I hope it was for something good!"

"Oh yes," the first guy confirmed. "She brings such a positive vibe to the place."

Hearing this touched my heart. Stella had brightened my life, but now she was also bringing joy to others. I was learning how dogs can break down barriers between people, allowing them to connect in ways they otherwise wouldn't. The nearly universal love for animals that people share can help bridge the social and personal gaps that so often keep us apart.

But I also had to laugh when Stella's true impact was brought home to me one day. I was on my way home from an appointment without Stella, and I popped in to Kroger's to pick up something for dinner. I stopped by the butcher's counter to say hello, but Stella's favorite butcher just looked at me, confused.

"Juan, it's me—Marika." I stepped closer to the glassed-in case so he could get a better look at me.

"I'm sorry—Do I know you?" He looked a little embarrassed as he weighed some cubed steak for a customer.

"It's me. Marika. You know—Stella's mom?"

"Ah! Ah! Stella's mom!" Now his face lit up with pleasure and recognition. "Of course! How are you? And where's our Stella today? She's not sick, is she?"

I quickly explained that Stella was fine and waiting for me at home. He gave me a little "something special" to take back to her, and I left the store shaking my head, thinking, *Stella and I are here just about every day, working on training. I talk to Juan several times a week, and yet he doesn't recognize me without Stella at my side. Stella's become my conduit for human interaction. People are inspired to open up and share when they meet Stella. That's the power of this wonderful dog.*

The more joy that Stella brought to our lives, the more I looked for ways to pay it forward. There had to be more I could do to help other people and animals reap the benefits I was experiencing from having adopted Stella. That's when I saw that the Fort Wayne Pit Bull Coalition were looking for volunteers to help foster dogs. I didn't know much about fostering at the time, but the more I learned, the more interested I became.

Basically, foster parents take in homeless dogs

for a temporary stay until the dogs are matched with a "forever family." Fostering can be as short as an afternoon or overnight, or as long as several weeks. Sometimes foster parents are needed just to help out with an emergency transport or to take a dog to be neutered when no one else is available.

Fostering doesn't only get dogs out of shelters (a very stressful environment for animals where there is a high rate of disease transmission due to the close quarters), it also gives dogs a chance to learn how to live in a home, be potty-trained, and get used to interacting with adults, kids, and other animals.

One of the primary reasons why dogs are surrendered to shelters is because of destructive behavior, and fostering can help mitigate some of these behaviors by socializing the dogs before they are adopted. Also, the better the foster family gets to know the fostered dog, the more information they can pass along to the forever family about that dog's preferences, issues, and behaviors, thereby increasing the odds of a successful long-term placement. And if the foster family happens to fall in love with the dog they are fostering and can't bear to see him or her leave, then adoption is always an option.

Fostering also provides a vitally important "decompression" period between the shelter and the forever home. The shelter environment is so stressful for dogs that it takes them some time to wind down, relax, and get back to their "normal" state. Too often families adopt a dog from a shelter and then end up bringing the dog back within the first few days because the animal is so nervous and wound up and seems unmanageable, when in reality, the animal simply needed more time to "come down" and adjust. Living in a more relaxed foster home environment between the shelter and the forever home means that these animals are in better shape, and better prepared, when they do transition to their forever family.

Another benefit of fostering is that it saves two lives for every one dog that is fostered. Each time a shelter dog is fostered, the space that dog was taking in the shelter is freed up and becomes available for another homeless dog. The statistics are shocking: according to the ASPCA, approximately 1.5 million shelter animals are euthanized each year (670,000 dogs and 860,000 cats). The majority of these are healthy, well-behaved, loving creatures that would make excellent family pets but instead are being put down simply because there just isn't enough space to house them. What an absolute tragedy.

When I saw a post on the Fort Wayne Pit Bull Coalition's Facebook page in March 2016 looking for families to foster some needy puppies, I saw my chance to start paying it forward. First I had to convince Brian, though, which I knew might not be easy. He never wanted to have even one dog (although I must say, he and Stella were getting along famously), and now I wanted us to take on puppies, albeit temporarily.

Happily, Brian said yes, and we went to pick up two puppies from a litter of six-week-old pit bulls that had been seized from a neglectful breeder in a county outside of Fort Wayne. It was important to foster the dogs somewhere other than the county where they'd been born because the law stated that, if the dogs stayed in their home county, the breeder would have the legal right to take them back.

I was so excited to meet our "new additions," but once we got to the shelter, my heart fell. The pups we were fostering, Booker and Cena, looked so tiny, so fragile and vulnerable, it was hard to believe they could be separated from their mother. Booker was russet colored with a white chest, white paws like little booties, and a white teardrop just above his nose. Cena was nearly all black with round, sad black eyes, a white chin, and a white bib across his chest.

"Come here, little guy," I said as I picked up Cena and gently tried to cuddle him. His thin coat of fur was cold to the touch and he shook with fear. I was afraid I might hurt him—he was so thin, I could feel every rib beneath his skin, and every bone of his back and spine.

"Who would be so cruel to treat puppies this

way?" I asked Brian as tears filled my eyes. "They are just innocent babies."

"I don't know," he replied sadly. "I can't imagine." Booker, being carefully cradled by Brian, looked even smaller, thinner, and frailer than Cena. *What are we getting ourselves into?* I wondered. *We could say no, but these little guys really need us.*

When we brought the foster pups home, Stella was so excited! I worried how she'd react to them, if she'd be jealous or too energetic with them, but she immediately took them under her wing, becoming super protective and acting as a foster mom. They were "her" puppies as much as ours, and when we put the puppies' crate in the basement, Stella would lie next to the crate, to keep an eye on the babies and keep them company. If she heard them cry, no matter where she was in the house, she would run downstairs to comfort them and keep them safe.

By the second day, we knew that not only were the pups malnourished, they were very ill. We took them to the vet, where we learned they had worms and tested positive for parvovirus, a potentially deadly viral infection that causes severe gastrointestinal issues including dehydration, vomiting, and bloody diarrhea. I worried about Stella catching this highly contagious disease, but the vet said that since Stella had been vaccinated against parvo, she'd be fine. Even so, she did get ill for a few days with mild digestive issues, and that was very concerning.

"Do you want to take the puppies back to the coalition?" Brian asked carefully once we knew how ill Booker and Cena really were. "This might be too much for us . . ."

"No. We made a commitment to care for these little guys until they're ready for their forever home. Let's make that happen," I replied.

Thus began an all-out, round-the-clock effort to nurse the puppies back to health. We fed the pups at regular intervals, weighed them every day and charted their growth, washed and bathed them repeatedly as needed. (Too young to be potty-trained, puppies generally pee and poop all over the place. Now imagine two puppies with nonstop diarrhea and you get a sense of what we were up against.)

Because the pups were so sick and so small, they struggled to maintain their body temperature, so Brian and I would hold the pups on heating pads on our laps to try to keep them warm. At one point, I looked over at Brian and thought, *There's the guy who didn't want to have a dog, and now he's sitting at the table eating dinner with a fork in one hand and warming a tiny puppy with the other.* He was so gentle and tender with the puppies, it was beautiful to behold.

Even with all our care, their health was so precarious. When Cena took a turn for the worse, we took him to the vet and he ended up spending three days in the veterinary hospital. The first morning he was back home with us, it was still dark out when I heard Brian stirring, getting up to get ready for work. He hadn't even taken Stella out for her walk yet, so she was still downstairs in her crate. "Brian," I asked softly. "Can you do something for me?"

He looked up, surprised to see me awake. "Sure. What is it?"

"Can you go downstairs and check that the puppies are all right?" I couldn't bear the thought of going downstairs myself and finding one or both of them lifeless in the crate. I needed Brian to be a buffer for me, to shield me from that potential pain.

"I'm sure they're okay," he said, sounding confident. He went downstairs and I waited anxiously, holding my breath and feeling my heart pound through my ribs as I lay in bed, the covers pulled up tight to my chin. It seemed to take forever, but at last I heard his footsteps coming back up the stairs.

Please, God, oh please let them be okay, I prayed. Brian popped his head in the door, and his smile told me all I needed to know. "They're fine," he confirmed, and finally I was able to breathe again.

We fostered Booker and Cena for three weeks and by the end of those three weeks, they had gained weight and were healthy and stable, ready for their new homes. Stella had even taught them how to bark for the first time, which was so cute! They tried so hard to bark like Stella, but they nearly toppled over, wearing themselves out just to produce a high-pitched little "woof."

Letting them go to their new homes was tough because we'd become so attached to them, but I was comforted by the fact that they were both going to people in our inner circle. Cena was adopted by a young man who worked for us at Jimmy John's and Booker went to a friend of a friend. Today, two and a half years later, both dogs are happy, healthy, and doing great.

I had tears in my eyes as we said good-bye to the pups for the last time. "That was harder than I thought it would be," I admitted to Brian. "I knew I'd get attached to them, but I didn't realize how much in such a short time."

"We don't have to foster again if you don't want to," he said. "Stella's enough to keep us busy."

"No, I want to do it again," I said through my tears. "Because we didn't just save Cena and Booker, we also made room for the two dogs, whoever they are, that took Cena and Booker's place at the shelter. What we're doing is important and worthwhile, even if it hurts."

It felt really good to have helped, but I still wished I could do more. I was starting to think bigger, wanting to save more dogs, and to raise money to help animals and their owners. But how? We could only foster a few dogs a year at most, when thousands of healthy animals are being euthanized for no reason other than that there's no place for them. And my primary focus was still rebuilding my health after surgery and radiation, not to mention the fact that we were in the process of selling our restaurants and planning to move to Arizona full-time.

Still, the seed of an idea had been planted, and now that seed was germinating. *There's something bigger down the road for me,* I thought. I realized with a start that I was visualizing the future in a way I hadn't for so long, picturing not just the days and weeks ahead but months and even years. I saw a future version of myself who was healthy, happy, productive, and contributing to society.

When I was at my sickest, my world was so small, it was defined by a hospital room, the radiation center, or my own bedroom. That was as far as my horizons extended. I couldn't see any future for myself at all. Death felt imminent, stalking me at every turn. I tried never to think ahead but instead just lived in the moment, because when I did imagine the future, it was with dread rather than hope. The only future I could see was one that I was no part of—I pictured my family struggling to cope without me; Brian widowed, moving through an empty house, spending long days and nights alone; and my girls without a mom, envying their friends who had moms to go to for advice and support, or just go shopping and hang out with. I saw my elderly parents without their daughter, struggling with the guilt, grief, and sorrow of having outlived their youngest child.

That future was so bleak. I had lived from treatment to treatment, appointment to appointment, scan to scan, fighting that constant battle to secure just a few more days of precious time, a battle that left me exhausted and overwhelmed. But now, it felt so different. The future seemed fun and exciting and challenging, offering me all kinds of possibilities. *I've got the passion, the energy, the commitment, the drive to do so many things that will have an impact, that will make a difference,* I thought. *And to think, all this started with Stella. A seven-month-old pit bull puppy set me on this brand-new path.*

Marika, Brian, Stella, and Caitie with Marika's parents, Peter and Marian Harrison, Florida, spring 2016.

CHAPTER EIGHT

Stella's First Flight

April 2016

Sending Booker and Cena off to their new homes broke my heart, but it also warmed my soul to know we'd helped get them healthy and ready to join their forever families. I was committed to helping as many dogs and people as possible, and I knew we'd be fostering again sometime soon. But before then, in the break before we welcomed another foster, we decided to fly down to Florida to spend spring break with my parents.

To be honest, I was a bit nervous about the trip, not just about how Stella would handle her first time on an airplane and nervous in general because I'm anxious about flying, but also nervous about spending time with my parents. *Maybe Stella can help me reconnect with Mom and Dad?* I wondered. *Maybe she can work her magic on my parents, just like she's worked her magic on Caitie and Brian and everyone else.* It was a lot to ask of one not-so-little dog, but I certainly hoped so. My faith in Stella's ability to touch, and change, the hearts of everyone around her was growing by the day.

I never had the easiest relationship with my parents and grew up feeling a little bit like I was in their shadow, struggling to live up to their shining example. My dad is a brilliant man, a defense contractor who founded Britannia, a multi-million-dollar office supply software company, in the late eighties, years ahead of the curve, and Mom was every bit his equal as she did the legwork to make the business fly. They were so focused, driven, and ambitious, while I was a sickly kid, didn't like school, and always struggled with my confidence and self-esteem. I often felt lonely and isolated growing up. Not only were Mom and Dad so busy with Britannia, my middle sister, Michelle, was seven years older than me and my eldest sister, Martine, was nine years older, so they were already out of the house while I was still in grade school, so I didn't share with them the common interests and peer group that so many sisters do.

When I was diagnosed with cancer, I thought that might bring my parents and me closer together, and it did, at first, until we fell out over my decision to forgo chemotherapy. Eventually we forged an uneasy peace, but there was still something unspoken between us, something awkward and uncomfortable that hadn't been resolved, even as I recovered from cancer and time went by.

Fast-forward to April 2016. We'd only had Stella for two months and we were preparing to take her with us to visit Mom and Dad in Florida, where by now they had retired permanently. I couldn't wait to share Stella with them in person so they could see what a beautiful dog she was and what a powerful and positive effect she was having on me and on my life.

Even so, I was like a worried, overbearing mama, praying Stella would be on her best behavior, both during the flight and once we arrived. How would Mom and Dad relate to Stella? How would she relate to them? We hadn't had dogs when I was growing up, so Mom and

Dad weren't used to being around them. Not only that, Dad had recently been diagnosed with Parkinson's disease and had trouble with his balance. I worried that Stella, in her excitement, might accidentally knock him over and cause him to fall.

So I made a commitment to prepare Stella for this trip the best I could, and to make sure everything went smoothly. I felt like it was a privilege to travel with Stella, and I believed we had a duty and a responsibility to make the whole experience as stress-free as possible, for Stella and for everyone she came into contact with.

First, Stella needed to be ready to handle the airport and then the flight. As an Emotional Support Animal, she'd be allowed to fly in the cabin with Brian, Caitie, and me rather than having to travel in a crate below in the cargo hold, so she really needed to be on her best behavior if she was going to spend several hours surrounded by dozens of strangers in very tight quarters.

Ever since she'd gotten her ESA certification, I'd been working hard with her on training, building on what we had accomplished in the obedience classes. I focused especially on the commands *down, sit,* and *stay.*

Okay, Stella, I tried to explain to her, *you have to be on your best behavior. You're not just representing yourself and representing our family on this trip, you're representing the entire pit bull breed. People will judge other pitties by what they see in you.* That's a lot to put on one pup's shoulders, but I had confidence she could handle it.

To help prepare Stella for the trip, I took her to malls, hotels, restaurants, hospitals, any new environment I could think of where we'd encounter lots of strangers, along with endless new sights, sounds, and smells. She constantly amazed me with how well she adapted to these new and different situations and circumstances.

When I first started training Stella in public, I worried that her being a pit bull might cause some problems based on people's often negative perception of the breed, but she almost always received a positive response wherever we went. There were just a few exceptions. For example, one day I was at Costco training Stella when a little girl in a stroller nearby kept reaching out her arms and saying, "doggie, doggie," while trying to pet her.

The mom quite rightly said, "You can't pet her, honey, because she's working."

But then a wise guy behind the woman sneered, "Yeah, you can't pet the dog because that dog'll eat her." Rather than lose my temper, I saw this as a "teachable moment" for all involved.

"That's right, Stella is training right now, so you can't pet her," I explained to the little girl, but loud enough for the man to hear. "But she's perfectly safe—she won't hurt you."

"Hurt you? That dog's gonna eat you," the man taunted again. At that point, I just gave up and walked away. Sometimes, it's just not worth it.

Fortunately, incidents like that were rare. As we got closer to our departure date for the Florida trip, I began taking Stella on short visits to the airport so it would be a familiar location to her by the time we left. The biggest challenge was the baggage claim. It's often said that dogs "see" with their noses more so than with their eyes, and the conglomeration of different smells in people's luggage in such a concentrated space was overwhelming.

Stella was like a drug-sniffing K-9 once she got around people's suitcases and travel gear! She'd go completely crazy, nose poking everywhere, sniffing up, down, and sideways, trying to take it all in. I suppose it's not surprising, when you think of all the uniquely and powerfully odored items people pack for a trip—clothes, shoes, food, shampoo, perfume, medication, and so on.

As we got closer to departure day, I was feeling pretty confident. The only part of our trip that we couldn't train for was going through security, since no one is allowed in that part of the airport without a ticket, so that's what made me the most nervous. I could only hope that Stella was comfortable enough with the rest of the airport that going through security would be a breeze.

We were all up early on the morning of April first, the day we were leaving for Florida. I must have gone through our paperwork a dozen times, making sure everything was in order—Stella's ESA certificate, her vaccination record, and her license. I'd worked so hard on training Stella, I wasn't going to let us get tripped up on a technicality. *Stella's ready, but am I?* I worried. *Not just flying to Florida with a pit bull, but flying at all.*

I'm an anxious flyer, one of those people who is convinced she's going to die every time she steps foot inside an airplane. The last thing I did before we left the house was to take a good look around, casting a critical eye upon the bedroom, bathroom, living room, and the rest of the house, thinking, as I always do, *Okay, if the plane goes down, this is how everything will look to whomever is tasked with sorting out my things . . .*

Once we got to Fort Wayne International Airport, the final time Stella could go potty would be before we went through security, because once we passed through the metal detectors, there'd be no place for her to relieve herself until after we arrived in Orlando several hours later. So after we checked in and got our boarding passes, I waited until the last possible moment and then I walked Stella outside, past the drop-off lane, and across the parking lot to find a suitable patch of grass.

The sky was overcast and it was cold and damp; spring had been a shy performer that year, teasing us from the wings but not yet announcing itself and taking center stage. I looked around at all the flags on flag posts, whipping in the wind, and felt the chill echo in my bones. My stomach was churning and I felt sick with dread, thinking about boarding that plane. Stella seemed more interested in her surroundings than in doing her business. I glanced at my watch. *The gate will be closing soon; let's hurry it up, Stella.* Finally, Stella did what we were there for, and we rushed back into the terminal building, catching up with Caitie and Brian just before they went through security.

My anxiety, which had been at a ten, ratcheted up to eleven as soon as I stepped into the security line. I didn't just dread getting on an airplane; I also dreaded going through the security scanner. Before my mastectomy, when I still had the lump in my breast, the tumor would show up on the screen, outlined in red on the left side of my chest when I passed through the scanner. (Tumors aren't normally visible on airport scanners, but it's thought that mine was detected because it was so close to the skin rather than being embedded deeply within the tissue, so the machine was reading it as an object separate from my body.)

Even though the tumor was gone now, passing through the scanner still terrified me and made me feel sick. *What if something new shows up? What if I have a tumor I'm not aware of? And if so, what a horrible way to find out, at the airport on the way to a vacation.*

That's the thing about cancer—you may be what doctors consider NED (no evidence of disease) from a clinical standpoint, but once you've had cancer, the disease is with you always, casting a shadow over everything you do. For me, passing through the scanner brought back terrible memories and reminded me that no matter what happened, I'd never be completely beyond cancer's reach.

When we were next in line to go through the scanner, I knelt down close to Stella, massaged her ears between my fingers, closed my eyes, and pressed my forehead to hers. I took a deep, calming breath, drawing strength from her strong, steady presence. *Okay, Stelly. Help me through this. I need you now.*

I walked through the metal detector with Stella, and the alarm went off. *Great! Like I wasn't anxious enough . . .* The TSA agent pulled us aside and patted us down. I was okay, but it seemed the metal in Stella's ESA vest and her two collars set it off. "Ma'am, can you take off her collars and vest?" the Transportation Security Administration agent asked.

"Of course," I replied. I quickly removed the items. Poor Stella looked so "naked," so exposed without her clothes, but she behaved beautifully.

"Please maintain control of your animal, ma'am," the agent said as he waved me through the machine while Stella stayed behind, sitting in position as I had commanded her. I was a little uneasy leaving her, unleashed and alone, but I was confident in the training we had done. She was absolutely calm, keeping her eyes on me at all times.

Once I had passed through, the agent told me to call Stella.

"Stella—come!" I commanded, and she trotted through the machine and right to my side without incident. "That's my good girl!" I said, slipping her a treat. I glanced around and saw so many people looking at Stella, amazed at how well she behaved. I loved having the opportunity to show pit bulls in such a positive light.

I got her dressed and on her leash, and we hurried to our gate to board the flight. I expected to get some stares, maybe even some critical looks, from other passengers when they saw us boarding with a pit bull, but no one said a thing and several people even smiled. Stella was a little nervous at first, especially as Caitie, Brian, and I took our seats in an economy-class row of three across, and positioned Stella in the very narrow space on the floor between our legs and the backs of the seats in front of us. All I could see was her head, and her slightly worried expression, poking up between our knees.

Fortunately, I was carrying plenty of cooked chicken, and the steady stream of treats seemed to keep her mind occupied as the engines roared to life beneath our feet, preparing for takeoff. As I fastened my seat belt and stroked Stella's smooth head, it suddenly occurred to me that I had put so much energy and effort into getting Stella ready for the trip, I hadn't had time to worry about seeing my parents and wondering if it would be awkward.

I also hadn't spent as much time as I normally did worrying about the flight itself. Stella helped lessen my anxiety about flying by redirecting my attention. Those learned patterns of worry, fear, anxiety, and helplessness that were so deeply engrained in my brain were gradually being rewired by Stella, as she gave me something so much more positive to focus on.

"Thank you, Stella," I said, and slipped her another piece of chicken. "Thank you for being the exact distraction I needed, and at the precise moment I needed it."

After we landed in Orlando, my parents were there to meet us, and they immediately wrapped the four of us—Brian, Caitie, Stella, and me—in an embrace as warm as the sunny Florida weather. I think every adult child has experienced that moment that takes your breath away, when you see your parents again for the first time in a while and realize how they have aged while you were apart. Suddenly, you see them as they must appear to other people—not as Mom and Dad but as an elderly couple, Dad tall and mostly bald, Mom slim with chic, bobbed blond hair. I reminded myself how precious every moment with them is, especially when they live so far away and visits are both rare and brief.

Having cancer at forty-one forced me to face my own mortality in such a shocking way, it was easy to lose sight of the fact that my parents were getting older and dealing with health issues, too. *It doesn't matter anymore if we disagreed on my cancer treatment,* I realized. *That was then, this is now. I'm here, I'm fine, and we are all together. Let's just enjoy it.*

Stella helped to break the ice as Mom and Dad petted her and stroked her head, lavishing her with love, and Stella's tail wagged madly while greeting them. "Oh, Marika, she's lovely," Mom said in her gentle English accent that had softened only slightly during her four decades in the States. Dad appeared a little less steady than the last time I had seen him, but Stella seemed to sense that, and she was careful not to jump up on him or be too energetic as they got to know each other.

As we walked to the car, I linked arms with

Mom and leaned my shoulder against hers. *I'm so glad we made the trip,* I realized. I watched Brian, Caitie, Stella, and Dad walking ahead of us, Stella trotting faithfully at Dad's side as Brian held the leash. *Thanks, Stella, for once again being that conduit for human interaction and making everything easier for me. What would I do without you?*

Our six days on Lake Harris in Tavares, about forty minutes north of Orlando, were wonderful and relaxing, especially seeing Stella react to such a new environment. Prior to the trip she had spent her whole life in Indiana, heart of the rugged Midwest, damp, gray, and industrial, and now she was experiencing palm trees and citrus groves and bracing inland lake breezes that seemed to delight her senses.

My parents lived near an orange grove and sometimes when we walked Stella along the road, oranges would roll off the trucks transporting the fruit and Brian would pick one up, peel it, separate the slices and give one to Stella. I didn't think dogs ate citrus fruits, but Stella loved it!

She also saw her first lizards, and she became fascinated by these quick, quirky, stealthy little creatures. She chased them everywhere and was determined to catch one, but they were always just a bit too fast for her.

200

We were excited for Stella to play in the pool because she loved puddles and creeks and couldn't wait to jump in, soak herself, and get absolutely filthy. But she was afraid of water, too, in other circumstances. She would get so nervous at home when I took a bath that she would burst into the bathroom and try to "save" me from drowning if she heard any splashing.

We thought she might love my parents' pool, but nothing could convince her to jump in, even when tempted by her favorite toys. So Brian took off her collar and very gently tried to carry her into the shallow end of the pool, thinking she'd feel safe in his arms, but as soon as her paws touched water, it was as if she were being tortured; she cried bloody murder, jumped out of Brian's embrace, and ran into the house as fast as she could.

We were still laughing when, moments later, she darted back out of the house toward the pool, grabbed her collar from atop the lounge chair, then ran back inside with the collar firmly clamped between her teeth and with a very annoyed look on her face. Apparently, Stella's fear of the water was trumped only by her fear of being naked in public!

It was so nice to spend time with my parents in such a relaxed atmosphere, without the stress of my illness or the pressure of choosing a treatment plan. I had always admired my parents for being so brave and following their dreams, even though it wasn't easy for me to be in their shadow, trying to live up to their example of being so bold and decisive.

Mom and Dad were living in their native England, and in their mid-thirties with three young daughters, when they decided to leave everything familiar behind—job, home, extended family—and emigrate in 1978 to the United States when a company in Fort Wayne offered Dad a job as a defense contractor and agreed to sponsor him. Those early years in this country were really tough for us, especially after Dad lost his job and couldn't get work since he no longer had the sponsorship of his employer and therefore couldn't get a work permit. He had worked here under U.K. security clearance, but he didn't have the necessary U.S. security clearance that would have made it easier to get another job in his field of expertise.

We basically had to go into hiding to avoid deportation, and it took a long time to get the legal issues resolved. At one point, my bright, brilliant dad was reduced to selling vacuum cleaners to try to support the family. We moved around a lot, too, from Indiana to Florida to California and eventually back to Indiana. Moving so much added to the stress we were under as a family and I think also contributed to me feeling lonely and isolated during much of my childhood.

What started as basic software applications written by my dad developed into a new company, Britannia, when we moved to California in 1989. Things also became more stable for us as a family at that point. Mom and Dad were so far ahead of the curve in developing this software company during a period when personal computers were still a novelty, and the Internet was something only Al Gore and a few other people had even heard of. Dad wrote the software applications while Mom handled sales.

Eventually, my first husband, Don, and I became co-owners of the company with my parents. I was tapped to take over once they retired, but I had other plans. You might think that working so closely with my parents made us close emotionally as well, but that wasn't always the case and there was often tension between us, especially right before I left the company in 2005 to open my first Jimmy John's franchise.

We'd been through so much as a family, and when I got sick, cancer threatened to drive a permanent wedge between us. But now that I was well and forging my new "best life," I promised never to let that happen again. Life is too short and too precious not to make the most of the time we have with our loved ones.

On our final day in Florida, Mom and I were in the kitchen preparing lunch, Dad was in the living room watching TV, and Brian and Caitie were out near the pool. Mom and I had just been making small talk, when suddenly, her voice turned serious. "Marika, you look wonderful. You seem so happy. What a joy to see you like this after . . ." Her voice trailed away.

"Things are good," I replied, quick to fill that awkward pause. "Brian and the girls are doing great, and Stella has given me so much. She's changed my life, Mom. I finally feel like I'm living again."

"Your dad and I were so scared when you wouldn't do the chemotherapy, but I realize now that you made the right choice. I'm proud of you. I'm so glad you stuck to your guns," she said softly. I was so touched and so surprised by her words, I didn't know how to respond.

Suddenly, we heard my dad laughing in the other room, a deep, rolling belly laugh unlike anything we'd ever heard from him. I looked at Mom and Mom looked at me and we hurried into the living room, where we found Stella on top of Dad in his recliner, licking his face and trying to squeeze herself onto his lap. "Okay, Stella, okay," Dad pleaded, helpless with laughter, only pretending to try to push her away.

I wrapped my arm around Mom's shoulder and she slipped her arm around my waist as we watched the sweet scene unfold between Dad and his grand-dog. We were all laughing now, but I also felt tears prick the corners of my eyes. *Thank you, my darling Stella,* I mused, *for the gift of precious moments like these. You've given all of us more than you will ever know.*

Caitie and Stella with foster dog G.I. Jane, spring 2016.

CHAPTER NINE

Stella and G.I. Jane

May 2016

My phone pinged. I set down the stack of boxes I was carrying, wiped the sweat from my forehead, grabbed my phone from the back pocket of my jeans, and quickly scanned the message: URGENT NEED: FOSTER FAMILY FOR SHELTER DOG. The Facebook notification came from the Fort Wayne Pit Bull Coalition and was labeled "highest priority."

"Guys, there's a dog that desperately needs help," I announced to Team Meeks. Brian, Caitie, Stella, and I were helping Carly move into a new apartment for the summer, and we'd already spent most of that sunny Saturday afternoon cleaning, lifting, carrying, assembling furniture, and filling up drawers. Even so, we still had a few hours of work ahead of us.

"What's the dog's story?" Caitie asked, looking concerned.

I leaned back against the stack of boxes I'd just set down and read the complete post. The details were heartbreaking—a young female pit bull mix had been brought to the shelter as a stray, and after being held for seventy-two hours as a ward of the county, they were trying to evaluate her for possible adoption. She was so traumatized, however, and so terrified, they couldn't even get her into the exam room to begin the evaluation. If they weren't able to evaluate her, that would be an automatic fail, which meant she'd be placed on the E List—E for euthanasia. This pup's only hope was to be taken in by a foster family who would work with her to overcome her fears and get her ready to transition to a forever home—no small task when a dog is so deeply damaged.

207

"Apparently, she's so scared, she doesn't even walk like a normal dog—instead she drags herself along the ground, as if she were crawling. Like they do in the army, when they crawl under wires," I said, paraphrasing as I read. "That's why they call her what they call her—G.I. Jane." I felt my eyes fill with tears and I swallowed hard.

"You want to go get her, don't you?" Brian asked gently.

"Yes, I do," I admitted. "I'd like to go get her out of that shelter this minute." I glanced down at my watch. "But it's too late. By the time we finish here and drive three hours back to Fort Wayne, the shelter will be closed for the day." I couldn't bear to think of that scared little dog spending the night in the shelter, confused and overwhelmed. *But at least she's off the streets now,* I told myself. *At least she's safe and receiving care. I'll get to her as soon as I can.*

Once we had Carly settled into her new apartment, we began the long drive home, which gave Brian and me plenty of time to talk. It had been less than two months since we said good-bye to Booker and Cena and only a month since we visited my parents in Florida. Were we ready to foster again? Especially a dog that, even before we met her, seemed to offer so many challenges?

"The decision is up to you," I told Brian. He drove and I sat in the passenger seat, looking out at the highway lined on either side with flat, open fields, and occasional billboards advertising gas-food-lodging. "I know you never wanted us to have a dog, let alone foster other dogs, so if you think this is too much, just say so."

In my mind, I was crossing my fingers and toes and every other appendage, hoping he'd say okay to us fostering G.I. Jane. But as always, I didn't want him to feel pressured or railroaded. His feelings mattered, too.

He shrugged. "If you really want to take her, I guess it's okay."

Yes! As usual, it wasn't exactly a ringing endorsement, but it was good enough for me. "Do you hear that?" I called to Caitie and Stella in the back seat. "We're getting a new addition to the family, at least temporarily."

"Yay!" Caitie cheered, and Stella, as if she understood, excitedly wagged her tail.

The next morning, Sunday, I took Stella with me to the "Pack Walk" sponsored by the Fort Wayne Pit Bull Coalition. The walk was designed for dogs that had already been adopted (and their owners!) to network, socialize, and give and receive support to other foster and adopting families that had received dogs from the coalition. I had arranged with Megan, the president of the coalition, that she would pick up G.I. Jane from the shelter and bring her to meet us at the walk.

I needed to make sure that Jane and Stella could get along in a neutral environment before we brought Jane home. Jane had obviously been through so much already, I didn't want to add to her stress and despair by inadvertently making a bad match.

When we got to the walk, I caught sight of Megan, her brown ponytail bobbing in the wind, and with her on a leash, Jane. As soon as I saw Jane, I felt that familiar rush of emotion that told me this dog was special. She was adorable—approximately a year old with a short, black-and-white coat, including a black patch over her right eye, one black ear, one white ear, and a round black nose. Her proportions were a bit unusual—her block-shaped head was the same size as Stella's, but her legs were very short, so she only stood about two-thirds of Stella's height at the shoulders. She was so short, in fact, she was later able to walk under Stella's hips and butt when Stella was standing.

I wasn't sure if Jane's unusual size and shape were caused by some chromosomal differences, or perhaps she was just an uncommon mix of dog breeds. She was so sweet, but I could tell she was in bad shape and had been through a lot. The skin on her stomach and chest, really her entire underside, was scraped raw from dragging herself along the concrete when she had been too scared to walk when she was at the shelter.

Brian took Stella's leash and I took Jane's, and we joined the other pack members. Jane was very fearful, sticking close to the ground, but at least she was walking, not crawling or dragging herself. She seemed to do better outside and around other dogs rather than being in the shelter. Stella and Jane seemed fine together—they didn't interact much but gave each other space. I think Stella must have sensed that Jane was a fragile soul and not quite ready to be friends yet. The four of us made a long, casual trek around Lindenwood Cemetery, one of the most beautiful cemeteries in Fort Wayne, a grand, nineteenth-century resting place full of majestic granite headstones and simple crosses, with trees and bushes just coming into full bloom.

"I can't imagine what people have done to Jane and how they have hurt her," I said to Brian. "I can only hope that with enough love, we can bring her around." I was already envisioning this little dog as part of our family. Stella seemed to accept her, and that was what sealed the deal for me.

We took Jane home and started working with her immediately. We only had three weeks to get her ready for her forever home, or at least get her stable enough to be fostered by another family, since we'd be leaving then for a wedding in Arizona.

Jane had a sweet-natured disposition, but with a spirit that was so, so broken. She was so fearful of everything, especially people. When we took her out for a walk, all she wanted to do was go back inside the house so she could hide away from the world.

We did everything we could for her, but it was Stella who helped her the most. Jane didn't trust humans, but Stella was able to connect with her, dog to dog. Stella taught Jane how to be a dog again (or maybe she was learning for the first time), playing games with her, teasing her, comforting her, showing her how to run and bark, how to retrieve a ball, how to jump, roll over, ask for treats, and play. Stella demonstrated what joy in action really looked like, and tentatively, Jane was beginning to follow.

The two girls had so much fun together and gradually, Jane began to emerge from her shell. I know everyone believes their dog is special, and every dog *is* special. But Stella is something different—a wise old soul. She seems to sense things, to understand and intuit things from the people and animals around her. I saw how she was with my dad when we were in Florida, how careful, gentle, and respectful she behaved, mindful of his issues with balance, and I saw how she was with children, getting down to their level, lowering her head and shoulders so she could be petted.

So it should have come as no surprise to see how she "adopted" Jane, taking the smaller, more nervous creature under her protective wing. Maybe I was one of Stella's "love projects," too. Since we'd met that first day at the meet and greet at Rural King, she'd sensed I was a bit of a lost soul, a woman struggling to find herself, to deal with overwhelming fear and anxiety and forge a new identity post-cancer. It was as if she'd said, *Come on, Marika. We can do this. We'll fly together. Follow me, and I'll teach you to soar.*

Jane had only been with us for a day when I noticed a few drops of blood on the white fur of Stella's tummy. I checked her thoroughly for any injuries, but she was fine. Then I thought that the blood might have come from Jane, so I checked her as well but didn't find anything. Both dogs had very short fur, and not only that, both Stella and Jane were predominantly white in color, so even a very small injury should have been visible. "Maybe just something she picked up outside," I decided.

We had made a pen for Jane on the tile floor in the foyer, so when Jane was inside the pen, I sat down beside her and stroked her shoulders and tummy, helping her relax. I was working to get her comfortable with human touch. She was still so scared, she was panting and her whole body shook, but the longer I sat with her, the

213

calmer she became. While petting her, I suddenly noticed a few drops of blood on the tile beneath her chin. *Oh no—the blood* was *coming from her. Something is really wrong.*

I looked more carefully and saw that a small trickle of blood was dripping from her nose. Not a lot, just a few drops. Otherwise, she seemed fine, but I knew this wasn't normal. I checked Stella again, too, even more carefully this time, but she was fine. I phoned the emergency vet's number and they said to bring Jane in first thing Monday morning.

Please don't let it be something serious, I prayed. Even though she wasn't "my" dog, I had become so attached to Jane in such a short period of time. I couldn't bear the thought of losing her. When we went to the clinic the next day, the vet took her temperature and discovered she had a fever of 104. The vet diagnosed a pretty serious upper respiratory infection and prescribed a course of antibiotics. The vet checked Stella, too, but fortunately, she hadn't caught the infection from Jane.

If Jane had stayed at the shelter rather than coming to us as a foster, she probably would have died, I realized with a start. Not that she wouldn't have been cared for at the shelter, but the bleeding from her nose was so minimal, it's unlikely anyone there would have noticed a few drops of blood, especially with so many dogs in that very busy and sometimes chaotic environment. *Fostering Jane likely saved her life,* I thought. *This beautiful little girl came to us for a reason. She's going to be amazing for the forever family that ultimately adopts her. But for now, she's mine.* I tried not to think about that inevitable moment when we'd have to let her go.

We nursed Jane back to health, and Stella was the best assistant nurse imaginable. She watched carefully as I gave Jane her meds and stayed by her side while Jane was napping, playing only gentle games while we waited for Jane to get back to one hundred percent.

Once Jane recovered from the infection, she really started to improve in other ways, too. She was happier, less fearful, and much more relaxed. She not only accepted affection from me, she let me embrace her, wrapping her up and cuddling her like a baby in my arms. I treasured these close moments, especially when I curled up with Jane and Stella was stretched out behind me, pressed against my back. Is there any warmer, safer, cozier place to be than sandwiched between two happy pups? It was absolute bliss, but tempered by the reality that soon we'd have to say good-bye and let Jane go. We couldn't keep Jane longer than the three weeks we committed to—we had that wedding in Arizona to get to.

Hands down, this is absolutely the single

hardest part about fostering—bonding with an animal, allowing them into your home and your heart, building a loving, trusting relationship, and then having to let them go. The experience can be emotionally devastating. As we grew closer to the end of our three weeks, I dreaded that day coming, and found myself frequently in tears and not able to sleep. Finally, one night before we went to bed, I was upset and weepy and Brian asked me what was wrong.

"It's Jane," I explained. "I feel like we're betraying and abandoning her. It's like we're teaching her that she's loved, cherished, and cared for here, and then I'm going to go and dash all her hopes and dreams by just sending her away to someone else. I can't explain to her that we aren't dumping her. She'll just think we don't want her anymore. And she'll think this is what humans do—they take care of you for a while, then they hand you off to someone else, who might love you, but also might not. How is she ever truly going to learn to trust?"

Brian reached over and wrapped his arms around me, holding me close. "I know how hard this is," he said. "Do you want to adopt her? Are you thinking of keeping her forever?"

"I wish we could," I admitted. "I would love that, and I've considered it so many times. But we've got so much going on right now." We were in the middle of trying to sell our Jimmy John's

216

restaurants and preparing to leave Indiana and move to Arizona full-time.

"And it's not just that," I continued. "If we adopt Jane, then we won't be able to foster any more dogs—Stella and Jane will be all the dogs we can handle. And that means the dogs we might have fostered could end up spending their lives in shelters, or even being euthanized, because we didn't have a place for them. The reality is, if Jane goes to a loving home, we have room with us for another foster, and another after that, and so on."

My deepest commitment was to helping dogs find permanent homes, and this was the best way to make that happen, even if it was just on an individual, case-by-case basis. *Someday I will be able to do more,* I vowed. *I just don't know how yet.*

As we moved into our third and final week of fostering Jane, I started posting information on Facebook, looking for a forever family for her. A family that we knew from Michigan responded, and after we talked extensively, it seemed like they would be a great fit. The mom, Kim, and one of their daughters, Ally, along with their dog, drove down to Fort Wayne to meet Jane. I knew they were a kind, loving family, but when we all went for a walk, Jane and their dog did not get along. The dogs weren't wagging their tails, and they weren't interested in getting to know or acknowledge each other. Pretty soon it was clear that this match was not going to work out, for Jane or for them. Kim and Ally were so sad and disappointed, they cried. I felt so bad that they had driven all that way and gotten their hopes up, and then were leaving empty-handed.

As I watched them pull out of our driveway without Jane in tow, I burst into tears. My emotions were in a jumble—on one hand, the selfish part of me was glad to have more time with Jane, but on the other hand, I had prepared emotionally to say good-bye to her, I had started to accept that she'd be gone (a process therapists call "anticipatory grief"), and now, suddenly, she wasn't going anywhere. The worst part of all was knowing that I'd have to go through this whole process again with the next prospective family, preparing for Jane to leave and then not knowing if it would work out or not.

"This is so, so hard," I sobbed on Brian's shoulder. "I don't know if I can do this again. My heart can't take it."

A few days later, we had a second meet and greet with another family, and, just like the first time, it didn't work out. Again, I was devastated, and now the clock was ticking as we only had a few days left until we had to leave for Arizona.

Deb from the Pit Bull Coalition very gently said to me, "Marika, let's do Jane's next meet and greet without you and Stella present, okay? Let's see if that works out better." I knew Deb was right. The last thing in the world I wanted was to be a factor in Jane not connecting with a new family. Jane and I had really bonded, and maybe Jane was picking up on my anxiety, sadness, and uneasiness around the potential foster families and that was affecting how she acted around them. Or maybe the families weren't able to connect with Jane because they sensed how close I'd become to her.

On the Tuesday night before our trip, Deb came and picked up Jane to take her to a new foster home and continue the process of finding her a forever family. Her toys were all packed up, along with her dish, leash, and other items. Saying good-bye was one of the hardest things I've ever done as I cradled her in my arms, rubbed her ears, and kissed her forehead, whispering "I love you," into her fur. I wanted to pull her deep inside me so I could remember forever how she felt, how she smelled, how she wiggled in my arms.

She had made so much progress with us, and I wished more than anything that I could explain why she was going away. "Be a good girl," I told her. "Be good for your new family."

I barely slept that night, wondering how Jane was doing in her new temporary home, wondering if she missed us and was waiting for us to come get her. I also worried how Stella would cope. She had grown so close to Jane, and now her best buddy was gone. There was no way to explain to Stella why Jane had left, and not only that, in the morning Brian and I would be leaving Stella for the first time since she joined our family.

We flew out early Wednesday morning. Caitie would be taking care of Stella while Brian and I were gone, and I had arranged for my friend Alana to check up on Stella during the day while Caitie was in school. Our flight was about three hours, and as soon as we landed in Arizona, I turned on my phone to find I'd missed several messages from Alana. *Oh no, oh no.* My mind raced. *Something's wrong with Stella, and now I'm halfway across the country. I never should have left her. She wasn't ready for it, and neither was I.*

When I finally got a hold of Alana, she said that when she got to the house to check on Stella, she found that Stella had had explosive diarrhea in her crate. Not only was Stella a dirty, smelly mess, she was so ashamed and upset about fouling her crate, she was inconsolable. "I cleaned her up the best I could and she seems okay now," Alana explained. "She's upset, but she doesn't seem to be ill. I'm going to stay here with her until Caitie gets home, so I can keep an eye on her, just in case."

"Thanks, Alana. Call me right away if there's any change."

If it had been up to me, I would have gotten on the very next flight back to Indiana, but we had a wedding to attend, and I didn't want to disappoint Brian's family. "And maybe it's good for Stella, too," I reasoned, "to get used to us not being home all the time."

Stella's diarrhea continued. It got so bad that Caitie ended up sleeping on a rug on the tile floor next to Stella's crate in the foyer near the front door. Caitie had to be that close in case Stella needed to go out because otherwise, there wouldn't be time for Stella to get outside to do her business, and if she soiled her crate, she'd be desolate with shame again. Stella was a wreck, Caitie was a wreck, and I was a wreck. The girls were both exhausted, and so was I, trying to monitor the situation from eighteen hundred miles away.

By Saturday morning, Stella's diarrhea was bloody and she had lost five pounds in the three days we'd been gone. I told Caitie to take Stella to the vet, which she did. The vet did a thorough exam and couldn't find anything physically wrong with Stella. She chalked up the diarrhea to separation anxiety. I was hugely relieved that it wasn't something worse, but it also made me feel terrible that by leaving, I had inadvertently caused Stella all this stress and discomfort.

There's a saying that as a parent, you can only be as happy as your least happy child. I would amend that to include, "You can only be as happy as your least happy dog." I was finding it difficult to enjoy anything knowing that Stella was so far away and so distraught.

The one bright spot in all this was Caitie. She was so mature and responsible in how she handled Stella. If I didn't know better, I would not have believed that this was the same young woman who had been feeling suicidal only seven months earlier. Stella had helped her grow into a stronger, more confident person.

Once Caitie and Stella had gotten home from the vet, Caitie sent me a video of Stella howling, sounding so sorrowful, a sound I'd never heard from her before. It just about broke my heart. "Tell her I'll be home tomorrow," I pleaded. "It's only one more day," hoping in vain she'd understand.

The wedding was beautiful, but to be honest, my mind was elsewhere, stuck firmly back in Indiana, worried about Stella, and also worried about Jane, wondering if she was doing okay with her foster family. I wouldn't be able to relax until I was back home and could see Stella again with my own eyes.

When Caitie came to pick us up at the airport, she had Stella with her on a leash at her side, and as soon as our eyes met, Stella bolted straight toward me, tail wagging a hundred miles a minute as she jumped up and covered me with kisses.

I knelt down and threw my arms around her. "I missed you, too, Stelly," I told her, burying my nose in her neck. "And I don't ever want to leave you again." Miraculously, her diarrhea stopped almost immediately, once we got home.

The next morning was absolute bliss. Brian was up early as always and took Stella for her walk, then let her loose to run upstairs to our bedroom, where she catapulted herself onto the bed, demanding love.

She and I were still cuddling under the covers when Caitie tiptoed in to see if we were awake. I tossed back the edge of the quilt and invited her to join us. She jumped into the bed, too, and the three of us just snuggled, enjoying each other's company. These moments were so precious to me. I had Stella to thank for being the glue that brought Caitie and me back together when our relationship had been so fractured and fraught.

"I'm so proud of you," I told Caitie as Stella repositioned herself between Caitie and me. "I know this was hard, but you took such good care of Stella. I couldn't have coped if you weren't here with her."

She shrugged, in that way teenagers do when they know something important is being said but they don't want to admit it. "I'm just glad she's better," she said. "I do miss Jane, though," she added.

"I do, too," I agreed. The house felt so empty without her.

"Mom, I think you should take a break from fostering for a while," she said softly. "It's too hard on you, and all the stress isn't good for your health."

I was so touched and humbled to think that my daughter had grown up so much and become such a thoughtful and caring young woman. *When did this happen? It seems like just yesterday she was a round-faced, serious little baby who loved books and puzzles and games . . .*

Inside, I felt torn. I couldn't imagine taking in another foster dog and having to again endure the pain of saying good-bye. But, on the other hand, if we had the opportunity to possibly save a dog's life, how could we say no?

Okay, intuition, tell me what I'm supposed to do now. I know I'm meant to do more, but I'm still searching for that missing piece. No doubt there will be another dog in trouble, another pit bull on the verge of being put down, and I'll feel the urge to foster again. But for now, I'm going to take Caitie's advice and give my heart time to heal. Let this fresh wound scab over and close up before I put myself through that again.

Brian and Stella.

CHAPTER TEN
A Dog Dad Is Born

2016

Since adopting Stella, one of the most beautiful and moving things has been watching the relationship she's developed with Brian, the guy who was sure he "didn't want us to have a dog."

You'd never believe that today, because Brian's the best and most devoted "dog dad" I can imagine, and as much as Stella loves me, there's no doubt that Brian is her father figure, her alpha, the leader of her pack, the one she instinctively goes to when she's hurt or scared. Stella also helped Brian and me grow closer as a couple and revitalized our marriage after my cancer treatment created an emotional and geographic barrier between us that threatened to send us spinning off in different directions.

Before Brian came into my life, I had just about given up on finding true love. I was enjoying a busy, fulfilling career, a home of my own, and two fantastic daughters—shouldn't that be enough? Wasn't I as blessed as I dared hope to be? *"Happily ever after" is just for books and movies,* I thought, *Real life is nothing like that.*

I think, to truly understand what Brian has meant to me, and how our relationship has changed my life, you need to know a bit more about what I went through with my first husband, Don. It's a challenge to talk (or write) about this time in my life and my relationship with Don. I have no desire to embarrass him or our families, especially since he is and always will be my daughters' father. On the other hand, this is part of my journey, a painful part of my experience that I need to own fully by speaking my truth. Through Stella I've become a much more public person, giving speeches, presenting at seminars and conferences, talking to the media, and I've learned the importance of being authentic and revealing your true self to the audience, warts and all. People are perceptive, and they know when you're holding something back. So it is with that spirit of honesty and humility that I share my story here.

When Don and I first met, I was nineteen, living in California, and working for a small, four-person, family-owned company that sold police products. This company was located in a large warehouse building that was part of a much bigger industrial complex. It was a lonely place to work, so visitors were both rare and exciting.

Don, a tax accountant, was hired to audit the company. I can't say it was love at first sight, but I found him interesting. At twenty-eight he was nine years my senior, and he was about my height, average build, with sandy brown hair and blue-green eyes. He was so serious, so professional, with a stern, no-nonsense attitude. He came to the office twice a week for several weeks during the audit, and I found myself looking forward to his visits. I made it my goal to charm him, or at least break through his cool exterior and get him to loosen up a bit.

Alas, nothing I did seemed to attract his attention, and I figured he just wasn't into me. I had almost given up on reaching him, but then one day I brought him some homemade chocolate chip cookies. He thanked me and as we shared the cookies and talked, I felt like we were finally connecting. *Yes! Success! All hail the seductive power of chocolate chips!*

Don asked me out and we started dating. I can't honestly say I was head over heels, but Don seemed to offer me answers, and a way forward, especially since he was older and seemed so mature and settled compared to me. My late teens were such a lonely, confusing time in my life. I'd grown up feeling so isolated, invisible and insignificant, overshadowed by my parents and older sisters, never quite finding my way. I'd hated high school and only finished one semester of college before realizing college wasn't for me. There was so much pressure on me to go back to college, get a degree, get established, have a plan, and just "do something" with my life.

After only three months of dating, Don took me to dinner one night at a nice restaurant by the ocean and asked me to marry him. It wasn't a complete surprise, because we'd talked about getting engaged and had even picked out a ring. Even so, it was thrilling to actually hear a man speak the words, "Will you marry me?" and I immediately said yes.

But then I excused myself and went to the ladies' room, where I peered into the mirror and saw staring back at me the pale, worried face of a confused teenage girl with long brown hair and big, sad brown eyes. My head was swimming, my stomach in knots, and I knew deep down that I had said yes not out of love but more because I didn't want to disappoint him, and because it seemed like what I was "supposed" to do. *But Don cares about me,* I reasoned. *He's interested in me and keeps track of everything I do. No one else has ever been interested in me in this way. That's love, isn't it?*

Don and I eloped on August 4, 1991, when we were still only nineteen and twenty-eight, respectively. I soon realized that what I had interpreted as love, especially the way he made me feel before we were married—relevant and important—was really just a means of controlling me. After we were married, I began to see the truth. Our life together was so regimented and everything had to be done his way. For example, the light switches had to be just so: "up" for on and "down" for off. The light in the upstairs hallway could be turned on or off either downstairs or upstairs, so Don installed a device to prevent the switch from ending up in the "wrong" position, even though this meant Carly and Caitie sometimes had to go upstairs to bed in the dark.

I deferred to Don in so many ways, and let go of the things that were important to me, sacrificing my own wants and needs in order to keep the peace. I stopped hanging pictures and photos on the wall because I knew I would do it "wrong." I stopped bringing in the mail from the mailbox; instead I would go to the box when Don wasn't home, riffle through the mail and see if there was anything important for me, then leave the rest there for Don to bring in later and deal with "his" way.

I even had to negotiate with him about giving me attention and affection. "Why don't you come and sit with me here on the couch?" I asked one night, patting the spot beside me as we sat in the living room watching TV, me on the sofa and him in his recliner. "Just for a little while."

"I'm comfortable here," he replied, eyes glued to the screen.

"Oh. Well, would you be willing to sit with me on the couch and watch TV three nights a week?" I asked softly.

He shook his head. "I can't commit to that."

"How about twice a week, then?"

He scowled. "I'm not prepared to agree to that."

"Once a week, maybe?"

"I can't say."

I felt so shamed and humiliated. What kind of woman has to beg her husband to sit next to her? I felt so disempowered, so unworthy and unloved.

Our finances were strictly controlled as well:

I had to provide receipts for everything I purchased, and the budget we had agreed on allowed us each just one dollar for lunch and a dollar fifty for supper each day. My lunch at work consisted of one can of Campbell's Chunky Vegetable Soup—it had to be vegetable, because the soups that had meat in them cost more.

We bought a house during the first year of marriage. As we were driving home from the loan closing, I was so excited, talking about getting a few small things to make the house feel like home, when Don slammed his hand down on the steering wheel and yelled, "Are you kidding me? Don't you ever think about retirement?" At nineteen, it wasn't exactly at the top of my list of concerns.

In that moment I had a flash of reality: *Seriously, you're going to fight me over a couple of knickknacks?* We were on such different pages, not just about money, but about everything. How was this ever going to work, long-term?

We weren't poor, and in addition to owning a home, we both had good jobs and some money in the bank. But if we reached the end of the budget before the end of the month, we just had to make do until the calendar turned another page. Our vastly differing views on money came to a head when I was eight months pregnant with our first daughter, Carly, and we ran out of milk before we ran out of month.

I told Don I needed money for milk and he said firmly, "No. No milk until next month." *What? This is crazy.* I wasn't going to deprive our unborn baby of vital nutrients over a dollar-fifty quart of milk, so I went out and got the milk anyway. I think I knew then that things would never get better, but I felt stuck. *There's nothing I can do,* I told myself. *I have to stick it out. I'm married, I'm pregnant, I've got to make this work.* I died inside a little bit that day, and the prospect of having a marriage based on love, mutual respect, and partnership slipped further out of reach.

In addition to issues with money, Don had a drinking problem that got worse when we moved from California to Fort Wayne in 1996. When he was sober, he was cold, indifferent, and withdrawn, but when he'd been drinking, his personality would change completely and he'd be friendly, happy, chatty, at least until he sobered up again.

I was walking on eggshells, constantly holding my breath, not sure which Don I'd be dealing with that day. I kept count of the beer cans in the fridge so I'd be able to gauge how much he'd drunk that day and modify my actions accordingly. One day, when Carly was still a toddler and I was eight months pregnant with Caitie, Don went to run an errand at Home Depot. As soon as I saw his taillights disappear down the road, I opened the fridge and counted the beer cans. *Four less than this morning. He's too drunk to drive—I've got to stop him before he kills someone!* I tried to call his cell phone but he had it turned off as usual. He'd use the phone to make calls, but refused to take incoming calls, so there was no way to reach him.

Hours went by with no sign of him. I was worried sick—there was no way he could still be at Home Depot, if he had even gone there in the first place. Had he had an accident and been hurt or killed? Or had he hurt or killed someone else?

Finally, I opened the garage door and sat on the step with Carly on my lap, just waiting for him to come home, sick to my stomach with worry. Eventually he did, with no word as to where he'd been. When I tried to tell him how scared and worried sick I had been, he blew up at me, accusing me of overreacting and being unreasonable. At that moment, I just shut down and stuffed my feelings, afraid to provoke him or make things worse. I was dying inside in ways I didn't even realize until years later, when Brian, and then Stella, opened my mind and my heart to what true love really was.

By 2005, Don and I had been married for thirteen years; Carly and Caitie were nine and six. Things hadn't improved between Don and me and I felt so lonely and unhappy, but when I raised the prospect of therapy, Don shut me down, saying, "I'm happy with the way things are; why would I go to therapy?" *Well, that's nice for you,* I thought. But feeling ashamed and embarrassed, I retreated further into myself and didn't dare ask again.

Being married to Don made me feel like I was in high school gym class, sprinting around the running track, while Don was the grumpy coach in the middle of the track with a clipboard and whistle, timing me with his stopwatch, goading me on and yelling abuse while secretly hoping I would trip and fall so he could relax and wash his hands of me, confident that I had proved his belief about me to be true: that I was an utter and absolute failure at everything I attempted.

By this time, Don and I had bought into Britannia and were co-owners with my parents, who were getting older and preparing to retire. There was no official succession plan in place, but the unspoken understanding had always been that I would take over and run Britannia once Mom and Dad had stepped aside. But I had different ideas.

For a long time, I'd been nurturing a secret dream to own a restaurant, and after much searching, I'd found an amazing opportunity to open the first Jimmy John's sandwich franchise in Fort Wayne. It was exactly what I was looking for, but I was scared to tell my parents, Dad in particular because I thought he'd be angry and disapprove. Even at the age of thirty-three, I couldn't bring myself to defy my parents or go against their wishes. Since the four of us owned the company, my leaving would have a big impact. I knew they hadn't planned for a future that didn't include me, so by leaving the company, I would be jeopardizing their ability to retire.

I had decided to move forward with the franchise opportunity and I needed to let my parents know, but I kept procrastinating about telling them. I felt awful, so nervous and stressed about breaking the news and fearing how they'd react.

I remained trapped in that terrible dance we do with ourselves when we're trying to avoid something unpleasant: Every day I'd wake up and tell myself, *Right, today's the day. Today I will tell them.* But then, invariably, I'd find a reason to put it off. *Today's not good; tomorrow will be better,* I reasoned. *Tomorrow the stars and planets will align in my favor.*

Eventually, after much delay, I reached the absolute, end-of-the-line, now-or-never deadline. If I didn't tell them today, it would be too late to sign the franchise paperwork and my chance to open the Jimmy John's would be gone forever. My heart was pounding and my hands gripped the steering wheel as I drove to work that morning, rehearsing in my head the best way to break the news. *Mom and Dad, this might be difficult, but I've got something to tell you . . . Mom and Dad, do you have a moment? Can we talk?*

Suddenly, my cell phone rang. I glanced down and saw that it was my eldest sister, Martine. *Hmmm. That's strange. Why would she be calling?*

"Hey, Martine, what's up?"

"Marika, it's Mom." Her voice sounded nervous, rushed and breathless. "She's been taken to the hospital with chest pains."

I swerved, nearly hitting the car in the lane beside mine. "Oh my God! What happened? Is she going to be okay?"

"They don't know yet. They're still doing tests. I was just there; I'm on my way back to the office. Dad's with her now."

"I'll be there as soon as I can," I promised, and ended the call.

My mind was a blur as I turned the car around at the next intersection and headed for the hospital. All I cared about was making sure my mom was okay, but in the back of my mind was a tiny voice saying, *You screwed up, Marika. You waited too long. There's no way you can tell them now.*

When I got to the hospital and hurried inside to the ER, I found Mom stable, awake, and talking. All her test results came back normal and

236

she hadn't had a heart attack. The preliminary diagnosis was that her chest pain was caused by stress. *She's under so much pressure at the moment,* I realized, *and I had been about to add to it by announcing out of the blue that I was leaving the company. I feel like such a total jerk* . . .

Mom didn't want us fussing over her, and Dad was by her side, so once it was clear that she was going to be okay, I headed back to the office. On the way, I phoned Martine to give her an update on Mom's condition. Martine hadn't known about Jimmy John's or that I was considering leaving Britannia, so I told her everything. I was so sad and frustrated and just needed to vent.

"It's my own fault," I admitted. "I put it off and put it off, and now it's too late—I've missed my window of opportunity. There's no way I can tell them now—what am I going to do, kill Mom with my selfishness?"

"Marika, you need to do what you need to do for yourself, not for Mom and Dad," she counseled. "If you need to tell them today, then tell them today. Don't let this chance pass you by."

Her words of support made me feel hopeful for the first time that day. I realized I would never have given myself permission to talk to my parents under these circumstances, but hearing it from Martine gave me the strength to believe

I could. *Why can't I ever believe in myself for myself?* I wondered. *Why can't that confidence come from inside me; why does validation always have to come from some external source?*

Okay. Martine is right. It's now or never. I turned the car around yet again and drove back to the hospital. By this time, Mom had been admitted for observation, so I went to her room, where my parents were surprised to see me back so soon.

"Marika, what's wrong?" Mom asked as I strode into the room feeling pale and shaky. I was so nervous, I could barely speak. I didn't want to scare them, there'd been enough stress for one day, so I forced myself to push out the words that I had rehearsed in my head so many times.

"Mom, Dad, I have something to tell you that you probably don't want to hear. I wish it didn't have to be today, but I can't afford to wait any longer. I know you've been assuming that I will take over Britannia after you retire, but I've decided I don't want to do that. It's my dream to own a restaurant, and I've got a chance to start the first Jimmy John's franchise in Fort Wayne."

I was still shaking as I finished speaking and waited, trying to gauge the expressions on their faces. *Well, at least I told them,* I thought. *The worst is over, and I got that off my chest.* For the first time in days, I inhaled deeply and felt like I could breathe again.

Neither Mom nor Dad said much after my announcement other than to acknowledge that they'd heard and they understood, but as I drove back to work later that afternoon, I knew Dad would be returning to the office soon, once Mom was settled for the night, and I dreaded that confrontation. I was certain that Dad would be angry, disappointed, or, worse, he'd give me the cold shoulder and shut me out completely.

When I arrived at my office, I walked around the corner and saw a beautiful bouquet of flowers waiting for me on my desk. I was so surprised. I knew they couldn't be from Don—he would never spend money on something so clearly not in our budget. When I unwrapped the flowers and opened the note, it read, "Go for it, honey! Love, Dad." I burst into tears. It was such a surprise and relief to know that I had his support. *Now I can do it,* I thought. *I can really work on making my dream come true.*

I left Britannia at the end of 2005. Without me in position to assume control of the company, my parents decided to sell it, and they closed on the sale in the summer of 2006, which allowed them to retire immediately, and Mom never had any stress-related health concerns after that. In a strange way, my leaving the company when I did was the best thing that could have happened, because if I had stayed on board, my parents would have continued to be involved with the company, and the stress on them would have continued as well.

After my Jimmy John's franchise application was approved, I needed to secure a location to build my restaurant. I had never done anything like this before, but then I found a spot at a local shopping center that seemed like the perfect fit. The developer of the shopping center was a guy named Brian Meeks. We spoke on the phone several times as I was working to get the location, and I was impressed by how kind, patient, and helpful he was, always taking time to answer my questions in depth, and never making me feel silly or stupid for not understanding something.

Then, the time came for us to meet in person. I wasn't expecting the meeting to be life-changing in any way; it was just an ordinary business meeting, like so many I was attending at the time. And yet, looking back now, the details of that day are cemented in my mind, as fresh as if they'd happened yesterday.

The sky was a brilliant electric blue as I drove to Brian's office, where we met in a conference room. I can still picture how I looked that day, dressed casually in sandals, brown pants, and a linen coral shirt. He came in and introduced himself and I was immediately taken by his warm smile, blue eyes, and firm handshake. I could see he was several years older than me, but his down-to-earth personality made me feel at ease. He was dressed business casual in dress slacks and a button-down Nautica shirt with a patchwork design.

As we talked about the restaurant space, he was all-business, quite serious, and as is typical for me, I challenged myself to break the ice and get him to loosen up. This time, I didn't have to resort to chocolate chip cookies—he relaxed a bit and we talked about stuff other than business. I learned that he was married and had grown-up children. I told him about Don and the girls, but I left out the details about how much I was struggling in my marriage. When the meeting was over, he shook my hand warmly and said, "If you need anything, Marika, or have any questions, just give me a call. I'm always here to help."

As I gazed into his eyes, I knew instinctively that he was someone I could trust, especially during this difficult period of building the restaurant. To be honest, the attraction, the desire to make this something more than a friendship, was already there, but there was no way to act on it. We were both married to other people, and our lives were complicated enough. *So, a friendship it will be,* I thought as I climbed into my car and drove away. *I'm so glad I've finally found someone I can count on. I've never needed a friend as much as I need one now.*

• • •

Once I'd been approved for the Jimmy John's franchise in early 2006, the real work began. Building and opening the restaurant was a multi-month process with new challenges every step of the way. Brian was there whenever I needed him, whether it was helping me go over contracts and lease documents, read and interpret blueprints, or, once we began the build-out, hiring contractors and electricians and making sure everything was going according to plan.

The learning curve was sharp in those early days, and I had no idea how much work would be involved in running a restaurant. We opened in October 2006 and for the first eighteen months, I worked seven days a week, often working until well into the early morning hours, and every day brought new and unexpected challenges. The original plan was for Don to help me run the restaurant by handling the bookkeeping, but he was so difficult and such an obstructionist, I finally had enough and told him just to stay home. From that point on, he didn't help or contribute to the business at all. Fortunately, I had Brian to rely on for support and advice.

Over time, Brian became my best friend, and I wished it could develop into something more. I remember him walking into the restaurant one day, in the middle of winter when it was freezing cold, and he was wearing a long wool winter coat. I took one look at him and all I wanted to do was to be curled up inside his coat. I had such a strong image of him wrapping that coat around me and pulling me in close, where for the first time in my life I could relax and feel truly warm and safe, protected from the outside world.

Brian and I often bumped into each other at the coffee shop inside the shopping center where my Jimmy John's was located. We were there one day, sharing coffee and discussing something about the restaurant. I don't recall how we got on the topic, but at one point I made the offhand comment, "Don is my rock."

"In what way is he your rock?" Brian challenged. He had a fiery look in his eye that I wasn't used to seeing from this normally laid-back, placid guy. "From everything you've told me, he's never there for you; he doesn't support you in any way. That doesn't sound like a 'rock' to me."

I mumbled something about accepting Don for who he was and that, after so many years of marriage, at least I knew what I was dealing with when it came to Don.

"Don't you think you deserve better than that?" Brian posed.

No. I guess I don't, I admitted to myself.

The morning after one particularly bad encounter with Don, I ran into Brian again and we sat down to talk. When I told him what was going on, he slammed his hand down on the table and said sharply, "For God's sake, Marika, when is enough enough?" I had never seen him react so emotionally before, and at first, I regretted telling him. *Now Brian's pissed off at me, too,* I thought as I drove home that night, but the more I thought about it, the more I realized, Brian wasn't angry *at* me, he was angry *for* me. No one had ever supported me in this way before. He had cracked that door open, just a little bit, and allowed in the first bit of light toward my own empowerment.

By 2008, Don and I were divorced and Brian's marriage had ended as well. Our friendship remained strong, but there seemed little chance of it developing into something more than just friendship when Brian moved from Fort Wayne to Indianapolis, 126 miles away, to pursue better opportunities in commercial real estate. He had been married for twenty-four years, so he wasn't looking to start another serious relationship right away, and I totally understood. I was still dealing with the emotional fallout of my own marriage ending as well.

Even after he moved, Brian and I kept in close contact, talking on the phone every morning, texting throughout the day, and video-chatting in the evenings. Sometimes we'd leave our computers open on video-chat while we watched a movie together, long-distance, him in Indianapolis and me in Fort Wayne. That way, we still felt connected, even when so far away. We also visited each other on weekends, but it was a long two-and-a-half-hour drive each way, and especially hard in winter on icy roads.

After two years, I had to be honest with myself that this relationship wasn't going anywhere; because of the distance, we seemed to be stuck in one place emotionally. One Wednesday morning in the summer of 2010, I just thought, *That's it; I'm done. I don't want to do this anymore. We both need to move on. We're together, but not together. There's no future in this for either of us.*

When I talked to Brian that morning, I expressed what I was feeling. He didn't say too much, but he didn't argue, either, so I assumed he felt the same way. I was sad, but I truly believed it was for the best.

After work that evening, I was curled up on the couch in sweats, binge-watching *Seinfeld* and eating leftover Chinese food straight from the container when the doorbell rang.

I peeked out the window and saw Brian standing at the door, looking nervous, straightening his jacket and finger-combing his sandy-gray hair. *What the heck? Why is he here?* I opened the door with one hand while still holding the container of leftover General Tso's Chicken in the other.

Meanwhile, on *Seinfeld*, Jerry was being heckled about his puffy shirt.

"Brian? What are you—"

"Marika, will you marry me?" he blurted out.

"What?" I wasn't sure I was hearing correctly. *Did he just propose?*

"Will you marry me."

"Oh. Wow." I pretended to search for the words. "Wasn't expecting that. Ummm, can I think about it?"

His face fell a thousand feet. He looked like one of those characters in a cartoon who has his heart ripped out, trampled on, and then handed back to him in a bloody pulp. I knew I had to put the poor guy out of his misery.

"I'm kidding. Of course I'll marry you." I threw my arms around him (being careful not to spill the General Tso) and hugged him for the first time not as his friend but as his fiancée. When I stepped back, he reached into his pocket and pulled out a ring. I held out my free hand, straight and steady, so he could slip it onto my finger. "Wait a minute." I leaned forward and peered more closely. "Is that my ring? The one I accidentally left at your place?"

He smiled sheepishly. "Yes. It's all I had on such short notice."

When I was still married to Don, I didn't like to wear my wedding ring to work because it would get in the way or snag my rubber glove, so I bought myself a plain gold band to wear instead. As a woman working long hours, often alone, wearing what looked like a wedding band also helped me fend off unwanted male attention. I had accidentally left the ring at Brian's during one of my visits, and now, here it was again.

"So, let me get this straight—you're proposing to me with a wedding band from my first marriage?"

"Yep."

"Hmmm."

"We can go get you a 'real' ring tomorrow," he quickly promised. How could I say no to that? I imagined that our phone call that morning had jarred something for him and made him realize he didn't want to lose me. I felt the same way. I hugged him again and invited him inside to join me in finishing off the leftover Chinese takeout.

The topic may not have come up in conversation that night, but if not, then it was sometime very soon after, when we were discussing plans for our lives together, that he spoke those fateful words, "I just have one request: I don't want us to have a dog. That's a deal-breaker for me."

At the time, it was so easy to agree. I had no intention of ever getting another dog, and I couldn't imagine that would ever change. Then again, I couldn't possibly have imagined Stella. Or should I say, I couldn't have imagined Stella until I—we—met her, and she changed both of us forever.

When we first adopted Stella, I understood that Brian said yes to having her not because he wanted a dog but because he wanted to make me happy. We were still in the phase of getting to know each other again as a couple after I'd been away undergoing treatment in Arizona for seven months. At times, it was a struggle to find that "new normal" that would take us forward. When cancer happens, it doesn't just strike the person who is sick, it strikes the whole family. We all had cancer, in a sense, and now we had to figure out what our post-cancer relationship would look like as husband and wife. I never dreamed that getting a dog would be something that brought us together, but there was Stella, working her magic yet again.

To Brian's credit, once Stella came home with us, he put aside any reservations he may have had about getting a dog and accepted her right away, taking her for walks every morning so I could sleep in, joining the obedience class with me and Stella, serving as our cameraman when I needed someone to film a video of me with Stella.

It may have taken him a little time to warm up to her on a personal level, but once he saw how open and loving she is, how intelligent, patient, and loyal, his respect for her really grew. And over time, that respect blossomed into love. Now, when Stella gets hurt or scared, she'll run straight to Daddy Brian, bypassing me completely. If she gets a thorn in her paw, she goes to him to take it out. It's like she knows, "Okay, Mom will freak out if she sees this, but Dad will help. I can count on Dad to take care of me." Brian has always been our rock, the girls' and mine, and now, apparently, he's Stella's rock as well!

Last year, Stella sprained her tail (I'm not sure how, could have been overly enthusiastic wagging and inadvertently hitting the wall). She was in agony, turning in circles and circles, and couldn't stop crying. I gave her some medication for pain relief, but that didn't seem to help and she was so distraught. I was so upset, I didn't know what to do, so she went to Brian, jumped up on his lap, and rested her head right on the center of his chest. Only then did she settle down and stop crying, as Brian put his arms around her and held her close in a warm, strong embrace, gently stroking her head and telling her he'd make sure she was okay.

When I watch the two of them together now, I can feel their great mutual love and companionship. They are buddies, playmates, pals, just a grown-up boy and his faithful dog. They have developed their own relationship, completely separate from me, and I wouldn't want it any other way. When we first got Stella, Brian loved Stella because he loved me. Now, Brian loves Stella because she is Stella, and nothing could be better than that.

CHAPTER ELEVEN

Stella the Social Media Star

Summer 2016

A fter the heartbreak of saying good-bye to our foster girl G.I. Jane in May, we received some very good news when the Fort Wayne Pit Bull Coalition invited Stella to appear as Miss September on their 2017 calendar. I was touched and honored to think this "throwaway dog" that had been abandoned and left to die by the side of the road just a few months earlier was now being asked to model for a calendar, appearing as the public face of a much-maligned and often misunderstood breed. Of course, I knew Stella was beautiful, but this was a wonderful opportunity to show her off and share her beauty with the world.

Meanwhile, as Stella was beginning her modeling career (and I was committing to making sure she didn't turn into a total diva who insisted on no blue M&M's and who refused to get out of bed for less than ten thousand dollars), as a family, we were making some major life changes. We decided to sell our Jimmy John's franchises in Fort Wayne and move to Arizona permanently to follow our dream, which was for Brian and me to begin a new career flipping real estate properties. In other words, buying properties that weren't in prime condition and needed some work, then updating and refurbishing them before selling them at a profit.

I had fallen in love with Scottsdale while I was there undergoing treatment, and so far we had bought three investment properties in the area. Our plan was to spend the summer in Arizona working on developing our properties, then go back to Indiana in the fall to pack up, sell the house, and move to Arizona permanently by early 2017.

We planned to leave for Arizona on June 12, as soon as we came home from Stella's calendar photo shoot. When Caitie and I arrived at the photo studio, I was worried Stella might be shy in front of the camera and I'd have to coax her to perform. It turned out, I needn't have worried—she was an absolute ham! Deb from the Pit Bull Coalition was there to direct the shoot, and she explained that they wanted Stella to jump up on the platform they had assembled, which had drapes on either side.

Once Stella was in position on the platform, she acted like she'd been doing this forever. She was so dramatic, turning around, lying down, posing this way and that, showing different angles and profiles, mugging for the camera, just generally strutting her stuff and commanding the stage with her signature moves. I could almost hear her saying, "Hey, I've got this, Mama." Honestly, Tyra Banks would have been proud, and I felt like I had "America's Next Top Canine Model" on my hands.

Stella was still striking different poses and hogging the spotlight when Deb looked at me and said, "Umm, okay, Marika, that's good. I think we have enough pictures of Stella now."

"All right, Stella, c'mon, girl," I coaxed, but she did not want to come down off that stage! It was only a serious bribe of baked chicken that convinced her to relinquish the spotlight.

As we were packing up to leave, we came across the Miss October pit bull and her people waiting in the wings. The lady holding Miss October's leash touched my arm and smiled. "We were watching Stella modeling," she confided, "and I can tell you, we'll never get our dog to pose like that! Our girl is nowhere near so animated."

I felt myself blush. "What can I say? My Stella's a natural!" Overall, the photo shoot was a fun, and funny, experience, but it did get me thinking. *Stella's so outgoing, and so good with people. She's not shy at all, and doing stuff in public doesn't faze her in the least. Maybe this is part of my mission, to share her with the world, using her to promote the causes we believe in.*

As soon as Caitie and I got home from the photo shoot, we dropped Caitie off (Caitie would be spending the summer at camp) and then Brian, Stella, and I climbed in the SUV to begin the long drive cross-country to Arizona. It's just over eighteen hundred miles from Fort Wayne to Phoenix, so the trip would take several days. I worried how Stella would do, cooped up in the car with us for so many hours, and how I would keep her entertained while Brian drove. I also seriously hoped she wouldn't get carsick! A vomiting dog would make a tough trip unbearable.

As it turned out, Stella did great. She fell in

love with McDonald's ice cream, so whenever we stopped for gas or food, we'd get her some ice cream and feed it to her by the side of the road. She could be fast asleep snoring, dead to the world, but the moment she heard a seat belt click, she'd bolt upright and stand to attention, awake and alert, and hoping for ice cream, most likely.

Stella loved the hotels as well. This was her first time staying in a hotel, and she loved to jump between the two Queen-size beds before curling up with me under the covers.

I sat in the back seat with her and played games, which kept her focused and occupied. She also had her toys to play with, including a cow toe, which was the actual hoof of a cow, that we picked up at a pet store and thought was a good idea. She took to it immediately, but the more she chewed on it and played with it, the more she slobbered all over it and the wetter it got, releasing the most pungent odor of fresh cow manure. It smelled up the car so badly, we had to throw it away when she wasn't looking. But that didn't alleviate the horrible smell, which lingered all the way across Oklahoma and into the Texas panhandle, making Brian and me feel sick. Upon further investigation, we realized that the slobber from the cow toe had dripped into her bed that we'd laid out in the back seat, and now that was saturated with the foul-smelling fluid. We had to take the bed out of the SUV and strap it to the roof of the Durango so it could air out while we were driving. I can only imagine how we must have looked to other drivers, tooling down I-40 at seventy-five miles an hour, with a dog's bed strapped to the roof and flapping in the breeze!

When we arrived in Phoenix three days after we left Fort Wayne, Betsy and Randy were there to meet us at one of the condos we had purchased, and where we planned to stay while we renovated the other two. It was the first time we were seeing this unit (we had bought it sight unseen), and Betsy and Randy had gotten it all set up for us, making up the beds, putting towels in the bathroom, everything. It was such a thoughtful touch from two very fine people.

The four of us ordered a pizza and had dinner in our "new" kitchen. After Betsy and Randy left, Brian and I sat talking, finishing a bottle of wine and admiring our temporary new home as Stella lay curled up at our feet.

"What do you think?" Brian asked, nodding toward the freshly painted walls.

"I think I'm happier than I've been in years. Maybe happier than I've ever been in my life. A new start, a new home, new possibilities." I nudged Stella with my foot. "And one amazing dog." I wondered if I had to reach rock bottom, if everything I had thought was important had to be stripped away by cancer, bringing me to the point where I truly believed I was going to die, in order for me to have the strength and courage to make this new start. I suppose I will never know for sure. All I knew then was that I was going to treasure every minute and never squander this gift of a second chance.

We soon got to work on our other two condos, doing construction and making other improvements. Stella came along with us to help every day while we were working, but soon it seemed like she wasn't feeling well. Normally, she loved our daily morning trips to Starbucks for a puppuccino, but now she just wanted to stay on the couch and I had to coax her into the SUV to come with me. Then she threw up all night and was just generally sick and listless. *Maybe she ate something that disagreed with her,* I thought. *Tomorrow she'll be better.*

But then she lost her appetite and I had to feed her by hand to get her to eat anything at all. *She'll be better tomorrow,* I kept telling myself, wishing and hoping and crossing my fingers that nothing was seriously wrong. A couple of days before she got sick, we'd had a rare desert monsoon that resulted in flooding. The back lot had filled with water and I had let Stella play off-leash in a puddle, but then I took her home and bathed her in the shower right afterward. Maybe the water was dirty, I thought, and maybe she picked up a bug or something from that. I couldn't bear the thought that I might have unwittingly exposed my baby girl to something dangerous.

On the fourth or fifth day that she was under the weather, we went to Home Depot around seven p.m. and brought Stella with us as I didn't want to leave her alone. Brian and Stella were walking ahead of me and Stella's head was bowed, and she had that look that could only be described as a "hang dog" expression. I had just stopped to ask one of the Home Depot workers a question when Stella started violently vomiting. *She's really sick,* I thought, and knew I couldn't ignore it any longer. *Could it be the flu? Or could it still be something she picked up from that flood water?*

Stella was sick all night, and I took her to the vet first thing the next morning. This was the first time we'd been to a vet since our experience with Josie back at the clinic in Fort Wayne, and the first thing I told the vet was, "She's a pit bull mix. You can muzzle her if you have to."

"That's okay, we don't need to do that," the vet reassured me. After an initial examination, the vet said the symptoms suggested she might have an obstruction. That stopped me cold. An obstruction in dogs could be fatal. *I can't lose Stella—I just can't.* She'd become like one of my children in the time I'd had her. All the fear and anxiety and powerlessness I felt with my cancer came rushing back to me. We're never totally safe, or totally free. Maybe fear is the true price of love.

"We'll need to do an X-ray to see if there's an obstruction," the vet explained, and I quickly agreed, then called Brian to give him the update.

The X-rays seemed to take forever while I was in the waiting room, praying, *Please, God, let Stella be okay. I need more time with my precious baby girl. Please let her be okay.*

When the vet returned, she said, "Well, there's no obstruction that I can see, and I can't find any other cause for her vomiting and lethargy. It might just be some type of tummy bug. I'm going to prescribe a course of antibiotics and see if that helps."

I drove home thanking God that the news wasn't worse. I got Stella home and started her on the medication, and slowly she began to improve. It was a long recovery, and she was sick for nearly two weeks before I could say she was fully back on her feet.

We never were able to pinpoint what caused the illness, but after that I was so careful about where I let her go, what I let her eat, and so forth. This whole experience was another scary reminder of how precious and fragile life is, and how quickly things can change. I vowed to treasure Stella every day that I was lucky enough to have her in my life.

By early 2017, Stella had recovered from her mystery illness and we had sold our house in Fort Wayne and completed the move to Scottsdale. I loved working with Brian on the real estate projects, but I was getting antsy to do more, career-wise. I was feeling great in terms of my health, but I still had that nagging voice in the back of my head, asking what I was doing with my life and if I was really making the most of my second chance, post-cancer. *There's got to be something else for me,* I thought. *I must do more.*

I dusted off and updated my résumé and started to explore various career opportunities. I had worked for myself for so long, I didn't remember what it was like to enter the job market. Also, things had changed a lot since I first started working right after high school in the early nineties. Now everything was online, Monster.com, CareerFinder, LinkedIn, et cetera.

I started sending out applications for professional jobs in and around Scottsdale, but I was dismayed to find that I wasn't called in for a single interview. All my old insecurities bubbled back to the surface. *Am I not smart enough? Skilled enough? Don't I express myself well enough on the application? Was my first husband right when he said I'd never amount to anything?* It turned out that the companies I was applying to filtered applicants by education, not by skills and work experience, and since I had left college after the first semester without a degree, I wasn't making the first cut, even though I had twenty years of work experience.

Frustrated, I instead began applying to places like Costco, Trader Joe's, and Whole Foods, but was turned away there, too, because I was overqualified. It seemed I was caught in a classic catch-22: Although I had the right experience, I didn't have enough education for the jobs that required a college degree, but I had too much experience for the lower-level jobs, and the way the application systems were automated, I was filtered out before I could even put myself forward for a position.

Hmmm, I thought, listening again to that powerful intuition, that deep and steady inner voice that guided my life. *Maybe this is the universe's way of telling me these jobs aren't what I'm supposed to be doing right now.* It was true that I really didn't want to be away from Stella every weekday at a nine-to-five office job, and possibly with a commute that would keep us apart even longer, but it was unnerving to think that I was unemployable.

I've been an entrepreneur all my life, beginning at age nineteen, when I started my first company, The Specialty Shop, making and selling personalized products, then was a co-owner of Britannia with my parents and was key in helping that company grow and prosper, and after that, I was a single mom of two pre-teen girls launching the first Jimmy John's in Fort Wayne essentially on my own. *If I did it before, I can do it again,* I told myself. *But what? Okay, universe, if I'm ready to go out on my own again, give me some clue as to what my new venture should be . . .*

I was seeing how much joy Stella brought to people everywhere we went, and I felt I had a responsibility to share that joy with the world. But how, exactly? *Maybe Stella should be a therapy dog,* I considered. *She has such an amazing ability to make people smile and forget their troubles, at least for a little while when they are with her.* I could picture us visiting hospitals and clinics and rehab centers, spending time with people who were scared, lonely, and in pain and brightening their days.

I started working with Stella to get her ready to be certified as a therapy animal. She did great, but me . . . not so much. I had so much anxiety, panic, and PTSD related to my own experiences in medical settings, I worried that going back to that environment, even in the role of a helper, not a patient, would be very triggering for me. Just being in a medical setting (even only to visit) brought back the sights, sounds, smells, and emotions from the past, like a flashback to my surgery, radiation, PET scans, endless appointments and consults, experiences that left me terrified and shaking. I felt torn. How could I find a way for Stella to help people in need without it becoming emotionally and psychologically unhealthy for me?

The answer to this conundrum came from the unlikeliest of places: the Internet. One day my daughter Carly said to me, "Mom, you should do more with Stella on Instagram. She's so cute, people would really love to see more of her."

I hadn't really considered that. I had started Facebook and Instagram pages for Stella at the end of June and was posting sporadically, gathering a few likes, comments, and followers here and there, but nothing significant. "You need to do more than what you're doing if you want to build a following," Carly explained. "You need to post more, and engage more directly with your audience." Carly's generation knew a lot more about these things than I did. I thought, *Why not? Stella is super-cute and very photogenic, if I make more of an effort, then more people might follow her.*

It was January 7, 2017, when I made a conscious decision to start building Stella's online audience, sharing her with other people and positioning her as a breed ambassador for pit bulls. I started looking at other dog accounts that were successful and studied what they were doing right and what I could learn from them.

With Carly's help, I started posting more cute photos and engaging more with Stella's followers. It worked! Stella's account grew quickly, and soon she was averaging one hundred new followers a day or more. I was humbled and amazed when I saw that people literally all around the world followed and loved Stella. That may sound funny; how can you love a dog you've never even met, but people were falling in love with her just based on her pictures and her inspiring story of overcoming the odds.

Her followers started sending us messages to share photos of their own dogs, especially pit bulls, and their stories about how their dogs had changed their lives, just like Stella had transformed mine. A true community was being built, photo by photo, like by like, post by post.

Now that we were tapping into a large dog-loving audience, the question became, How could we best share our message with others? I felt my passion developing, along with the sense that I had discovered "my thing," the thing I was meant to do. My goal became to share Stella's story and to educate people about the powerful and positive role that pets can play in our lives. Also, I wanted to share with people the health benefits of pet ownership (benefits that have been scientifically proven) and show the love these animals can bring us. We wanted to encourage people to rescue, adopt, and foster animals like Stella to improve and even save dogs' lives. We also wanted to lead the charge in pit bull breed awareness and acceptance, changing the negative stereotype of these dogs as violent, dangerous, and unpredictable.

Before long, I realized that managing Stella's affairs was a full-time job. Somewhere along the line I quit worrying about what I was going to do career wise or trying to hop back on the corporate ladder, and I just embraced what was right in front of me . . . Stella. Next thing I know, we had created the IncrediBullStella brand, and Stella had her own LLC, credit card, and checking account!

While we were building the brand and Stella's audience, I also found a new passion: I began writing and designing an IncrediBullStella coloring book for adults, all about how I had adopted Stella and how she had changed my life. The simple act of coloring, formerly thought of as solely a children's pursuit, has been shown to have relaxing and therapeutic benefits for adults as well. Not only that, I saw the coloring book as another venue to hopefully start to shift people's perceptions about the pit bull breed.

Finally, the universe seemed to be aligning in my favor, and I committed myself to working on this cause every day. I felt more energetic, optimistic, and focused than I had in years, and certainly more than I had since before my cancer diagnosis.

Every night before I went to bed and then again when I woke up the next morning, I would ask for direction and awareness as to what I should do next. Some people may have thought I was a little nutty, but I didn't care. I had such a sense of purpose and felt so engaged with what I was working on, it didn't matter what other people thought. My intuition told me a couple of different things: One—keep showing up, keep throwing down seeds, something will bloom. Two—something from nothing. Something from nothing, I repeated that like a mantra—every day I would work on my next steps, which seemed to arrive out of thin air . . . and something would come from nothing.

I felt my perspective shifting in other ways as well. Even though I had been an entrepreneur since I was nineteen, I had never actually enjoyed playing that role, and having to constantly pretend made me feel stressed out and afraid. The chronic anxiety it caused me left me so drained and exhausted that I thought about dying. If I were dead, it would all go away and the battle would be over.

I was never suicidal; I didn't actually want to die, I just wanted to disappear for a while, to have a break from the fear and stress. Before I opened my first Jimmy John's, I sometimes felt trapped working with my family at Britannia, and I so longed to make a career change but I feared taking that first step. I recall once saying, "Staying here is like a cancer eating away at me." I knew how overly dramatic that sounded, but as it turned out, if the doctors were correct and I had had cancer for six to eight years prior to my diagnosis, then it was during that period of my greatest fear and anxiety that the cancer was actively growing inside me, threatening to make a reality the death I had sometimes imagined.

In addition to the stress I experienced in my past businesses, I also so often felt like a fraud. It didn't matter how vulnerable or scared I felt, I had to constantly maintain an air of confidence. There was no one to confide in. I couldn't share my feelings with my staff, and certainly not with our customers, industry partners, or competitors. It seemed I just had to make everyone else feel things were all right, even though my knees were knocking most of the time.

And now . . . now, suddenly, everything was so different. Not only did I have Brian's love and support to guide me and back me up, I had Stella to keep me focused on the positives rather than any dark thoughts. I had such a passion to share Stella with the world, it far exceeded any fears or anxieties I had about going public and putting myself out there in scary or nerve-racking situations. *I'm ready at last,* I thought. *Bring it on.*

Marika and Stella with foster dog Roxy, late 2017 *(photo courtesy Brian Meeks)*.

CHAPTER TWELVE

Stella, Roxy, and The Dodo

Spring 2017

Stella's online presence was growing by leaps and bounds as we moved into the spring of 2017. I still struggled with occasional dark thoughts and anxieties, but most mornings I woke up in bliss: opening my eyes to a full day's schedule of events and meet and greets and opportunities for Stella to pair with local companies and organizations to promote their products and causes, along with our mission. It also didn't hurt that I woke to a big, happy, goofy, wet-nosed puppy jumping into my bed, demanding cuddles. With her smiling face, lolling tongue, and furiously wagging tail, how could I be unhappy about anything?

We also started doing media appearances on local news shows, sharing our personal story of how Stella's love and companionship changed my life, and also talking about pit bulls in general, hoping to dispel people's numerous myths and misconceptions about the breed.

I was way out of my comfort zone now, and sometimes my nerves did get the best of me, but as long as I had Stella to focus on, my anxiety remained manageable. *I'm doing this for a higher purpose,* I told myself, and those words always gave me hope and strength.

Meanwhile, my heart had finally healed, at least a little bit, after saying good-bye to our foster G.I. Jane, but I wasn't sure I felt ready to take in another foster dog yet. But then fate intervened with different plans.

Stella had started having some incontinence problems, which was highly unusual for her. The vet put her on hormone medication, which took care of the problem, but had the effect of making her behave strangely. Suddenly, my bright, bubbly, happy girl was nervous and fearful. She would try to sit on top of me, looking for a place where she could feel safe. Deeply concerned, I took Stella to Jose and Monique, two trainers I knew who had their own training facility. They took one look at her and said, "Hmmm, I think Stella needs a friend."

"A friend? What kind of friend?"

"Having another dog in the house would really help Stella settle." That was still sinking in when Monique added, "And we have just the dog for Stella. Her name is Roxy. She's looking for a forever home, but you could foster her until then."

Jose smiled. "Roxy and Stella would make a good pair," he added.

I was feeling a little skeptical, until they brought out Roxy and it was another one of those love-at-first-sight moments for me. *Oh damn,* I thought, *she's got me good.* Roxy was a big girl, a pit bull mix that looked like she might be part boxer, and maybe a few other things thrown in for good measure, with a large, square head, a short coat in a warm shade of tan, and deep, soft, coffee-colored eyes.

Stella and Roxy hit it off immediately, and they were hilarious together. Roxy was very chill, just going with the flow, but she was also a total clown, big and boisterous, like a bull in a china shop but with a wicked tail wag. If she caught you across the shins, you certainly felt it! She also had a bad habit of peeing on the floor, and we weren't sure why that was an issue for her.

We didn't know much about Roxy's background, but she didn't know how to play typical doggie games, especially fetch, so we worked to teach her. During one of her lessons, Brian was outside working with both dogs. He threw a ball for Stella, then threw one for Roxy, but both dogs dove for the same ball and one hundred fifty pounds of fast-moving dog collided in midair. Brian heard a blood-curdling cry as both dogs hit the ground in pain. Roxy took the brunt of it, ending up with a deep gash in her front leg. I held Roxy in my arms as Brian assessed the damage. "It's bleeding pretty bad," he said. "It looks like she needs stitches." Fortunately, Stella escaped with only scrapes and bruises.

We took Roxy to the vet and were shocked when, during the exam, the vet told us that Roxy had a serious heart murmur. The worst murmur is grade six; Roxy was a four. *Oh no. She's such a good, sweet girl.* I fought back tears as I rubbed her ears and stroked her shoulders. *She doesn't deserve this.* And I worried about her future, too. *Who will want to adopt a dog with a serious heart defect?*

"There is a surgical procedure that can fix

this," the vet offered as she finished stitching the gash in Roxy's leg. "But we'd need to do an ultrasound first, to better assess her condition."

"She's not our dog," we explained. "But we'll let you know what we decide."

It was a quiet journey home as we pondered the devastating news. While Brian drove, I sat in the back seat between Roxy and Stella, petting both girls, but holding Roxy especially close, my arm draped over her shoulder and my hand pressed to her chest, where I could feel her heart beating fast beneath my palm. "All this time, we had no idea something was wrong with your poor little heart. Maybe we could have helped you earlier if we had known."

I had fallen deeply for this girl in the short time we'd had her, and I couldn't bear to think that she might not survive because she didn't have a forever family in a position to pay for what sounded like very expensive treatment.

We got in touch with Jose and Monique to give them the update on Roxy. They were shocked and contacted Mollie, the woman who had originally found and rescued Roxy. Mollie wanted Roxy to have the procedure necessary to fix the murmur, and she volunteered to pay the three-thousand-dollar cost. Roxy had an ultrasound, and then a second ultrasound to confirm the findings of the first.

The ultrasounds revealed that in addition to

the heart murmur, Roxy had BB pellets lodged all down her side. I was shocked and horrified. I thought, hoped, that the worst she'd been through with her original owners was that they hadn't taught her how to play games or fetch. Now I knew that the truth was so much worse.

We scheduled Roxy for the procedure, and I was a very nervous mama on the day we took her in to the clinic, but she came through with flying colors. The vet used a catheter to open up the blockage, and the fix was instant, immediately resolving the problem. I thanked God that it was so simple. And interestingly, Roxy never had another accident in the house after that.

By the summer of 2017, I was ready to self-publish my IncrediBullStella adult coloring book, so I hired a local marketing company to help me market it and spread the word. They came up with an excellent plan to land me interviews with the media and other outreach efforts. One day I got a very excited phone call from Mychael, the manager of my campaign. "Guess what, Marika?—I contacted 'The Dodo' and they want to do your story!" he said breathlessly.

"The Dodo?" I asked.

"Yeah. You know, the people who produce those cute, funny, touching, animal-themed videos you see on Facebook and other places online?"

I had seen the videos; I guess I had just never

thought about where they came from or how the producers found their subject matter. "They want to interview Stella and me?" I asked.

"Yes! Marika, this is an amazing opportunity."

I was excited, too, knowing the reach of an online video could go so much further than any press we might do locally. So I began putting together clips and sending them to the Dodo producers, and then we did a two-hour Skype interview so they'd have plenty of material for our story.

When I saw the finished product, I was so touched. The one-and-a-half-minute video really packed an emotional wallop, beginning with a scene of me massaging Stella's head between my bare feet, my toenails painted bright orange as Stella's smushed face shows absolute bliss.

I was grateful to be alive, I guess, but I had forgotten how to live . . . my voiceover began. Over photos and live-action footage of me and Stella, I went on to describe how I'd gotten wrapped up in fear and anxiety, almost like an obsession, until Stella helped show me a better, happier path.

Here I am, stuck in the dichotomy of actually overcoming cancer, I said, *but I was trapped in this really miserable space, and Stella shifted me out of that.*

I didn't know when the video was going to be released online, but on July 21, I was in the living room with Stella, folding laundry, when Carly, who was sitting at the kitchen counter with her laptop, suddenly called me over, very excited, saying, "Mom, Mom, The Dodo video just came out!" I went over and watched it play on the screen, but while I was watching the video, Carly was watching the "views" start to rack up. Three thousand, four thousand . . . now it was fifteen thousand views! Within a few hours, our little video had been viewed more than one hundred thousand times! I was absolutely floored. I thought our story was important, but I had no idea it would touch so many people, most of them strangers, people who had never met us in person, and probably never would, but who had been moved by what we'd gone through.

Most humbling for me was the number of people, especially fellow cancer survivors, who contacted me directly after seeing the video to say they understood. My words enabled other people who were struggling to come forward, while helping me to realize that I wasn't alone.

The one-minute version of the video was posted on Instagram while a longer, three-minute version was posted to Facebook. Soon it was picked up by other platforms as well and posted to numerous other sites such as Snapchat, Pittie Nation, and Instagram again.

By now, our story has been viewed more than

ten million times. When I think of the number of lives this has allowed Stella to touch, it's overwhelming. I was so moved by our experience with The Dodo video that I decided to donate one hundred percent of the proceeds of the coloring book to the Arizona Humane Society, as a small gesture of giving back.

Things were going so well with my IncrediBullStella venture, I decided it was time to start challenging myself on a personal level as well. January 2018 would mark the five-year anniversary since I was diagnosed with breast cancer. I had my yearly exam with my surgeon that month, but assuming I got the all-clear (fingers crossed), I was going to make 2018 my year.

I was feeling so much better mentally, I wanted to reflect that physically as well. I hired Bob, a personal trainer, to lead me through a new, more intense workout routine. I had been working out three days a week, but now I wanted to double that to six. But that first session was so hard, I thought I was going to die. I told Bob after the session finished, "This is too hard. I can't do this. It's not worth it, if I'm going to be miserable for days afterward."

"Stick with it. It will get better," he promised, and slowly but surely, it did. At first, I didn't tell anyone other than Bob about my new workout regimen because I didn't want to be judged, but after three or four weeks, I was looking and feeling better, and I found the strength to share what I was doing. Everyone was so supportive, and I felt I had the space to explore this new area.

In October 2017, I saw an ad on Instagram announcing the 15th Annual Hero Awards, sponsored by The Arizona Pet Project. This event was designed to celebrate both human and animal heroes who represented stories of survival, companionship, and heroism while raising much-needed funds to pay for spay and neuter initiatives and intervention programs to keep pets at home and out of shelters. *This is perfect for us!* I told Stella.

When I read through the nomination form online, I realized that Stella would be a perfect candidate for the Loyal Companion award, given to the animal "who acted in an extraordinary way and stayed by their loved one's side during a difficult time" (such as a person with a terminal illness, or provided comfort during the passing away of a spouse or family member, etc.).

While I didn't adopt Stella until after I finished my cancer treatment, I never could have gotten through the aftermath of cancer if she hadn't been by my side. But then my negative self-talk started casting doubts; *If I apply and we're chosen, we'll have to go up onstage, maybe give a speech, talk to the media, all the things that make me nervous*. And then that voice inside said, *Wake up, Marika! This isn't about you; this is about Stella. You're doing this for her.* So I filled out the nomination form, put together some articles and links, and sent it off with a prayer for good luck.

Determined to move further and further outside my well-established comfort zone, I signed up for dancing lessons, something I never would have even considered pre-Stella, pre-cancer, pre- any earlier time in my life. Brian had wanted to learn how to dance, so when our friend Betsy signed up for lessons, I surprised Brian and signed him up, too. Shortly after he started, we went to an event at a dance studio that offered a free swing lesson. On a whim, I took the free lesson. I had no idea what I was doing and frankly felt like an idiot. But I kept at it; I kind of had to since everyone else was doing it, too, and slowly I started to pick up the steps.

In that moment, my belief system around my abilities shifted a bit. It was exciting to think that maybe I could learn to dance. I had always assumed that dancing was for other people, not for me. But why not? Why shouldn't Marika be able to dance?

After that class, I decided to sign up for actual dance lessons. I loved it, and it blew my mind that I loved it and that I was able to learn a little more each lesson . . . I was learning how to dance!

At home I would practice my steps with Stella as my only audience. She may not have understood what I was doing, but in her calm, steady, amber eyes, I saw patience, acceptance, support. It made me wonder, not for the first time, why we can't see ourselves the way our animals see us—as amazing creatures deserving of devotion and unconditional love.

I just couldn't believe it. The belief that I couldn't learn how to dance was so strongly embedded within me that finding out that I could in fact dance tipped my world a little sideways. I saw so clearly that my own beliefs about what I could and couldn't do were creating my reality. Now my mind was asking, how many other things could I do if I changed my mind-set, threw away my preconceived notions and deeply held negative beliefs, and just did it?

After dancing for a couple of months, I took part in a mock competition that included the waltz, tango, and foxtrot. I, Marika Hamilton Meeks, she of the formerly two left feet, was able to dance all of those!

I thought I would be nervous during the competition, but I wasn't. I was ready to dance, and I think I danced better at the competition than I ever had during our lessons.

Brian recorded my dance on his phone and I

was able to watch my performance. When he saw me playing back the video yet again, he said to me, "How many times are you going to watch that?"

"As many times as I need to!" I joked. I watched it over and over; I just couldn't believe that strong, graceful woman gliding across the stage was actually me!

It might sound silly, but I actually believe I have Stella to thank for giving me the courage to take up dancing. The more I worked on sharing Stella's story with the world, the more relaxed and content I felt overall. I woke up with her beside me, and I felt inspired and confident that the next opportunity, the next idea, the next person I needed to meet would show up and be waiting for me.

Not only that, if something didn't work out, I was okay with that, and simply chalked it up to the divine plan that none of us can really understand while it is unfolding. The universe was starting to shift from a scary, hostile place to one that was loving, supportive, and nurturing. But of course, it wasn't the universe that was changing, *I* was changing.

For the first time in my life, I was living my purpose and I was living it with ease. Ease. I like the way that sounds. Sometimes I have moments of doubt and I think, *Am I just being unrealistic? Is this really my purpose? Am I being an idiot to think that I can really make a difference, have an impact on the world? Or am I just wasting my time, effort, money, and energy? Maybe I'm just a fool?*

Then I take a deep breath and try to remember what my priorities are. To enjoy what I'm doing. That's it, if I can keep it fun and inspiring for me, that is worth more than any money I could earn. I have something that money can't buy; I am engaged and passionate and I wouldn't change that for all the money in the world.

I had almost forgotten about nominating Stella for a Hero Award with The Arizona Pet Project, but then in November, I got the call letting us know that not only had Stella been chosen to receive the Loyal Companion award, the judging committee had made her a unanimous choice!

I was so excited for Stella, and excited for our whole family. *This will give us the chance to share Stella's story with a much broader audience,* I thought. Of course, I also realized that I had nothing to wear . . . well, the dinner wasn't until March, so I had some time to figure it out.

When January 2018 rolled around, I felt that familiar dread, that sick feeling in the pit of my stomach as I faced my yearly checkup with my breast cancer surgeon. This year was especially significant as it was now five years exactly since

I had first been diagnosed, and that's a major milestone for every cancer survivor.

Usually, scheduling this appointment sent me into a tailspin of fear, anxiety, worry. The previous year I took an anti-anxiety pill before the appointment, just to help take the edge off my fear, but this year I said, "No. I want to actually experience it this year. I will face whatever happens. I don't want my senses to be dulled by medication."

I was feeling stronger, more confident than in the past, but then I decided to slip the pills into my purse, just in case. *Just knowing they are there might make me less likely to need them,* I reasoned. At the last moment, I decided to bring Stella to my appointment as well. *You're my Emotional Support Animal,* I told her. *And today, more than any other day, I really, really need your emotional support.*

As Brian drove me to the appointment, my mind was racing. *The past eleven months, since we adopted Stella, have been the best time of my life. I have hope now; I have a purpose; I have passion and a reason to get out of bed every day. But cancer can change that in an instant. If the cancer is back . . .*

It seemed so cruel, so unfair to think that just when my life was back on track, it could all be torn away from me. I've been told that, with the kind of cancer I had, if I have a recurrence, that will pretty much be it for me—there won't be any treatment to stop the disease the second time around. *Please, God,* I prayed, *let today go okay. Let me be healthy.*

We arrived at the clinic and while Brian went to park the car, Stella and I took the elevator up to the second floor to check in for my appointment. As soon as the elevator doors closed, I felt intense waves of dizziness and nausea that sent me reeling. I had to hold tight to Stella and brace myself against the wall in order just to stay upright.

I recognized this response as something called "anticipatory anxiety," which means when going into a situation that is triggering, the body responds to the feelings and expectations tied to that place from past experiences. Now that I understood where this reaction was coming from, I felt better. At least a little bit.

My knees were shaking and my heart pounding as I entered my surgeon's office, checked in, and took my place in a chair in the waiting room. Brian came in soon after and sat down beside me. I started playing with Stella's ESA vest to distract myself, and it worked. Suddenly, I was more aware of her than I was aware of my fear. Stella has that ability to soften everything. It's not about me anymore, it's not about the scary stuff, I'm thinking about something other than the very, very scary reason why I am here.

Stella's my shield; with her, I feel safe, and not so vulnerable.

I felt like I sat there waiting forever, those interminable, agonizing minutes, both fearing what came next but also wanting to get it over with. At last, we were called into the exam room. *It's showtime,* I told Stella, as she rose from her haunches and fell into step at my side.

"How are you, Marika?" Dr. Herbert asked, gently taking my hand.

"Pretty nervous," I admitted. "But I've got Stella here to help me through it." After all my terrible experiences with the medical community, I truly found an angel in Dr. Laura Herbert. She was the kindest, most patient, and most empathetic surgeon I could have found. When she performed my mastectomy in 2015, she did everything she could to make it easier on me, so unlike the nightmare I'd experienced when I had my first surgery, the lumpectomy in Indiana in 2013.

For example, she performed my surgery at an orthopedic hospital, rather than the regular hospital, because it was smaller, friendlier, and had a better nurse/patient ratio. Before I had the anesthetic, she had come into my room, sat on the edge of my bed, put her hand on my knee, and just talked to me, woman to woman, human being to human being. She made me feel safe, protected, cared for. She made me feel like I mattered.

As she performed the exam today, I was nervous, but she did everything she could to put me at ease, talking me through each step of her exam. I had made a decision after I had my mastectomy and finished radiation that I was not going to have any more mammograms, scans, or other tests; I was going to have my yearly exam with my surgeon and that was it. Dr. Herbert supported this decision. For me, it was a conscious choice not to live from appointment to appointment, from test to test, from scan to scan. Undergoing that type of testing pushed me to the edge of a nervous breakdown, and I chose not to live that way anymore.

"Everything looks good, Marika," Dr. Herbert said at the end of the exam. "I don't feel anything suspicious or concerning. I look forward to seeing you next year."

Yes! My relief was immense. I immediately hugged Stella and kissed her forehead. "Hear that, Stella? We're good for another year! And what a year I have in store for us!"

My excitement over getting the all-clear from my doctor was tempered by having to say good-bye to Roxy in February. We had kept her longer than we kept most fosters, because we wanted to get her to her three-month checkup after her heart procedure. Once she got the all-clear back in September, I started posting on Facebook and

Instagram that we were looking to find her the perfect home. A young woman named Hannah saw the post, started following me, and sent me a message saying she was interested in adopting Roxy.

In September we invited Hannah to meet Roxy, and it was a great match, right from the first moment. These two really "got" each other, but Hannah wanted everything to be perfect before she brought Roxy home. So we agreed to keep Roxy until February, so Hannah could be in the best possible position to complete the adoption.

On a Friday afternoon, Brian and I helped Hannah move into her new apartment, and Roxy moved in as well. I loved Hannah and had every confidence in her as an adoptive pit bull mom, but I was so worried about Roxy. After living with us for so long, I feared she'd be heartbroken, believing that we had abandoned her to a relative stranger.

At eleven a.m. Sunday morning, we received a phone call from Hannah, sobbing and hysterical. "Hannah, calm down, what's wrong?" I was terrified that something terrible had happened to Roxy. *And she's only just left us . . .*

When Hannah was finally able to speak, she explained that she had gone to start her washing machine, but the water valve was broken, and her kitchen was quickly filling with water, which was now up to her shins.

"Hang on, we'll be right there," we told her, but it was a twenty-minute drive to her apartment, and by the time we got there, we were sloshing through water. I couldn't help wondering, *Will Roxy be excited to see me? Will she think we've come back to pick her up and take her home? Will Hannah feel bad that Roxy is so bonded to us?*

Brian figured out that the break was in the wall behind the stackable washer/dryer unit, and it would take some work to repair. Roxy, for her part, completely ignored us, looking through the window and crying for Hannah. She'd apparently forgotten about us completely, even though we were her parents for more than half a year!

Wow, Hannah is really her person, I realized. And Roxy figured that out in a day and a half. That's the true beauty of fostering—you can love a dog, but you are not necessarily that dog's person. As a foster parent, you are helping an animal find that forever family, giving them the chance to find "the one."

Roxy's life today is amazing: She goes hiking and on vacation with Hannah. Hannah will do anything for Roxy, she'll move if she has to, she'll do anything to protect her. This also demonstrates how, when someone adopts one of our foster dogs, we don't lose a dog, we gain a new family member. We adopt that person, too. Hannah will be part of our life forever.

We recently had a little scare when Hannah phoned to tell us she had to take Roxy to the vet, but our fears were allayed when the vet diagnosed Roxy with acid reflux from eating too much strip steak.

"If all we have to worry about is Roxy being too well fed, things are going very well indeed," I told Brian with a laugh. And then I looked at Stella, snoozing, curled up around my feet as we cuddled on the couch. "Stella gave me back my family when you all felt so far away. And she gave me a focus other than fear and anxiety. But she's done so much more than that—she's given me new friends and new family, a whole circle of people and animals I never otherwise would have met. That's pretty powerful for a homeless pup who was abandoned and left to die by the side of the road. Isn't it amazing, what love can do?"

The Meeks family today: Marika, Carly, Stella, Caitie, Brian.

EPILOGUE
Stella (and Marika) Just Getting Started

Autumn 2018

Thanks to Stella, today I find myself a forty-six-year-old wife, mother, and cancer survivor who is living her best life ever. Stella and I are on a mission, to spread her key messages about pit bull breed awareness and acceptance, the health benefits of pet ownership for people, the importance of spaying and neutering, and the wonderful, lifesaving opportunities that come with fostering.

We've also become deeply involved in fighting Breed Specific Legislation. Pit bulls, sadly, are often discriminated against, and Breed Specific Legislation (BSL) impacts pit bulls and other similar dogs more than other breeds. For example, in Montreal, if you have a pit bull, it must be muzzled even in your own fenced backyard. Insurance companies often don't provide coverage if you have a pit bull, and many landlords specifically exclude tenants from having pit bulls, so between insurance not covering homeowners and landlords not allowing them, shelters are overflowing with pit bulls just like Stella. It breaks my heart to think how many beautiful dogs like Stella that would make kind, loving, gentle family pets are instead euthanized every year simply because of myths and misunderstandings about the breed. Stella and I are committed to helping change that.

Meanwhile, Brian and I have been happily married for almost eight years, and we've settled in Arizona's beautiful Paradise Valley. My health is great, and my daughters are happy and healthy, focusing on their education. Caitie, who was once so lost she contemplated ending her life, now volunteers as a peer counselor, talking to other kids and young adults about suicide prevention.

I had a rough start in life, and Stella did, too, which may partially explain why we were so drawn to each other. I never thought I was worth much, and I accepted the little that people gave me, in terms of love, respect, and affection. I didn't believe I deserved anything better. Today, instead of being content with crumbs, I spend my life in pursuit of things that bring me joy. If something compelling comes across my path, I go for it, and if I fail, I chalk it up to experience and then go back and try again.

Getting to this point wasn't easy. In fact, I came about as close as you can get to losing my life before I realized that not being me was killing me. I had to come to understand and believe that I was entitled to be happy. Entitled to be and do those things that bring me joy, entitled to happiness. What are you entitled to?

In the pages of this book, I share how becoming an entrepreneur, leaving a failed marriage, dealing with my first husband's alcoholism, and navigating my Stage 3 breast cancer diagnosis all taught me, eventually, just what I *was* entitled to: finding true love, trusting my intuition, deep healing of body and spirit, faith in myself, and so much more.

It's taken me a long time to realize it, but I can finally say that I am so grateful for what cancer has taught me. I am so grateful I got this diagnosis/opportunity in my forties. What if I didn't get it until I was eighty? If my wake-up call came at eighty . . . what a waste that would have been. Being diagnosed at forty-one gave me the opportunity to live the second half of my life differently from the first. What greater tragedy is there than figuring out your passion in life when it's too late to act on it?

My journey is about so much more than my efforts to stay alive. It is *all* about how to *live* while you are still alive. Isn't that what we all should be focused on anyway, cancer or no cancer? This is my most important work; this is what my soul is calling me to do. This, come what may, is the path and life I have chosen.

And finally, there is Stella. When she wakes me up every morning by bounding into my room and into my bed, I stare into her deep amber eyes and I see reflected back to me nothing but pure love, patience, and acceptance. I see an idealized version of myself. I used to feel like I wasn't enough, but to her, I am enough, and so much more. I may not be a perfect person, but I'm *her* perfect person, and that's all that matters. Her love keeps me grounded, but her love also gives me wings to fly.

Thank you, Stella. You came along when I least expected it and you healed my broken spirit, you mended my splintered family, and you gave me something to focus on other than my anxiety, worry, and illness. You've opened my mind, my heart, and my world to new people and new possibilities. I can't wait to see where our adventures take us next!

ACKNOWLEDGMENTS

Many people were instrumental to us in the writing of this book. We would especially like to thank our editor, Michaela Hamilton, and everyone at Kensington for all their hard work and support.

Marika would especially like to thank her husband, Brian; her best friend, Betsy; and her mom for helping her with this undertaking.

Elizabeth begs forgiveness from her cats, Claudius and Calpurnia, for writing yet another "dog book." She trusts she will, in time, earn back their love.

FOR MORE INFORMATION

To learn about our mission, please visit www.incredibullstella.com.

Fort Wayne Pit Bull Coalition
www.fwpbc.com

The Arizona Pet Project
www.azpetproject.org

Arizona Animal Rescue Mission
www.azanimalrescue.org

Maricopa Animal Care and Control
www.maricopa.gov/3560/Animal-Care
-and-Control

With hundreds of dogs, and way over capacity, Maricopa Animal Care and Control has to make difficult decisions every day. Limited space and limited funds put an inordinate number of dogs, especially pit-bull-mix dogs, at high risk of being euthanized.

Sadly, this is the case in many places across the country. The only true solution to end the suffering of these dogs and the overpopulation problem is to spay and neuter as many pets as possible.

THE
KWAKIUTL

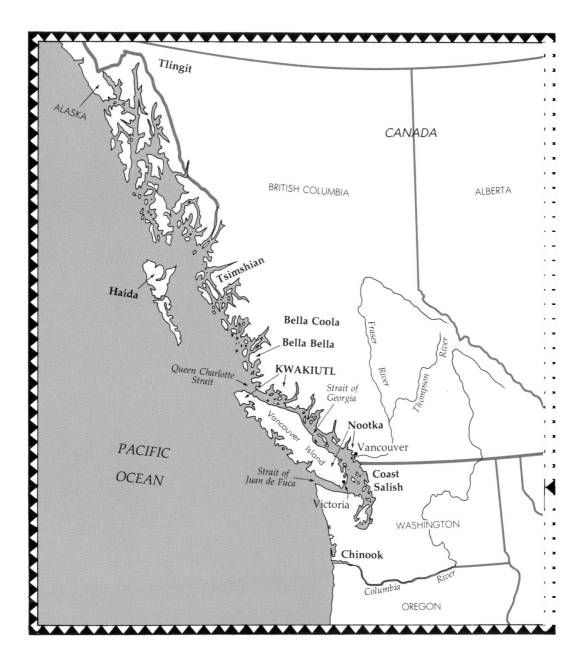

Tlingit

ALASKA

CANADA

BRITISH COLUMBIA

ALBERTA

Tsimshian

Haida

Bella Coola

Bella Bella

KWAKIUTL

Queen Charlotte
Strait

Strait of
Georgia

Fraser
River

Thompson
River

Nootka

Vancouver

Vancouver
Island

Strait of
Juan de Fuca

Coast
Salish

PACIFIC

OCEAN

Victoria

WASHINGTON

Chinook

Columbia
River

OREGON

THE
KWAKIUTL

Stanley Walens

Frank W. Porter III
General Editor

New Gloucester Public Library

CHELSEA HOUSE PUBLISHERS
New York   Philadelphia

On the cover   A 19th century Kwakiutl mask, representing a mythical female being named Dzonokwa.

Chelsea House Publishers
Editor-in-Chief   Remmel Nunn
Managing Editor   Karyn Gullen Browne
Copy Chief   Mark Rifkin
Picture Editor   Adrian G. Allen
Art Director   Maria Epes
Assistant Art Director   Howard Brotman
Manufacturing Director   Gerald Levine
Systems Manager   Lindsey Ottman
Production Manager   Joseph Romano
Production Coordinator   Marie Claire Cebrián

Indians of North America
Senior Editor   Liz Sonneborn

Staff for **THE KWAKIUTL**
Copy Editor   Christopher Duffy
Editorial Assistant   Michele Berezansky
Designer   Debora Smith
Picture Researcher   Sandy Jones

5   7   9   8   6   4

Library of Congress Cataloging-in-Publication Data

Walens, Stanley
  Kwakiutl/by Stanley Walens.
    p.   cm.—(Indians of North America)
  Includes bibliographical references (p.   ) and index.
  Summary: Examines the history, changing fortunes, and current situation of the Kwakiutl Indians. Includes a picture essay of their crafts.
    ISBN 1-55546-711-3
        0-7910-0384-1 (pbk.)
  1. Kwakiutl Indians. [1. Kwakiutl Indians. 2. Indians of North America.] I. Title II. Series: Indians of North America (Chelsea House Publishers)
                                                          90-2310
E99.K9W344   1991   CIP
970.004'979—dc20   AC

CONTENTS

INDIANS OF NORTH AMERICA

CHELSEA HOUSE PUBLISHERS

INDIANS OF NORTH AMERICA: CONFLICT AND SURVIVAL

Frank W. Porter III

The Indians survived our open intention of wiping them out, and since the tide turned they have even weathered our good intentions toward them, which can be much more deadly.

John Steinbeck
America and Americans

When Europeans first reached the North American continent, they found hundreds of tribes occupying a vast and rich country. The newcomers quickly recognized the wealth of natural resources. They were not, however, so quick or willing to recognize the spiritual, cultural, and intellectual riches of the people they called Indians.

The Indians of North America examines the problems that develop when people with different cultures come together. For American Indians, the consequences of their interaction with non-Indian people have been both productive and tragic. The Europeans believed they had "discovered" a "New World," but their religious bigotry, cultural bias, and materialistic world view kept them from appreciating and understanding the people who lived in it. All too often they attempted to change the way of life of the indigenous people. The Spanish conquistadores wanted the Indians as a source of labor. The Christian missionaries, many of whom were English, viewed them as potential converts. French traders and trappers used the Indians as a means to obtain pelts. As Francis Parkman, the 19th-century historian, stated, "Spanish civilization crushed the Indian; English civilization scorned and neglected him; French civilization embraced and cherished him."

7

Nearly 500 years later, many people think of American Indians as curious vestiges of a distant past, waging a futile war to survive in a Space Age society. Even today, our understanding of the history and culture of American Indians is too often derived from unsympathetic, culturally biased, and inaccurate reports. The American Indian, described and portrayed in thousands of movies, television programs, books, articles, and government studies, has either been raised to the status of the "noble savage" or disparaged as the "wild Indian" who resisted the westward expansion of the American frontier.

Where in this popular view are the real Indians, the human beings and communities whose ancestors can be traced back to ice-age hunters? Where are the creative and indomitable people whose sophisticated technologies used the natural resources to ensure their survival, whose military skill might even have prevented European settlement of North America if not for devastating epidemics and disruption of the ecology? Where are the men and women who are today diligently struggling to assert their legal rights and express once again the value of their heritage?

The various Indian tribes of North America, like people everywhere, have a history that includes population expansion, adaptation to a range of regional environments, trade across wide networks, internal strife, and warfare. This was the reality. Europeans justified their conquests, however, by creating a mythical image of the New World and its native people. In this myth, the New World was a virgin land, waiting for the Europeans. The arrival of Christopher Columbus ended a timeless primitiveness for the original inhabitants.

Also part of this myth was the debate over the origins of the American Indians. Fantastic and diverse answers were proposed by the early explorers, missionairies, and settlers. Some thought that the Indians were descended from the Ten Lost Tribes of Israel, others that they were descended from inhabitants of the lost continent of Atlantis. One writer suggested that the Indians had reached North America in another Noah's ark.

A later myth, perpetrated by many historians, focused on the relentless persecution during the past five centuries until only a scattering of these "primitive" people remained to be herded onto reservations. This view fails to chronicle the overt and covert ways in which the Indians successfully coped with the intruders.

All of these myths presented one-sided interpretations that ignored the complexity of European and American events and policies. All left serious questions unanswered. What were the origins of the American Indians? Where did they come from? How and when did they get to the New World? What was their life—their culture—really like?

In the late 1800s, anthropologists and archaeologists in the Smithsonian Institution's newly created Bureau of American Ethnology in Washington,

D.C., began to study scientifically the history and culture of the Indians of North America. They were motivated by an honest belief that the Indians were on the verge of extinction and that along with them would vanish their languages, religious beliefs, technology, myths, and legends. These men and women went out to visit, study, and record data from as many Indian communities as possible before this information was forever lost.

By this time there was a new myth in the national consciousness. American Indians existed as figures in the American past. They had performed a historical mission. They had challenged white settlers who trekked across the continent. Once conquered, however, they were supposed to accept graciously the way of life of their conquerors.

The reality again was different. American Indians resisted both actively and passively. They refused to lose their unique identity, to be assimilated into white society. Many whites viewed the Indians not only as members of a conquered nation but also as "inferior" and "unequal." The rights of the Indians could be expanded, contracted, or modified as the conquerors saw fit. In every generation, white society asked itself what to do with the American Indians. Their answers have resulted in the twists and turns of federal Indian policy.

There were two general approaches. One way was to raise the Indians to a "higher level" by "civilizing" them. Zealous missionaries considered it their Christian duty to elevate the Indian through conversion and scanty education. The other approach was to ignore the Indians until they disappeared under pressure from the ever-expanding white society. The myth of the "vanishing Indian" gave stronger support to the latter option, helping to justify the taking of the Indians' land.

Prior to the end of the 18th century, there was no national policy on Indians simply because the American nation had not yet come into existence. American Indians similarly did not possess a political or social unity with which to confront the various Europeans. They were not homogeneous. Rather, they were loosely formed bands and tribes, speaking nearly 300 languages and thousands of dialects. The collective identity felt by Indians today is a result of their common experiences of defeat and/or mistreatment at the hands of whites.

During the colonial period, the British crown did not have a coordinated policy toward the Indians of North America. Specific tribes (most notably the Iroquois and the Cherokee) became military and political pawns used by both the crown and the individual colonies. The success of the American Revolution brought no immediate change. When the United States acquired new territory from France and Mexico in the early 19th century, the federal government wanted to open this land to settlement by homesteaders. But the Indian tribes that lived on this land had signed treaties with European gov-

ernments assuring their title to the land. Now the United States assumed legal responsibility for honoring these treaties.

At first, President Thomas Jefferson believed that the Louisiana Purchase contained sufficient land for both the Indians and the white population. Within a generation, though, it became clear that the Indians would not be allowed to remain. In the 1830s the federal government began to coerce the eastern tribes to sign treaties agreeing to relinquish their ancestral land and move west of the Mississippi River. Whenever these negotiations failed, President Andrew Jackson used the military to remove the Indians. The southeastern tribes, promised food and transportation during their removal to the West, were instead forced to walk the "Trail of Tears." More than 4,000 men, woman, and children died during this forced march. The "removal policy" was successful in opening the land to homesteaders, but it created enormous hardships for the Indians.

By 1871 most of the tribes in the United States had signed treaties ceding most or all of their ancestral land in exchange for reservations and welfare. The treaty terms were intended to bind both parties for all time. But in the General Allotment Act of 1887, the federal government changed its policy again. Now the goal was to make tribal members into individual landowners and farmers, encouraging their absorption into white society. This policy was advantageous to whites who were eager to acquire Indian land, but it proved disastrous for the Indians. One hundred thirty-eight million acres of reservation land were subdivided into tracts of 160, 80, or as little as 40 acres, and allotted tribe members on an individual basis. Land owned in this way was said to have "trust status" and could not be sold. But the surplus land—all Indian land not allotted to individuals—was opened (for sale) to white settlers. Ultimately, more than 90 million acres of land were taken from the Indians by legal and illegal means.

The resulting loss of land was a catastrophe for the Indians. It was necessary to make it illegal for Indians to sell their land to non-Indians. The Indian Reorganization Act of 1934 officially ended the allotment period. Tribes that voted to accept the provisions of this act were reorganized, and an effort was made to purchase land within preexisting reservations to restore an adequate land base.

Ten years later, in 1944, federal Indian policy again shifted. Now the federal government wanted to get out of the "Indian business." In 1953 an act of Congress named specific tribes whose trust status was to be ended "at the earliest possible time." This new law enabled the United States to end unilaterally, whether the Indians wished it or not, the special status that protected the land in Indian tribal reservations. In the 1950s federal Indian policy was to transfer federal responsibility and jurisdiction to state governments,

encourage the physical relocation of Indian peoples from reservations to urban areas, and hasten the termination, or extinction, of tribes.

Between 1954 and 1962 Congress passed specific laws authorizing the termination of more than 100 tribal groups. The stated purpose of the termination policy was to ensure the full and complete integration of Indians into American society. However, there is a less benign way to interpret this legislation. Even as termination was being discussed in Congress, 133 separate bills were introduced to permit the transfer of trust land ownership from Indians to non-Indians.

With the Johnson administration in the 1960s the federal government began to reject termination. In the 1970s yet another Indian policy emerged. Known as "self-determination," it favored keeping the protective role of the federal government while increasing tribal participation in, and control of, important areas of local government. In 1983 President Reagan, in a policy statement on Indian affairs, restated the unique "government is government" relationship of the United States with the Indians. However, federal programs since then have moved toward transferring Indian affairs to individual states, which have long desired to gain control of Indian land and resources.

As long as American Indians retain power, land, and resources that are coveted by the states and the federal government, there will continue to be a "clash of cultures," and the issues will be contested in the courts, Congress, the White House, and even in the international human rights community. To give all Americans a greater comprehension of the issues and conflicts involving American Indians today is a major goal of this series. These issues are not easily understood, nor can these conflicts be readily resolved. The study of North American Indian history and culture is a necessary and important step toward that comprehension. All Americans must learn the history of the relations between the Indians and the federal government, recognize the unique legal status of the Indians, and understand the heritage and cultures of the Indians of North America.

A Kwakiutl chief making a speech at the November 1894 potlatch hosted by anthropologist Franz Boas at Fort Rupert. Boas was accepted by the Kwakiutl and given the name He'iltsakuls, meaning "the silent one," because he could not speak Kwakwala, the Kwakiutl language.

STUDYING
THE KWAKIUTL

In 1886, a German anthropologist named Franz Boas boarded a steamer in Victoria, Canada, and began a short trip up the coast of Vancouver Island. He was bound for an Indian village where he could study the languages of the region. Boas believed that if his work was successful he could establish himself as a scholar in his newly adopted country, the United States.

Boas soon reached Newhitty, one village of the Indian group identified as the Southern Kwakiutl, on the northern coast of the island. At first he was viewed suspiciously. The Indians thought that he had been sent by the government to force them to give up their traditional culture.

When the young scholar explained that he did not disapprove of their customs, the Newhitty invited him to a special ceremony during which Boas listened to speeches and songs and feasted on fresh halibut. The host dis-tributed gifts of money and blankets to Boas and other guests, who watched as the host proceeded to chop up a new boat and set the pieces ablaze.

Boas sat fascinated by the ceremony. He was so eager to learn more about the Kwakiutl that he would spend the next 50 years studying them. As a result of Boas's pioneering work, many anthropologists have since been drawn to the Northwest Coast to study the region's Indian residents. Although there are many Indian groups in the area, the Southern Kwakiutl (now more often referred to as the Kwakiutl) are still the most compelling to scholars. The vast amount of research they have inspired makes them among the most examined Indians in North America.

The Northwest Coast culture area is generally divided into three sub-regions. The northern region contains three tribes, the Tlingit, the Haida, and the Tsimshian. The central region in-

Boas in the pose of a participant in the traditional hamatsa *dance. This photograph was one in a series from which a life-size diorama of the hamatsa ceremony was created by the Smithsonian Institution. The diorama is now housed in the American Museum of Natural History in New York City.*

cludes the Kwakiutl, the Bella Bella (sometimes referred to as the Northern Kwakiutl or Northern Wakashan), the Bella Coola, the Nootka, and the Coast Salish people of southeastern Vancouver Island and the adjacent mainland. The southern region contains the Salish-speaking tribes from Puget Sound south, the Chinook tribes of the Columbia River area, and the tribes of coastal Oregon and northern California.

The Kwakiutl lived in the center of the Northwest Coast region in isolated villages accessible to one another only by the sea. The name *Kwakiutl* (pronouced approximately KWA-gee-oolth) loosely refers to the residents of originally about 25 to 30 large villages along the northern and eastern coasts of Vancouver Island and the adjacent mainland of British Columbia, from Cape Mudge in the south to Rivers Inlet in the north. Because of their isolation and separation, it makes little sense to talk about these different peoples as a single unified tribe. The names that have come to refer to the Indian groups of the Northwest Coast were not the names by which they referred to themselves. Instead they are artificial and often erroneous names given to Indian groups by government administrators at the end of the 19th century. The Kwakiutl thought of their villages as politically autonomous and thus they refer to them as separate "tribes." All these tribes together compose the Kwakiutl Nation.

The coast of British Columbia, Canada, has been the home of Indian peoples for thousands of years.

The basis of Kwakiutl social and political organization was the village, whose residents were allied by their common language, Kwakwala, and by shared participation in economic, social, and ceremonial activities. Each of the many Kwakiutl tribes had its own territory, winter village, and seasonal resource area. Each also comprised several large kin groups called *numayms*, the really important units of Kwakiutl society, in which the ownership of resources, living sites, and myths was vested.

There was a great deal of resettlement and migration among the peoples of the Northwest Coast during both the prehistoric and historic periods. For thousands of years, Northwest Coast Indian cultures have been engaged in a long, slow, and complex process of tribal expansion and contraction. After contact with European and American traders at the end of the 18th century, the peoples of the coast abandoned many of their more isolated villages and resettled in conglomerate villages near trading posts. Once disparate groups

The Kwakiutl village of Alert Bay, photographed in the late 19th century. The Kwakiutl originally lived in 25 to 30 villages, each of which was politically and socially autonomous.

A woman in ceremonial clothing, photographed at Fort Rupert in the late 19th century.

consolidated and artificially became tribes when the Canadian government created reserves and set up tribal agencies to administer their affairs.

Kwakiutl identity is strongly tied into their traditional names. The Kwakiutl feel that the misnaming of their tribes is one of the many ways by which non-Indians have tried to take away their sacred traditional histories and identities. History and its retelling are extremely important to the Kwakiutl. History for the Kwakiutl is a private family possession, a sacred treasure that began in ancient times and which

will continue far into the future. The right to tell the specific story of a person and his or her ancestors resides only with that person and only in the proper ceremonial context. An outsider cannot recount these events any more than he or she may dance one of the family's dances or call himself or herself by one of the Kwakiutl's names. Recently, as part of their revitalized cultural programs, the Kwakiutl have been recording this history for themselves, but it is generally not available to non-Kwakiutl scholars either for study or publication.

The Kwakiutl are a diverse group with a wide variety of experiences and opinions. There is no one single history of the Kwakiutl. Because of Boas's research, what is known of Kwakiutl history and culture is primarily that of the Fort Rupert Kwakiutl. (The village of Fort Rupert was the center of Kwakiutl mercantile and ceremonial life from the 1850s through the 1870s.) Not all Kwakiutl had the same historic experiences: Some became wealthy as others were relegated to poverty; some prospered as others suffered; and some found security and happiness in adopting white customs and religion as others found the same in rejecting non-Indians ways. Today, some Kwakiutl see the resurgence of traditionalism as a step backward, a retreat into a fantasy image of the past. However, others regard it as a blossoming of true Kwakiutl pride in their own remarkable social and religious creativity, a mark of their unique place in the world and the annals of humanity. ▲

An early-20th-century photograph by Edward Curtis of a Kwakiutl woman preparing a strip of cedar bark. Around her shoulders she wears a blanket woven from such strips.

2

PEOPLE
OF
THE SALMON

Along the Northwest Coast of North America—from Yakutat Bay in Alaska to the mouth of the Columbia River in Washington—stretches a narrow, rugged land with dense and impassable forests and steep mountains rising thousands of feet above tumultuous seas. Only in a few scattered and isolated sites along the many thousands of miles of coastline, both on the mainland and on countless offshore islands, is the beach sufficiently flat and protected from wind and waves that early people could build villages there. Yet for at least the past 8,000 years, wherever it was possible, humans have settled on the thin wedge between the oceans and the forests.

No one knows when the first Indians arrived on the Northwest Coast. About 20,000 years ago, groups of hunters of large land mammals crossed the Bering Land Bridge from Siberia into Alaska and headed southward along the Rocky Mountains until they reached the Great Plains of the central United States. Perhaps a few groups of these hunters then traveled westward across the Rocky Mountains, following the river valleys that run from the continental divide toward the Pacific Ocean. Or possibly groups of Indians who had already adapted to living by the ocean migrated along the coast from Asia to the Pacific Northwest. The coastline of the Pacific Northwest has changed greatly during the last 20,000 years, and many of the places where the earliest inhabitants might have lived are now buried beneath the surface of the sea.

The earliest known prehistoric sites on the Northwest Coast date from about 12,000 years ago. Archaeologists believe that the people who inhabited these sites probably were hunters of

19

By about 12,000 years ago, the great glaciers covering the Northwest Coast had melted enough to make the region suitable for habitation.

land animals, because the type of tools they made were not well adapted to fishing. These people's stone tools were fashioned from fist-sized pebbles. One end of the pebble was left smooth so that the tool would fit comfortably in the user's hand. Flakes of stone were knocked off the other end to produce a moderately sharp but strong cutting edge. A single all-purpose pebble tool could be used for such diverse tasks as cutting wood, butchering meat, and hunting animals. The flat flakes that were chipped off large pebbles could

as seals and sea lions. Because they did not have the tools to work wood well enough to make sturdy canoes, they probably fished only from land or from skin boats in waters near shore. The discovery of obsidian (volcanic glass) in sites hundreds of miles away from where it was quarried is evidence that there was trade among peoples throughout the region.

About 5,500 years ago, some major changes occurred. As the Northwest Coast Indians became more dependent on fish as their primary food, they began settling in those areas where the fishing was more reliable. Some villages, still inhabited today, have existed for thousands of years. The Indians also began developing the sophisticated woodworking technology that became a hallmark of their culture. Middens (refuse heaps) from this period contain many tools designed for very specialized tasks, such as fishhooks made to catch only a single species of fish. These objects indicate that a technological explosion had taken place in Northwest Coast life. The Indians had become much more effective at gathering the resources in their environment and learning methods of preserving and stockpiling food surpluses. As a result, their population rose and their villages grew larger. Political and social organizations were transformed: The accumulation of food and wealth enabled some people to become leaders, and the clan and tribe became important communal groups. Over the course of 5,000 years, the Northwest Coast Indians

themselves be made into razors, scrapers, chisels, knives, slicers, and other tools used to work animal skins.

Little is known of the daily lives of the inhabitants of the Northwest Coast during this earliest period. They probably lived in small houses made from poles over which skins and bark slabs were placed. They mostly hunted land mammals but may have fished for salmon and hunted sea mammals, such

gradually developed their own distinctive and remarkable way of life, one which in some ways continues today.

The climate of the North Pacific coast is milder than would seem warranted by its northern location. The mountains shield the area from the cold winter air to the east; the Japan Current, a current of warm water that runs across the northern Pacific, heats the atmosphere, creating dense fogs and heavy precipitation, especially in the winter. The average rainfall in some parts of coastal British Columbia is more than 160 inches per year. The coast is vulnerable as well to the vast weather systems that develop in the northern Pacific and the Arctic. These systems sometimes cause the weather to change at a moment's notice.

Archaeologists have uncovered much information about the ancient inhabitants of the Northwest Coast. The two men in this photograph are excavating tools used long ago by the Indians of Quadra's Island, British Columbia.

A Kwakiutl woman opening her harvest of clams. The waters of the Northwest Coast tradition-ally provided the Kwakiutl with most of their food.

The heavy rainfall and moderate temperatures of the Northwest Coast create a unique environment. The area is a dense rainforest with towering trees of many species. Everywhere the ground and the branches and trunks of trees are thickly covered with moss. A heavy tangle of undergrowth of shrubs and bushes grows wherever sunlight is able to penetrate the dense canopy of

vegetation. Passage through these forests is so difficult that overland travel was possible for early Indians only along a handful of trails. Although they sometimes journeyed a short distance into the forest to collect wood or hunt land animals, their lives were oriented almost exclusively toward the sea and its incredible bounties.

The cold, murky, deep waters of the Northwest Coast are one of the great fishing grounds of the world, exceptional for both the variety and abundance of marine life. The most important sea life to the Indians were the five species of Pacific salmon that appeared near the coast annually. Each year, millions of fish might collect at the mouth of a river at the start of their journey upriver toward their spawning grounds. Salmon, the staple food of the Northwest Coast Indians, was eaten fresh during the summer or smoked and dried for winter use.

Other fish were also important in the Northwest Coast diet, including eulachon (pronounced OO-la-ken), herring, smelt, cod, rockfish, lingcod, halibut, eel, sturgeon, dogfish, and dozens of other species. Of these, none was more valued than eulachon. These herringlike fish were also known as candlefish, because their fat content is so high that if a wick were placed in one's mouth and lighted, the fish would burn like a candle. The oil (often referred to as grease) of the eulachon was frequently a part of the Indians' meals. It was served in a special bowl into which a diner dipped his or her food. There were several major eulachon spawning areas in Kwakiutl territory. Access to these fish and their oil gave the Kwakiutl an important place in the trade network among tribes.

The sea also provided many other kinds of food: sea mammals, such as porpoises, seals, sea lions, sea otters, and whales; seabirds and waterfowl; mollusks, such as clams, mussels, oysters, limpets, and abalone; and crabs, octopus, squid, and sea urchins. The eggs of sea gulls, puffins, and other seabirds were gathered from the rocky offshore islands where these birds nested.

Although land game was plentiful, the difficulties of hunting on land made it a secondary part of Northwest Coast life. Deer and elk, the most common of the large forest mammals, and the mountain goats that roamed above the timberline were hunted by bow and arrow. Grizzly bears, black bears, and wolves were found throughout the forests and killed in baited traps. Many small mammals were hunted for their fur, especially beavers, raccoons, otters, weasels, mink, marmots, and squirrels.

Vegetable foods played only a minor role in the Northwest Coast diet. However, bulbs, roots, leaves, and shoots of ferns, nettles, clover, cinquefoil, skunk cabbage, lilies, and other plants were a welcome addition to the Kwakiutl food supply when they could be obtained. Even more prized were the many types of berries and other fruits that could

sometimes be found in the forest: salalberries, salmonberries, soapberries, huckleberries, blackberries, strawberries, cranberries, and crab apples.

The Northwest Coast Indians were fortunate in the overwhelming abundance of the natural resources of their land, but they would never have prospered if they had not developed the ingenious tools and technologies needed to take advantage of their environment.

Their dependence on salmon as a food source compelled the Northwest Indians to develop complex and highly effective ways of catching these fish. Salmon spawn (lay their eggs) in the shallow stretches of freshwater streams but live most of their life in the ocean. At the end of their life cycle, mature salmon gather at the mouth of the stream in which they were spawned to begin their final journey upriver. Because every stream or river has unique features—such as varying widths and depths and different currents and speeds—fishing technology had to be adapted to suit specific situations. For example, a net that might be very useful for catching fish in the slow, deep waters at the mouth of a river would not work well in a swift, shallow stream.

The most effective tools for salmon fishing were the stone trap and the weir. Both were built across streams to entrap migrating fish so that they could be caught easily. Stone traps were especially useful in areas where there was a significant tidal flow. Fish entered the

A Kwakiutl basket (made of woven cedar twine) used to carry a fisherman's catch.

area blocked off by the trap during an incoming flood tide, when the water was higher than the trap's walls. When the tide receded and the water level dropped below the height of the walls, they would be stranded.

Weirs were far more common as a means of concentrating the salmon. These fences were constructed by driving piles into a riverbed using large, flat stone hammers and then tying a woven lattice of wood slats onto this framework. Weirs were sometimes built with

gaps onto which the Indians would tie large basket traps. Fish would swim through the gaps directly into the baskets. More often, salmon concentrated by weirs or stone traps were then netted, speared, or harpooned.

Eulachon and herring, which in the spring appeared near the shore in immense shoals, were caught with large dip nets or with special toothed rakes onto which the fish were impaled when fishermen combed the rakes through the water. In the calm bays where the herring came to spawn, the Indians would set out special floating frames from which they suspended spruce or fir boughs. The herring would deposit their eggs onto these boughs, which could then be lifted easily from the water. The dried roe provided a tasty and nutritious food.

There were several other means of catching fish. Strong and flexible twines and ropes manufactured from braided strands of kelp, nettle, or cedar bark were used in various types of nets. Some fish—usually the larger species—were caught with hooks and lines.

The abundance of food from the sea would have been meaningless for survival if the Indians had not developed the means of drying and preserving their food surpluses for future use. During the fishing season, fish fillets were hung to dry in the sun on latticeworks of poles and smokehouses would be filled from floor to ceiling and wall to wall with the bodies of fish drying in the heat of an alder-wood fire. Because preserved, dehydrated fish could ab-

sorb atmospheric moisture and turn moldy during the wet winter along the coast, the Indians placed horizontal racks under the roofs of their homes where fish could be kept dry in the hot, smoky air rising from the cooking fire. Some kinds of fish and other foods were mixed with eulachon oil or seal oil to repel moisture.

The Northwest Coast Indians had three basic methods of cooking their food: grilling it over an open fire, steaming or baking it in a pit oven, and boiling it. Grilling and baking were done mostly during the summer, when the food was fresh. Boiling was used in the winter because the process helped reconstitute the moisture levels in the stored, dried foods. To boil food, the Indians placed it in a box or basket filled with water and then dropped red-hot stones into the container. Occasionally, fish was eaten raw. Some fish parts, especially fish heads, were immersed in oil and allowed to putrefy to create a dish that was considered a great delicacy.

The Northwest Coast Indians' proficient woodworking technology allowed them to take advantage of the natural resources in their territory. Although they made some implements from stone, rodent incisors, antlers, and shells, wood was the material from which the Indians manufactured most of their tools and utensils. Every part of Northwest Coast life involved the use of wood and wood by-products.

Perhaps the most important wooden object made by the Northwest

The Kwakiutl made canoes of many shapes and sizes, each suited for a specific task. Their smallest canoes were one- or two-person vessels used for navigating rivers; their largest could carry as many as 50 people on trade or war expeditions.

Coast Indians was the canoe, for living in the region would be nearly impossible without a means of traveling on the water. They manufactured canoes of many different sizes and shapes. Although most had high ends and low sides, each was tailored for use in a particular water condition or for a specific task. The population in a large village might possess several hundred canoes, ranging from small one- or two-person boats for navigating rivers to enormous vessels that could transport as many as

50 people on a war or trade expedition. The most common large-sized canoe among the Kwakiutl was about 35 feet long and was used for long-distance travel.

Canoes were fashioned by a master craftsman from a single cedar log—a lengthy and difficult process. Like all activities of the Northwest Coast Indians, canoe making had a spiritual dimension. A carver spent a great deal of time praying and singing sacred songs in order to seek the guidance and pro-

tection of the spirits from whom all power was thought to come. A canoe and the tree from which it was made were thought to be alive and to possess a soul. Both therefore had to be treated with the same care and respect that was due a human being.

The canoe maker first would select and fell an exceptionally large tree with an even, straight grain. He then would split the log in half lengthwise and begin to shape the outside of the canoe. Next, he would turn the canoe over and hollow out the inside, a task that involved slowly and carefully charring the wood with hot rocks and then using an adze (a cutting tool with a thin, arched blade) and chisels to remove the softened wood.

The roughly shaped canoe would be moved down near the water's edge to be finished inside and outside. The finished canoe had to be perfectly symmetrical along its center axis, and the wood had to be of even thickness or it would be unbalanced and unseaworthy. All of this precision work was carried out without the benefit of measuring tools. The canoe maker had to rely exclusively on his careful work and a practiced eye.

The final shaping of the canoe was accomplished by filling the vessel with water heated to a boil with hot rocks and carefully bending the wood after it had been softened by the steam. The canoe was then heated a last time in a dry fire to harden, sanded smooth, and covered in dogfish oil to seal the wood. Finally, the vessel was painted and dec-

orated. Canoes were propelled by short-handled paddles or, in shallow water, by long poles.

Although their woodworking and fishing technology allowed the Indians to harvest food resources very effectively, they could not gather food at all places or at all times of the year. The steep and rocky terrain of the coast made it possible to fish only at specific and often isolated spots when the fishing conditions were right. However, these areas were often not good places to live, so the Indians tended to occupy them just during the summer fishing season. In the winter, they lived in large villages, where they devoted much of their time to social and religious ceremonies.

Summer villages were built near prime fishing spots both along the coast and upriver and usually were composed of small, temporary wooden shelters and cabins. These structures were rectangular and had long, sloping or nearly flat roofs. At fishing camps, people sometimes lived in lean-tos with one or more sides open to the outside air.

Winter villages were built in sheltered locations that offered protection from high winter tides and the fierce storms that could blow eastward across the Pacific Ocean. They consisted of large houses that were sometimes elevated above the beach on stilts to raise them above the highest tides. In areas of steep terrain, the entire house might be built upon a platform raised on pilings. A boardwalk ran the entire length

of the village, in front of the houses. This area was the center of much of the Indians' outdoor social activity.

The wooden winter houses of the Northwest Coast Indians were impressive dwellings, the construction of which required an incredible amount of cooperative effort. A large Kwakiutl winter house might be 40 feet wide, 100 feet long, and 20 feet high. A house was always oriented so that its facade and entrance faced the beach and ocean.

The first step in constructing such dwellings was to make a frame by placing massive vertical support posts—

usually three along the front of the house, three in the center, and three in the back—upright in the ground. Heavy horizontal beams running along the long axis of the house were set into notches carved in the posts. Smaller beams were laid perpendicularly across the beams. Finally, a frame of rafters was lashed to the beams, which were then covered with overlapping planks and shingles.

The planks in the walls and roof were structurally separate from the framework of the house and could be moved apart to admit light or ventilate

An engraving of the interior of a Nootka house, after a 1778 watercolor by John Webber. The Kwakiutl lived in similar dwellings, which were large enough to house several families.

the house during hot weather. (To save work, each year these planks were removed, bundled up, and transported to the summer village, where they were used to form the roofs and walls of the small houses there.) In rainy or cold weather, with all the openings in the house closed up, these structures could become quite unpleasantly smoky and damp.

Inside each winter house, a raised platform ran along the walls. The space beneath the platform was used for storage, as was the space in the rafters and beams. The platform itself held the living areas of the house's occupants.

Several families lived in each house. Their living and storage areas were separated with plank or mat walls, affording each family a measure of privacy. A family's social status determined which area they occupied; for instance, the head of the household and his immediate family always lived along the house's rear wall. The center of the house was left open. In the middle of this communal area was a cooking fire used by all.

The status of a house's residents was often signified by a totem pole, a cedar pole decorated with elaborate carvings. Non-Indians have long been impressed and intrigued by these sculptures. Today they stand as a hallmark of Northwest Coast Indian culture.

When the Northwest Coast Indians first encountered Europeans in the late 18th century, there were few such poles because it was difficult to carve them

A totem pole outside a house in Alert Bay, 1895. The figure on the top of the pole holds a Copper, a ceremonial object treasured by the Kwakiutl.

using beaver-incisor blades. Only after the Northwest Coast Indians obtained iron-bladed tools from non-Indian traders were they able to produce a large number of intricately carved poles.

Totem poles were decorated with carvings of humans, animals, and supernatural beings (often referred to as spirits) and commemorated significant incidents in the mythic history of a family. The carvings often told of how supernatural beings gave the family's ancestors the spiritual power that justified the group's political power in the present. The right to harvest resources in specific locations was thought to have been awarded to some families long ago. By depicting the granting of such rights, the images on totem poles served to proclaim and validate the special privileges of such high-ranking families.

Totem poles were thought to link humans to the spirit world. The Indians also believed the poles had souls and could come to life in a supernatural dimension. Prayers to the spirits could be addressed to totem poles. Small offerings of food and tobacco were often placed in front of totem poles, and they were sometimes recarved or repainted to renew the connections between humans and spirits.

There were several types of totem poles. Probably the best known is the house frontal post. These sculptures were very tall, between 30 and 50 feet high, and were erected outside the front wall of a house. Often frontal poles were freestanding, erected as far as several yards away from the dwelling. However, sometimes they were placed against or partially integrated into the outside wall, and an opening in the bottom of the pole served as an entrance to the house during ceremonies. (Another, simpler entrance was used most of the time.) Among the Kwakiutl, this entrance might be carved to represent a creature's mouth or the opening of its body cavity, where the soul was thought to reside. As people climbed into or out of this entrance, they were spiritually transformed.

A more common type was the memorial pole, a 20-to-30-foot pole bearing only a few carved or painted figures. Such poles were erected in front of or to the side of a deceased chief's house within a few years after his death. The figures represented the chief and other symbols of his life and family history. The raising of a memorial pole was accompanied by a ceremony known as a *potlatch*, during which the chief's successor would assume his titles.

Interior house posts were the most widespread type of pole. Such poles were carved from the large vertical timbers that formed the frame of a house. They were often elaborately carved, either with geometric patterns, crest designs (visual images of creatures to whom one's ancestors were spiritually connected), or a combination of the two. A house might have as many as five interior house posts, but nearly every dwelling contained at least one.

The raising of a totem pole was a complex and festive process. First, the

A group of Kwakiutl exiting a house, the front of which is painted with an image of a mythical creature. The doorway forms the creature's mouth. The Kwakiutl believed that they could be spiritually transformed by passing through such doorways during ceremonies.

pole raisers dug a deep hole and erected a large scaffold over it. They then slung ropes up and over the scaffold and tied them near the apex of the pole. Hundreds of people pulled backward on these ropes to raise the pole upward from its tip; others held ropes to keep the pole from swaying or positioned and repositioned a large log crutch on which the partially elevated pole rested. When the pole was finally vertical, the hole was packed with large rocks and soil.

Canoes, houses, and totem poles were certainly the most spectacular products manufactured by the Northwest Coast Indians, but their woodworking skills also allowed them to create an immense variety of everyday objects and ceremonial items. The forests in the region contained trees of many species, including red cedar, yellow cedar, hemlock, and yew. Each kind of tree had its own unique properties, which determined how the Indians made use of its wood or bark. For

example, hardwoods, including yew and alder, were used for objects that required strength and flexibility, such as bows and harpoons. The soft wood of the yellow cedar was easily carved into spoons, dishes, and bowls. However, by far the most important tree to the Kwakiutl was the red cedar. Its soft, even-grained wood was relatively easy to split into long, even planks from which the Indians made many of their most essential possessions. In addition to canoes and housing beams and supports, red cedar wood was used for storage containers, cradles, weapons, and ceremonial paraphernalia. From its fibrous inner bark, laboriously beaten until soft and then twined and knotted, they made their clothing, many types of baskets, ropes, twine, and mats.

The Kwakiutl were renowned for their wooden boxes and bowls. These containers were produced in many sizes and shapes, a variety that reflected their importance in all aspects of Kwakiutl life. They were used as storage containers for food and other family valuables, as furniture, as serving platters at feasts, as drums, and even as coffins.

One of the most common types of Northwest Coast containers was the bentwood box. Its four sides were made from a single cedar plank. The plank was carefully shaped and cut, smoothed using sandstone blocks or dogfish skin, softened in steam, folded, and then joined at the ends. A skilled wood-carver could fashion a bentwood box so exactly that its seam was vir-tually watertight. Another type of container was a small bowl or box called a grease bowl. This vessel was used as a container for eulachon oil at feasts and potlatches. These grease bowls became so saturated that some collected by museums a century ago still ooze oil.

Boxes and bowls used for holding ceremonial items and for serving food at feasts were generally carved in the shape of, or with decorations depicting, crest animals. These objects were treated and handled with great protocol because they were thought to give a family a spiritual identity and to link it to its ancestral past. The families of the bride and groom at marriage ceremonies exchanged such boxes, a gesture that symbolized the new alliance between the two groups.

The Kwakiutl also manufactured many types of baskets. Basketmaking was exclusively the domain of the women. Most of the baskets they made were used to carry or store food and other objects. A skilled basket maker could weave one so tightly and evenly that it could carry water. Tightly woven basketry hats were worn in the rain. Baskets for everyday use were left undecorated, but those made for holding special materials and items were often quite elaborately woven and adorned with geometric or crest designs.

Mats woven from cedar bark and other fibrous materials had an immense variety of uses as well. In addition to serving as partitions inside houses, they often functioned as floor coverings or, folded, as cushions. During a cere-

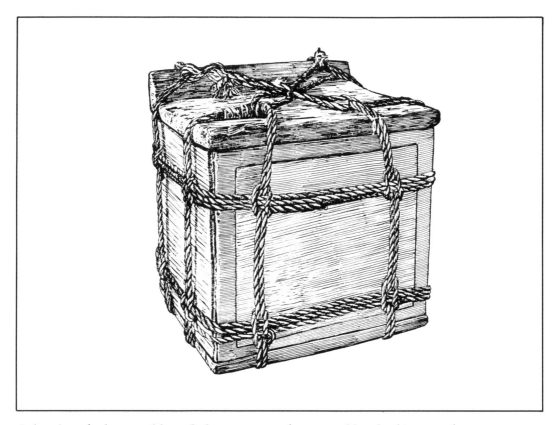

A drawing of a bentwood box. Only a master craftsman could make this type of storage container, the four sides of which were created from a single plank of cedar.

mony, a chief might stand on a mat while making a speech and a dancer or guest might be given a mat on which to sit. Ceremonial objects were wrapped in mats for storage.

Mats were also used as clothing. During cold and wet weather, warm and water-repellent clothing was essential. The simplest and most common garment was a woven cedar-bark cape, cloak, or blanket that the wearer wrapped around his or her body in a variety of styles and then tied or pinned

shut. The cedar bark was sometimes interwoven with the wool of mountain goats or the hair of a type of dog with an exceptionally woolly coat that the Indians kept just for that purpose. These poncholike blankets were often rubbed with fish oil to increase their water repellency.

During most of the summer, however, the peoples of the Northwest Coast donned few clothes. Men often wore just a small breechcloth or nothing at all, and women usually wore only a

small skirt. Although fancy moccasins were part of ceremonial dress, most of the time people went barefoot.

The Kwakiutl were known for their blankets made from the inner bark of the yellow cedar, which was softer than that of the red cedar. Some were decorated with painted, dyed, or woven designs. Other Northwest Coast Indian tribes often traded with the Kwakiutl for these valued blankets.

The Indians also made clothing from animal fur or skin. Chiefs and some other nobles had the privilege of wearing robes made from the pelts of sea otters, bears, wolves, and other ani-

mals. The skins of deer, elk, caribou, and sometimes moose were obtained from other tribes in trade and used to make body armor. (Armor was also made from wood slats or thick ropes.)

Personal adornment was quite varied. Nearly everyone wore ear pendants and nose rings made from shells, especially abalone or dentalia. Married women in some of the Bella Bella groups wore a lip plug, called a *labret*, made from wood, bone, or shell, which was inserted into a perforation made in the skin just beneath the lower lip. Necklaces made from shells or shell beads were very popular, and women

Garments made from cedar bark. Cedar-bark clothing was warm and water-repellent and therefore ideal for the Northwest Coast's cold and wet winters.

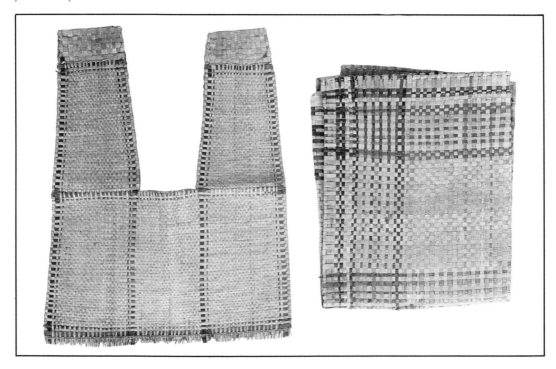

A Kwakiutl woman with an elongated forehead produced by head-flattening—the painless practice of strapping an infant's head between a pair of padded boards in order to flatten the front of his or her skull. Flattened heads were considered a mark of great beauty among the Kwakiutl.

often wore bracelets and anklets of fur. People painted their faces with a mixture of sooty pigment and fish oil or bear grease to protect themselves from wind, sun, and biting insects. During the ceremonial season, facial paint designs were often quite elaborate. Some facial tattooing was practiced and was considered a mark of high status.

The Northwest Coast Indians thought personal cleanliness and neatness were important. The region's climatic conditions presented a perfect breeding ground for head and body lice, so family members frequently combed and deloused each other's hair. Men cut their hair at shoulder length; women wore theirs in braids. Sometimes women wore combs or plaited strips of fur into their braids. Both sexes rubbed bear grease and ocher into their hair for cosmetic reasons.

People usually bathed and washed their hair only before rituals. However, men undergoing religious or military training took a bath every morning no matter what the air or water temperature. They often also took steam baths, which were believed to purify the body. Like many of the native peoples of North America, the Indians of the Northwest Coast had no soap. Instead, they used a mixture of stale urine and the sap of certain plants as a detergent. Such a mixture is a fairly effective cleansing agent.

Among the Kwakiutl and several other peoples of the southern Northwest Coast, head-flattening was one of the most favored means of making oneself attractive. The heads of some infants (most often girls) were placed between a pair of padded boards set at a tapered angle across the forehead and the back of the skull. As the bones of the skull grew, they hardened into an elongated shape above the face. The practice of head-flattening was painless and had no ill effects on the intelligence of the child.

The native peoples of the Northwest Coast lived in an area of abundant resources. However, although the Indians of the Northwest Coast were relatively secure and comfortable, theirs was not a luxurious life. The surplus of one local item did not free a group from worry or make them wealthy. It simply gave them a commodity that they could trade for other goods that were not locally available.

Not until after contact with non-Indians did the Kwakiutl make and use many of the sumptuous and extravagant material goods that are now showcased in museums. But the postcontact era was not just one of increased material and economic well-being. It was also an era of increasing economic competition, epidemic disease, resettlement, warfare, slavery, and social and political upheaval. In every aspect, it was a time of significant and powerful change in Northwest Coast life. ▲

The arrival of Captain James Cook and his crew in Nootka Sound, as drawn by John Webber, the expedition's official artist, in 1778. During Cook's monthlong stay in the region, many Indians canoed to the ship, performing ceremonies en route that signaled their eagerness to trade with the foreigners.

THE
SOFT GOLD
RUSH

Long before Columbus sailed to the New World, there existed a widespread international trade network among the peoples of Europe and Asia. Among the many goods that were exchanged were furs. Although several different types of furs were traded, by far the most important was beaver. The soft, woolly undercoat of beaver pelts was processed into a felt from which warm, water-repellent cloth and hats could be made. The demand for furs was so great in Europe that hunters eventually killed most of the beavers and other fur-bearing animals native to the Old World. In order to stay in business, fur traders then had to search for new areas in which these animals could be found.

Reports of early European explorers revealed that North America was just such a place. In the early 17th century, English and French fur traders began to journey to what is now the northeast-ern United States and southeastern Canada, attracted by the large popula-tion of animals—especially beavers—in this area's rich environment. At the same time, Russian fur traders traveled to present-day Alaska. When traders exhausted the population of animals in one area, they simply moved on to an-other—the English and French travel-ing westward and the Russians moving southeast.

The desire for many commodities—including gold, silver, sugar, spices, and slaves—led to exploration and eco-nomic exploitation of the New World by Old World peoples. The fur trade played a particularly important role in the history of interaction between the Indians of the present-day United States and Canada and the immigrants from across the Atlantic. In exchange for European goods, Indian hunters de-livered pelts to the foreign traders.

When Indian groups had hunted all the animals in their own territory, they either had to form alliances with groups whose lands still contained fur-bearing animals or take control of these peoples' territory by force. Such warfare destroyed or displaced entire Indian populations, sometimes long before white traders ever appeared in their lands. Although the fur trade brought many Indians some prosperity, it also produced vast social changes among the native peoples of North America.

By the 1770s, the world market for beaver pelts was glutted. White traders began to look for new furs that would demand high prices in the international fur trade. At the same time, political and economic changes in Europe were affecting the balance of power in North America. The influence of the Spanish, who claimed vast areas of territory in present-day Mexico and the southwestern United States, was in a steady state of decline. The Dutch, who had held great sway in the fur trade in the East, were losing much of their economic control of the world market. In addition, the long struggle between the English and the French for control of international trade, the world's oceans, and the natural resources of North America was growing more heated.

The Pacific coast of what is now the northwestern United States and southwestern Canada soon became a stage for the political and economic competition among these nations. The Pacific Northwest was inhabited by many fur-bearing species. However, rough waters, fog, and strong and variable winds made it difficult to sail along the coast north of San Francisco. In the late 18th century, an easily navigable alternate route to the Northwest via Hawaii was found. With this discovery, the large-scale fur trade in the Northwest was underway and the battle between European powers for control of the region began.

The most important animal for the Northwest Coast fur trade was the sea otter, whose warm and waterproof pelt was in great demand in Asia. The sea otter fur trade (also referred to as the maritime fur trade) had begun when Russian fur traders traveled south from Alaska to the Northwest Coast in the early to mid-18th century. By the end of the 18th century, however, the Russians ceased their movement into the area. Battles with the Tlingit Indians, the most northerly of the Northwest Coast tribes, and increased competition from other non-Indian traders discouraged the Russians from pursuing the maritime fur trade.

The first non-Russian vessel to contact a native Northwest Coast people was the Spanish ship *Santiago*. Captained by Juan Pérez, the *Santiago* sailed into the territory of the Haida Indians in 1774. The ship was approached by three canoes of Indians, who greeted Pérez with great ceremony. The next day, more than 200 Indians in 21 canoes encircled the ship. The Haida brought furs, blankets, mats, basketry hats, and carved wooden dishes, spoons, and boxes to trade for European goods,

A painting by John James Audubon of a Canadian sea otter caught in a trap. Trappers called the pelts of sea otters "soft gold" because they were worth a great deal of money in foreign markets.

such as beads, clothing, and iron. Pérez and his crew also traded with the Nootka Indians on the west coast of Vancouver Island. Several other voyages in the following years gave the Spanish a foothold with this Indian group.

The intensity of the maritime fur trade increased dramatically with the monthlong visit of English navigator Captain James Cook to Nootka Sound in the summer of 1778. Many hundreds of Indians came to see Cook's vessel. The Kwakiutl and Nootka were age-old trading partners; therefore it is possible that several Kwakiutl traders visiting the Nootka were present. Cook and some of his crew traded pieces of iron, glass beads, clothing, and knives to the Indians for about 1,500 sea otter pelts. The Englishmen later sold the pelts in China for an immense profit. Each pelt had cost them about 10 cents but was sold for about $100, nearly 10 times the annual wages of a sailor.

When reports of the value of sea otter furs (sometimes referred to as "soft gold") reached English and Amer-

ican merchants, a "gold" rush began. Numerous expeditions and traders immediately set sail from Boston or England for the Northwest Coast. There they traded European goods to Indians for pelts. The traders then journeyed to China, where they sold the pelts and bought valuable Asian goods, such as silk, furniture, porcelain, spices, and tea. From China, some sailed home and sold the Asian products they had obtained for enormous profits. Others spent the winter in the Hawaiian Islands or elsewhere in the Pacific and then returned to the Northwest Coast for another season of trading. Such a voyage took about two years. For the luckiest, cleverest, most aggressive, or most scheming traders, the profits from a single successful voyage might mean a lifetime of wealth and luxury. The lure of this soft gold was so great that within a few years of Cook's return to England, there were ships trading all along the Northwest Coast.

Hampered by rules and restrictions governing their country's foreign trade, the English initially were far less able to take advantage of the maritime fur trade than the "Bostonmen," as American traders who sailed out of Boston became known. In 1788, the first American ships arrived on the Northwest Coast—the 220-ton *Columbia Redivivus* (captained by John Kendrick) and the 90-ton *Lady Washington* (captained by Robert Gray). Whereas the *Columbia Redivivus* remained in Nootka Sound, the *Lady Washington* traveled up and down the coast. It is difficult to know exactly which Indian groups the Americans encountered; the crews of these and other trading ships purposely kept poor records to prevent competitors from obtaining any information about the best villages with which to trade. However, the crew of the *Lady Washington* possibly made contact with Kwakiutl living along the west coast of Vancouver Island and probably stopped at other villages along the island's north and northeast coasts.

White traders would sometimes cooperate, but just as often, they would rob each other. Some crews would "take prizes" from another nation's ship under the pretext that the ship had invaded waters claimed by the crew's mother country. For a brief period in the late 1780s, it appeared that Spain and England might go to war over control of the West Coast. But the situation was resolved in 1790, when a settlement called the Nootka Convention opened up the coast to traders of all nationalities.

Faced with increased competition, those European powers interested in the maritime fur trade sent out expeditions to the Northwest Coast. Their purpose was supposedly to survey the area or to collect scientific information about the environment and its peoples. Their actual goal, however, was simply to sail past as much territory as possible, thereby potentially establishing a claim to these lands.

In 1792, the Spanish commissioned such an expedition to sail around Vancouver Island. In 2 small schooners, 20

men left Friendly Cove, the Spanish base at Nootka Sound, in May. They sailed southward to explore land at the end of the Strait of Juan de Fuca and then headed north along the east coast of Vancouver Island, stopping at Gabriola Island in the territory of the Salish Indians. There, only a month after they had set sail, they met an English ship, the *Chatham*, captained by George Vancouver. Vancouver was on a surveying expedition for the British government.

The officers of the two expeditions spent several days honoring one another. Vancouver suggested that they cooperate on a joint survey of the area, but the arrangement did not work out for long. The Spaniards set sail alone, journeying north around the end of Vancouver Island and then southward along the west coast before returning to Nootka Sound. On the expedition, they passed through a significant portion of Kwakiutl territory. They stopped in at least one large Kwakiutl village in early 1792 and at several other Indian villages along the north and northeastern coasts of the island.

These Spaniards were not the first Europeans known to have contact with the Kwakiutl, however. Only two weeks before the Spaniards' encounter with the Indians, Vancouver visited a Lekwiltok Kwakiutl village on Quadra's Island at Cape Mudge. The journals of several of the crew's officers and of Archibald Menzies, the ship's surgeon and naturalist, provide the first written descriptions of the Kwakiutl people.

When the English ship arrived at the village, 18 small canoes paddled out to greet Vancouver. Relations between the English and the villagers were cordial during the few days they spent together. Vancouver noted the Indians' courtesy as the Lekwiltok presented the

The Kwakiutl village of Cape Mudge, drawn in 1792 by William Sykes. The artist was a crewman on the HMS Discovery, *the first European vessel to sail into Kwakiutl territory.*

Captain George Vancouver visited the village of Chief Cheslakees on the Nimpkish River in July 1792. The village was made up of 34 houses, many of which were painted with images that celebrated the inhabitants' status.

English with gifts and food and traded with the crew for European goods. Although it was probably the first time Europeans had ever been in a Kwakiutl village, the Indians knew all about the etiquette of trading. They had most likely learned how to deal with white traders from the Nootka. This Indian group probably had also been the source of the European goods that Vancouver recorded were already present in the Kwakiutl village when his ship arrived.

Menzies's journal reported that the Kwakiutl were physically similar to the Nootka and Salish Indians he had met previously. He described the Kwakiutl as slender and short limbed and of medium stature. Menzies also noted that they seemed to move stiffly, perhaps, as he surmised, because they spent so much time squatting on shore or in their canoes. Among the scientist's other observations were that the Indians had flat faces, small eyes, and small, poorly maintained teeth; painted their faces with red and black designs; wore copper and shell ornaments in holes pierced in their earlobes and in the septum of their nose; and decorated their hair with red ocher, soot, and birds' down. He also remarked on the lack of

shyness in Kwakiutl women and children and on the dress of both sexes, noting that women wore clothing made of fur, wool, or cedar bark and that men often wore nothing.

After the Vancouver expedition left the Lekwiltok village, it continued to sail north through Seymour Narrows to the main Kwakiutl territory. The Englishmen arrived among the Nimpkish Kwakiutl living near Alert Bay on the evening of July 19. This substantial village then comprised 34 houses, some quite large and decorated with painted figures, arranged in 2 rows parallel to the shoreline. The total population was between 350 and 500, probably swelled by summer fishing activities. The village controlled one major access route to the Grease Trail, a network of waterways and steep overland trails that connected Kwakiutl territory to the lands of the Nootka.

On the morning of July 20, a group of Kwakiutl in canoes paddled out to the ships and invited the English ashore. When the visitors arrived on the beach, they were received with a large, formal greeting ceremony. At the house of Chief Cheslakees, the Englishmen were further honored and entertained by the type of boisterous and energetic singing and dancing ceremonies that have been a part of Kwakiutl life for centuries. During the nine days the traders spent at this village, they were taken all about town, constantly surrounded by Indians offering them gifts and bits of food and asking for presents in return.

The visit was a ceaseless round of bartering. The sea otter fur trading was supervised by the chief, but villagers were allowed to negotiate minor exchanges for beads, buttons, or other trinkets on their own behalf. So much of this petty trading took place that the English soon had none of these objects left.

Vancouver wrote that the Kwakiutl seemed to be willing and capable negotiators who were "well versed in the principles of trade." He noted that they knew that they could get more for their furs by taking them to the Nootka than by selling them directly to the English. The captain estimated that he paid more than double the going rate for the 200 sea otter pelts he bought from the Nimpkish.

Metal cooking pots and other manufactured items from Europe were greatly desired by the Kwakiutl. To obtain these goods, they encouraged non-Indian traders to visit their lands in the late 18th and early 19th centuries.

Vancouver's observations on other aspects of his visit are scanty. His primary mission was not to study the Kwakiutl but to survey the coastline so that England could make a territorial claim to the portions of the Northwest Coast that had not yet been claimed by Spain. After Vancouver determined that he was exploring an area outside the realm of Nootka chief Maquinna, with whom the Spanish had already established a trade alliance, the Englishman set about establishing his own trade relationship with the Indians he encountered. His reports about the Kwakiutl were designed to show that the Kwakiutl had willingly become trading partners of the English and to thereby block any future efforts by the Spanish to trade with this group of Indians.

Many different types of European goods were desired by the Northwest Coast Indians during the period of the maritime fur trade. At first, they mostly wanted metal, especially iron (which they fashioned into tools and weapons) and copper (which they made into jewelry and ceremonial items). Cloth and objects made from it—including ribbons, blankets, and duffels—were also very popular. Tailored European clothing quickly replaced traditional clothes made out of the rough fibers of shredded cedar bark. Other desired items included tools, mirrors, cooking pots, musical instruments, and foodstuffs, especially flour, crackers, rice, potatoes, molasses, coffee, tea, and sugar. Tobacco and, after 1800, Indian brandy

(gin with brown coloring added) and Indian rum (cheap, semitoxic, diluted rum sweetened with molasses) were also in great demand.

The character of the ship-based traders varied greatly, ranging from fair-minded to rapacious. Their personalities often affected their approach to dealing with Indians. Some would trade only from the safety of their vessels, keeping their guns ready as they allowed only one or two Indians onto their ship at a time. Others invited groups of Indians aboard their ships for meals and entertainment. Still others would come ashore and stay in a village for a few weeks, an approach that usually promoted long-term trade alliances with specific Indian leaders.

When a ship arrived offshore from a village, it was greeted by a fleet of canoes paddled by Indians dressed in ceremonial war costumes and wearing body and face paint. As they approached the ship, the greeting party loudly sang ritual songs while beating the rhythm on the canoes' gunwales with the shafts of their paddles. One of the Indians—either a chief or a chief's representative—would perform a dance on the platform at the front of the largest canoe. While dancing, he scattered sacred red ocher or eagle's down onto the water, a gesture that indicated that he came in peace. Then, using the marked cadences of ceremonial speech, he would formally greet the visitors. Further trade rituals—including speeches, dancing, singing, presentations of gifts, and displays of

crests and other symbols of status— were sometimes performed for days before trading began. To the Indians, such rituals were as, if not more, important than the actual exchange of goods. The long rituals frequently exasperated white traders, however. They were eager to trade with one village and quickly move on to the next, for the more villages they visited, the greater their profits.

Whites also preferred to trade with Indians who had not previously had contact with non-Indians. Not only did they want to build an exclusive trade relationship with such groups, but also they knew they could take advantage of these Indians' ignorance of the prices of goods established elsewhere. For instance, a sea otter skin that cost a trader three to nine chisel blades in a village where Indians were experienced in dealing with white traders might be bought for only one blade from previously uncontacted people.

The Indians were just as good at maneuvering the trade to their advantage as the whites were. Indian traders often tried to monopolize dealings with a ship's crew by chasing off other Indians who came to trade with the vessel. The Indians also played trading ships off one another to keep the price of furs high and of European and American goods low. They often refused to deal with a white trader who did not have

Fort Vancouver, a post established by the Hudson's Bay Company in 1824 on the Columbia River near present-day Portland, Oregon. For decades, the company dominated the fur trade in the Pacific Northwest.

the exact goods they wanted or who was charging prices they felt were too high. Indian traders even resorted to trickery. Some agreed to trade only at night, when it was too dark to see the quality of the furs they were selling. Others painted their furs black to make them look more luxurious to their customers.

Although neither Indian nor white traders hesitated to cheat or rob each other, for the most part their relations during the maritime fur trade were peaceful. Both sides were always prepared for an armed conflict, however. Crews of wary white traders were ready for battle whenever they were near an Indian settlement, knowing that a poorly defended vessel could easily be overrun and its men killed or captured and sold into slavery. As the Indians approached a vessel in their canoes, they were never sure whether the visitors would honor them as guests or take them as hostages. Knowing that hostilities could break out even over minor incidents or misunderstandings, both sides were prepared to use force to avenge real or perceived injustices.

The relationship between Indian and white traders became more complicated after 1793, when Canadian trader Alexander Mackenzie reached the coast of Bella Coola territory via an overland route. Soon afterward, several land-based fur trading companies—the Hudson's Bay Company, the North West Company, and the Pacific Fur Company—set up permanent trading posts in the area and began competing with the maritime traders. At first, the competition worked to the Indians' advantage. They had even more white traders to play off each other in order to obtain the best price for their goods. The competition was short-lived, however. In 1814, the Pacific Fur Comany was taken over by the North West Company, which in turn merged with the Hudson's Bay Company in 1821. For decades to follow, the British-owned Hudson's Bay Company enjoyed a virtual monopoly over all trade with the Indians from present-day Oregon to southern Alaska.

During the winter of 1824–25, Fort Vancouver was founded on the Columbia River near what is now the city of Portland, Oregon. This post flourished as the headquarters of the Hudson's Bay Company's Columbia Department, which oversaw trade in what are now Washington, Oregon, Idaho, and British Columbia. Presiding over Fort Vancouver was John McLoughlin. In addition to keeping peace with the Indians, McLoughlin was charged with helping the British maintain their dominance in the Northwest by squeezing Americans out of the fur trade. Under his control were about 500 people, engaged both at the post and in the surrounding territory. Some whites working for the Hudson's Bay Company remained on the coast for decades and established long-term relations with specific Indian leaders. Some even married Indian women.

In the decades following the founding of Fort Vancouver, several forts

continued on page 57

OBJECTS OF POWER AND BEAUTY

The Kwakiutl believed that spirits came to earth each winter, dwelt among humans, and passed on spiritual powers to some young men and women. As members of special secret societies, these people then impersonated the spirits during a complex series of rituals known as the Winter Ceremonials. The cherished hereditary myths and dances enacted by the performers were thought to guarantee the Kwakiutl's spiritual renewal and economic prosperity.

The performances at the Winter Ceremonials were spectacular, filled with magnificent stage effects, sleight-of-hand magic, and visual trickery. The spirit impersonators would be killed in a violent and bloody fashion and then would be brought back to life. Statues would speak and move, magical objects would fly through the air, and creatures would appear and disappear miraculously.

The ceremonial paraphernalia that aided Kwakiutl ritual performers were not only ingenious implements of stagecraft. These objects, particularly the masks, were also intricate and beautiful works of art. Between 1897 and 1904, George Hunt, an employee of the Hudson's Bay Company who was of Tlingit and Scottish descent, collected nearly 2,500 such creations that were made and used in the 19th century. The ceremonial objects that appear on this page and the following seven are from Hunt's collection, which is now housed in the American Museum of Natural History in New York City.

A ceremonial bowl in the shape of a spoon, the handle of which represents Dzonokwa. A giant female monster, Dzonokwa was said to wander through the woods, where she kidnapped and ate children. She also had the power to bestow great wealth on people.

The mask of a fool dancer, one of the performers who kept order during the Cannibal dance. The long nose is an allusion to the A'las-iamk, supernaturals with huge noses who were thought to grant the fool dancers their power.

People imbued with the power of the Cannibal-at-the-North-End-of-the-World exhibited wild behavior that, through the Winter Ceremonials, members of the Cannibal Society sought to tame. Rattles in the shape of human skulls such as these were shaken by the assistants of Cannibal Society initiates to calm them.

A mask representing the assistants of the Cannibal-at-the-North-End-of-the-World, Ho'xuhok (a cranelike being), and two ravens. The beaks of the three avian creatures could be moved to clack in rhythm as the wearer danced.

The simple, subtly hued raven mask (above) dramatically opens to reveal another being, the brilliantly colored Raven of the Sea (right). Initiates into the Cannibal Society would often become uncontrollable at the sight of raven masks because of the raven's close association with the Cannibal-at-the-North-End-of-the-World.

A mask representing Sisiutl, an assistant of a female warrior named Tooquid. A snakelike creature, Sisiutl is shown to have a serpent's head at both of its ends and a human face at its center. The creature was thought to have the power to turn enemies to stone with its gaze.

A feast bowl in the shape of a two-headed wolf. Each wolf head holds in its teeth a Copper, an important Kwakiutl ceremonial object.

A mask composed of two octopus heads, one on top of the other. By manipulating the strings, which were probably invisible in the dark, the wearer could move the tentacles and open and shut the smaller head's mouth.

Wooden puppets depicting a ghost dancer and its two children.
These beings, who could bring the dead to life, were associates of
Tooquid. The puppets were manipulated during her dance to signify
her otherworldly powers.

continued from page 48

were built along the Northwest Coast. Among them was Fort Rupert, the first trading post in Kwakiutl territory. Built in 1849, this fort quickly became a major center of Kwakiutl trade. At the same time, villages, such as Newhitty, that had been important trade centers during the maritime fur trade lost their power and population.

In the 1820s, the Hudson's Bay Company succeeded in freezing most of the independent American traders out of the Northwest Coast fur trade. Indians who wanted European goods thereafter could only obtain them from the Hudson's Bay Company's forts. Among the items the company provided Indians were foodstuffs, tools, ammunition, clothing, blankets, furniture, and cookware. By eliminating their competition, the company was able to reap exorbitant profits: A sea otter fur worth $700 might garner only $2 to $4 in company goods.

Quickly, the forts became magnets that attracted Indians from many outlying villages and different tribes. For instance, the population of Fort Rupert at its height in the 1850s and 1860s was nearly 3,000, nearly 10 times the number of inhabitants of a large Kwakiutl village before contact with non-Indians. Sometimes the groups that immigrated to the forts forged new alliances with one another. But as the various groups struggled to dominate the others' access to white traders and their wealth, most of the areas around the forts became battle zones—as violent and dangerous as any frontier town.

Before contact, a chief's position was inherited. After the Indians began trading with whites, however, new avenues for obtaining prestige and power appeared. Thereafter, leadership fell into the hands of strong individuals who, through warfare or coercion, became influential in the fur trade. As the Hudson's Bay Company's monopoly developed, the main road to power for a chief was through controlling the flow of furs into the forts. A chief with this control could sell furs to whichever fort was then offering the highest prices. The chiefs of the four tribes of Kwakiutl who had moved to Fort Rupert were especially successful at collecting, hoarding, and manipulating the sale of furs that arrived along the southern coast. In this way, the Kwakiutl gained far greater economic and political power than they had during the era of the maritime fur trade.

Initially, the fur trade had little effect on Kwakiutl ways. The traders had had little intention of, or interest in, interfering with the Indians' culture. They only wanted the pelts the Indians brought to them and merely did whatever seemed necessary to keep the flow of furs at a maximum. Indian hunters participating in the trade did exactly what they had done before: hunt animals and trade the pelts to their allies for goods. Within a few decades, however, the population of sea otters on the southern Northwest Coast had dropped so low that the Indians had to find new ways of obtaining furs. Threatened with poverty after a time of

A posed photograph of a Kwakiutl man dressed in rope armor and armed with a stone club. These accoutrements of hand-to-hand combat became obsolete after the Kwakiutl obtained guns from non-Indians in the early 19th century.

plenty, the Indians became more willing to trade, steal, or kill to get pelts because furs were the only goods that they could use to buy the guns, metal tools, fancy foods, and cloth garments they wanted. Before contact, the tribes of the Northwest Coast had sometimes warred with each other, but at the height of the fur trade, military conflict was constant. European and American firearms increased the effectiveness of Indian warfare, and groups armed with guns sometimes wiped out entire villages.

The warfare propagated by the fur trade also altered traditional Indian living patterns. In the past, the Northwest Coast Indians had lived scattered throughout their entire territory and took advantage of all its resources. In the decades following contact, however, many isolated villages were abandoned. Their former inhabitants joined with people of other small villages to form new, larger villages at sites chosen because their geography made them easy to defend. Another tide of refugees became permanent residents of the villages that sprang up near the Hudson's Bay Company forts.

As villages became larger and more powerful, the nature of warfare changed. The small-scale raiding for revenge, glory, or profit practiced in the precontact period continued, but in addition, battles for territory were now fought. Dozens of villages might band together to wage a large-scale military campaign against a common enemy or competitor.

The most famous military raid in Kwakiutl history occurred in about 1835. After the Bella Coola had attacked a Kwakiutl village and killed many people, a party of 32 war canoes from all of the Kwakiutl tribes set out to seek revenge. As the Indians were paddling toward Bella Coola country, they met a party of high-ranking Bella Bella chiefs. The chiefs were on their way to a ceremony and were carrying some important ceremonial equipment. One Kwakiutl was so enraged by the Bella Coola's massacre that he lashed out at the Bella Bella chiefs, who had had no involvement in the slaughter. Once the killing began, everyone joined in.

For some Northwest Coast groups, the only way to remain in the fur trade was to prey on others. Some plundered any undefended and isolated village. Others settled along narrow waterways on trade routes so that they could rob traders journeying to and from the forts. Still others stationed themselves outside the entrance of a fort, exacting tribute from any other group that came to trade there.

By the 1830s, the sea otter population was so depleted that it was difficult for sea otter fur traders to make a living even using such drastic means. Coastal Indians then turned to trading with tribes living to the east, where other fur-bearing animals were still fairly easy to find. After obtaining furs from interior peoples, the traders would carry them to the forts along the coast. The Hudson's Bay Company encouraged this practice because it was easier to trans-

port the furs from the Pacific Coast by ship than to haul them across overland routes.

Another new way the Indians could participate in trading was to become dealers in slaves. Dealers either raided villages for slaves themselves or purchased them at major trading centers and then brokered the slaves to other tribes. Many groups were in need of slaves to perform menial labor because their own members were too busy trading to do such work themselves.

Some tribes became especially good at slave raiding. Parties of Tlingit and Haida raiders traveled annually to Salish territory and even as far south as northern California on slaving expeditions. The Nootka, whose supply of sea otter furs was among the first to be exhausted, turned to slave trading as a means of reestablishing their position of importance in the trade system. Among the Kwakiutl, those at Fort Rupert were especially successful as slave raiders and traders.

During the early 19th century, Northwest Coast Indians found still other ways of obtaining goods and cash. From the beginning of the fur trade, natives supplied non-Indian traders with food, water, wood, and other provisions for a price. They quickly learned that sailors would also be willing to pay for prostitutes, who were usually female slaves, and for objects crafted by Indian artisans. Eventually, some Indians were hired as wage laborers by European and American traders. Such laborers performed a

number of services, including constructing forts, repairing ships, mining coal, and acting as interpreters or guides. The Fort Rupert Kwakiutl once even offered to work as mercenaries for the British.

Not all of the many changes that took place in Northwest Coast Indian culture after contact were related to the region's economy. Through their social contact with foreign peoples, Indians were introduced to new customs. The Indians were fascinated by the unfamiliar behavior of non-Indian traders. Often, curious Indians sat on the ships' decks for hours at a time just to watch the strangers. Many Indians learned about Christianity from sailors, who urged the natives to adopt Christian values and beliefs. The sailors also taught the Indians about liquor and gambling—both of which had far-reaching effects on the way Indians saw themselves and others. Even the seemingly harmless activity of playing cards taught the Indians new ideas about competition.

Merely learning of the existence of non-Indians drastically changed the Indians' view of the world. Before contact, the Kwakiutl knew many other peoples, all of whom were Indians who lived more or less as they did. Whites, however, had a way of life that was startlingly different from their own. Each time the Indians were introduced to a new white custom or belief, they had to determine its worth and decide whether to adopt it themselves. Such decisions led to disagreements among

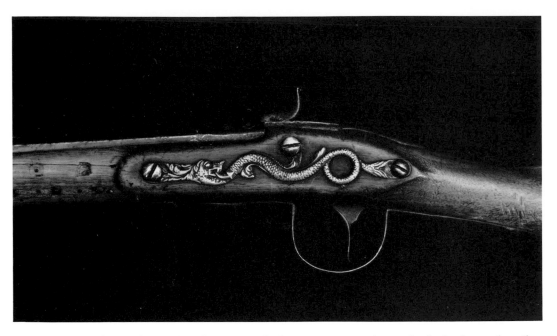

A gun sold by the Hudson's Bay Company. Such weapons were increasingly in demand as the Indians of the Northwest began to battle for control over hunting territory and position in the fur trade.

people within Indian groups. Those who wanted to take on white ways were accused of being too willing to forget their Indianness; those who did not were called old-fashioned.

Perhaps the greatest changes in Northwest Coast Indian culture were the result of disease. European and American sailors during the period of the fur trade were not a particularly healthy lot. Poor nutrition, unsanitary living conditions, and ineffectual medical treatments all contributed to their ill health. When the sailors came in contact with Indians, they often transmitted European and tropical diseases to which the natives were not immune.

In 1773, Captain Cook journeyed to Tahiti and found that the islanders were suffering from a host of European diseases that could only have been introduced to them by Cook's crew during an earlier trip. It is likely that they passed on these same diseases while visiting the Nootka five years later. Epidemics of smallpox, syphilis, measles, mumps, tuberculosis, cholera, scarlet fever, influenza, and chicken pox soon spread throughout the Indian population of the Northwest. Many tribes were destroyed by disease within a few years after contact; infected by Indian carriers, some were decimated even before they ever encountered whites.

LOCATIONS OF KWAKIUTL TRIBES AND VILLAGES IN THE EARLY 19TH CENTURY

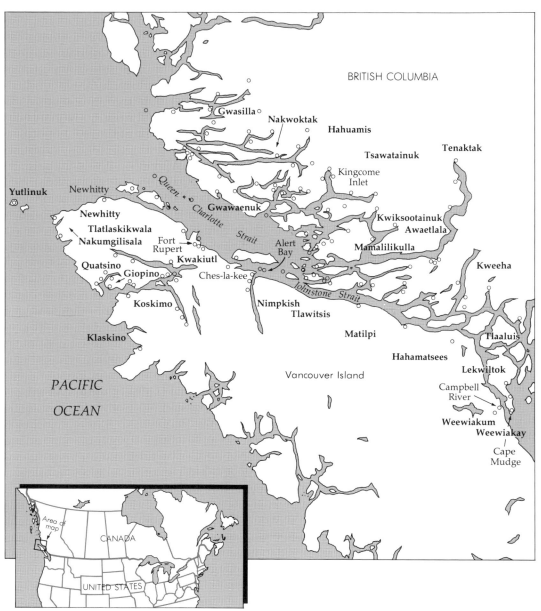

BRITISH COLUMBIA

Gwasilla
Nakwoktak
Hahuamis
Tsawatainuk
Tenaktak
Kingcome Inlet
Newhitty
Yutlinuk
Gwawaenuk
Newhitty
Kwiksootainuk
Tlatlaskikwala
Awaetlala
Nakumgilisala
Fort Rupert
Alert Bay
Mamalilikulla
Kwakiutl
Kweeha
Quatsino
Giopino
Ches-la-kee
Koskimo
Nimpkish
Tlawitsis
Klaskino
Matilpi
Tlaaluis
Hahamatsees
Lekwiltok
Vancouver Island
Campbell River
PACIFIC
OCEAN
Weewiakum
Weewiakay
Cape Mudge

Queen Charlotte Strait
Johnstone Strait

Area of map
CANADA
UNITED STATES

Smallpox epidemics were probably the most deadly. Early journals record several extreme outbreaks during the 1780s and 1790s among the Tlingit and Haida. Although it is not documented, an epidemic of smallpox probably hit the Kwakiutl at this time.

Two more major epidemics—one in 1836 and one in 1862–64—greatly thinned many tribes. The latter affected virtually every Pacific Northwest group, on the coast and in the interior, killing one-third of the remaining Indian population. A large number of whites recorded the horrors of this outbreak. Hundreds of Indians died in camps located near forts. Rotting corpses lay wherever the sick fell. Entire villages and tribes were destroyed. Survivors fleeing their ravaged villages often carried the disease with them, thereby spreading the epidemic to areas that were previously unaffected. The epidemics undoubtedly had a profound effect on the culture and psychology of the Indians who survived.

Although many old ways remained, the era of the fur trade reshaped the world of the Kwakiutl. Through their contact with whites, they had suddenly been introduced to entirely new possibilities for wealth and social advancement, coupled with substantial changes in their population and residence patterns. The Indians responded with intelligence, creativity, and energy to these unfamiliar circumstances, and they emerged from this period of crisis still masters of their own destiny. But the future would present them with new and even more difficult challenges as they encountered a new breed of whites, settlers hungry for control of the Kwakiutl's ancestral lands. ▲

A Kwakiutl man aboard an English ship, photographed in 1873.

4

SETTLEMENT
AND
DISPOSSESSION

Spurred on by visions of fertile land and gold in the western wilderness, swarms of new settlers descended on the Pacific Northwest in the 1840s. In the Oregon and California territories of the United States, the newcomers brought disaster to the natives of the region. The Indians were brutally mistreated by the settlers and the U.S. government alike. Many were massacred; many more were forcibly relocated to reservations far from their ancestral lands.

The British government was eager for non-Indian settlement of the lands it controlled north of present-day Washington State. However, it hoped to avoid the kind of social upheaval represented by the Oregon Madness by formalizing its colonial adminstration. In the process, Vancouver Island was named a colony and ceded to the Hudson's Bay Company in 1849. Richard Blanshard was named the island's first

colonial governor. Two years later, he was replaced by James Douglas, an experienced fur trader who had been based at Fort Victoria.

During Blanshard's brief administration, an important incident affecting the Kwakiutl occurred. In the summer of 1850, three British sailors deserted their ship, possibly to sneak off to the gold fields of California, and boarded a boat whose next destination was Fort Rupert. When the British asked the Kwakiutl to help apprehend the deserters, some Indians captured and executed the men. The Indians assumed that ordinary seamen were slaves of their officers and therefore dealt with the sailors as they would have any escaped slaves. It is also possible that the Kwakiutl had been offered a reward for the deserters, dead or alive.

In any case, to the Kwakiutl's surprise, Governor Blanshard declared that the Indians responsible were mur-

derers and vowed to avenge their action. Either out of intertribal jealousy or fear of the British, Indians from other tribes accused the Newhitty Kwakiutl of performing the executions. An investigator was sent to Fort Rupert and concluded that the Newhitty had not been involved in the killings. However, the findings did not quell the governor's determination to seek retribution against the Newhitty.

Blanshard boarded a gunboat, the HMS *Daedelus*, and sailed to a Newhitty village. There he ordered the Indians to surrender the killers. When he received no response from them, he had his crew destroy the village with artillery shelling. A year later, some Newhitty tried to calm the governor by delivering the bodies of two men, whom they claimed to have been the murderers. For no apparent reason, Blanshard then ordered a gunboat to destroy still another Newhitty village.

Douglas, Blanshard's successor, was less openly hostile to the Indians, but for the most part, the new governor simply followed the policies set forth by the British colonial government, many of which were designed to seize control of the Indians' territory and resources. The British held that the Indians had rights only to land on which they lived or farmed, and then only if they accepted British rule. Because the Indians of the Northwest were hunters and gatherers, not farmers, the British generally felt justified in denying that they had any claim to their homeland.

Douglas, however, was interested in negotiating treaties with the Indians that allowed them to retain control over a limited amount of land. He was not motivated by a sense of fairness or justice, though. He was trying to stabilize the relations between the British and Indians in order to prevent American settlers from moving north and disrupting the fur trade. To keep the fur trade profitable to the British, Douglas wanted to ensure that the Indians had enough land on which to hunt.

Douglas also wanted to help Indians prosper economically. Again, his reasons had less to do with the Indians' well-being than with fulfilling British goals in the region. The governor felt that if Indians became involved in the colonial economy, they would also become assimilated into colonial society, willingly giving up their culture, religion, and political structure and choosing to live like the British colonists. To accomplish this transformation and maintain peace at the same time, Douglas favored British law rather than military force as the tool with which to rule the Indians, a policy that brought him into conflict with both British settlers and the British government. They still supported the confrontational policies of Blanshard. Douglas, however, recognized that if the United States invaded the Canadian territories, the British would need the Indians to help defend their interests. It was clear to the governor that the Indians would not long remain politically and militarily

aligned with the British if they continued to be the victims of gunboat attacks.

Douglas's fears of an influx of Americans proved well founded soon after gold was discovered along the upper Columbia, Thompson, and Fraser rivers in the mid-1850s. Thousands of miners, many from California, began to arrive in Victoria. In 1856, the population of the city included about 500 whites; by the end of 1858, the number had grown to 25,000. Hundreds of new businesses opened to provide supplies for the miners. The Hudson's Bay Company made immense profits—far beyond what it had made from the Indian fur trade—by selling provisions to the new immigrants. The British government also acted quickly to secure a claim to the newfound mineral wealth in the region. It took control of Vancouver Island back from the Hudson's Bay Company and renamed all its territory west of the Rockies as the colony of British Columbia. Douglas was appointed the new colony's first governor.

During this period, several Salish groups living in southern Vancouver Island and near the Fraser River on the mainland were pressured to sign several treaties. In these treaties, the Indians purportedly renounced all claims to their land and its resources. In return, they were promised pitifully small amounts of cash or goods and tracts of land called reserves, which they would be allowed to occupy for eternity. The government, however, never made an

A white miner prospecting for gold in British Columbia, photographed in the late 19th century. The influx of thousands of prospectors to this region in the 1850s led to many conflicts with the native population.

attempt to honor the treaties. The Indians received only a small amount of the money they had been promised, and their reserves were left unprotected from encroachment by non-Indian settlers.

After 1859, the British government in British Columbia stopped bothering to negotiate treaties when it wished to take control of Indian land and relocate groups to reserves. The British saw no reason for dealing fairly with the natives. With the large influx of whites to the colony, the Indians no longer posed a significant military threat to non-Indian settlements. The new immigrants also provided a large pool of cheap labor. When the fur trade was central to the economy, whites relied on Indian labor, but now the Indians were viewed by the British merely as obstacles to unbridled economic development. By the early 1860s, Douglas's replacements had developed a policy of dispossessing Indians of their land by any and all means. Indians were often accused of being thieves and having no respect for British property rights, but it was the British who displayed no regard for Indian property rights during their wholesale theft of British Columbia from its native inhabitants.

Within a decade of the Fraser River gold strike, the colonial government had sold to whites tens of thousands of acres that had been set aside as Indian reserves. In 1865, a land ordinance established that no Indian family could be allotted more than 10 acres, causing the size of reserves to be even further re-

duced. At the same time, a white individual could own 640 acres.

As thousands of prospectors congregated along river valleys in southern and interior British Columbia, conflicts often arose with the native inhabitants. In some incidents, Indians were murdered by prospectors. More commonly, the newcomers engaged in less violent activities that were nevertheless extremely damaging to the Indians. The whites were poisoning salmon streams with mercury, which they used to process gold ore. The miners often took over riverside sites that had been important to Indian fishermen for centuries. Some whites began to compete directly with them by placing nets across the mouths of rivers to catch salmon as they swam upriver. Some of the salmon were eaten by the white fishermen, but most were used as fertilizer on farms that whites had established on fertile lands confiscated from the Indians.

The Indians also suffered from an increased interference in their lives by British and Canadian authorities. To enforce British law throughout Vancouver Island and the mainland, Douglas established a police force. By working actively to stop disputes between Indians and whites, he was able to prevent the widespread violence that had erupted at the same time in Washington Territory to the south. Indians were hardly treated with justice, however. When Indians were robbed or murdered by whites, the police were brought in to prevent riots but rarely to punish the perpetrators. When they defended

themselves against attacks, they were hunted down and executed. And when Indian leaders refused to surrender the accused criminals, their villages would be riddled by naval artillery. Afterward, whatever few Indian possessions were left untouched by the bombardment would be set on fire.

Naval bombardment became the standard policy for dealing with unruly coastal Indians who refused to submit to British authority. On several occasions, Kwakiutl villages were attacked by gunships. The village at Cape Mudge was shelled twice. However, the most dreadful attack was on Fort Rupert in 1865. The Fort Rupert Kwakiutl had been very successful in gain-

ing control of the interior fur trade and the intertribal slave-trade network. As a result, they had also been able to corner the market in bootleg liquor, which they purchased from American traders and sold to other Indian tribes at great profit. The colonial government took exception to this trade because it attracted American ships to British Columbia waters and gave the Indians profits that the government wanted for its own citizens. In order to end the Kwakiutl's control of the trade, the government fabricated an excuse to send gunboats to their village. The artillery completely destroyed the Indians' homes but left the Hudson's Bay Company's post there untouched. The Fort

The Hudson's Bay Company post at Fort Rupert in 1866. A year earlier, British gunboats attacked the Kwakiutl village that had grown up around the post in order to stop the Fort Rupert Kwakiutl from dealing with American traders. The artillery destroyed the village but left the British trading post untouched.

Rupert Kwakiutl built a new village a short distance away, but the attack dealt a severe blow to the status of Fort Rupert and to the morale of its inhabitants.

The gold along the Fraser quickly disappeared, and within a few years, most of the prospectors left the region. But many thousands of non-Indian settlers remained in British Columbia. Almost overnight, Victoria had become a cosmopolitan city populated by Europeans, Asians, and Indians. For the Salish Indians native to the area, the growth of Victoria was an immediate and unmitigated disaster. For the Kwakiutl, however, the influx of whites was at first a great boon. Relatively few non-Indians came into their territory, yet they were able to benefit from Victoria's economic prosperity. They began to take their goods into the city rather than to the Fort Rupert post. They could reap much greater profits by trading on the black market in the city than by dealing with Hudson's Bay Company traders, whose monopoly on legal trade allowed them to charge exorbitant prices for their goods.

Victoria acted as a magnet for the natives of coastal British Columbia. Large numbers of Indians, including

A panoramic view of Victoria, British Columbia, in the 1870s. To obtain wage work, many Kwakiutl settled permanently in the city. Living in an overcrowded Indian ghetto there, most were forced to contend with poverty, starvation, and the prejudices of Victoria's rapidly growing non-Indian population.

hundreds of Kwakiutl, traveled there each summer. Eventually, a group of Kwakiutl formed a permanent settlement there. These people came into frequent contact with members of other tribes and with non-Indians. Although there was some violence between different peoples, most of their relations were peaceful.

The Kwakiutl's survival in Victoria depended on their ability to earn enough cash to purchase food and goods. Because many neglected to gather food or make other preparations for the winter, they faced poverty and starvation if they were unable to buy supplies. In order to obtain a steady cash income, the Kwakiutl in Victoria often became wage laborers. Some worked as fishermen and hunters, joined logging crews, became field hands, or caught dogfish and sold their oil. The young and strong often became seal hunters or worked on the crews of whaling ships and commercial fishing vessels. Some women earned significant amounts of money as laundresses or as prostitutes, an occupation to which the Kwakiutl had no moral objection. However, as the population of immigrant laborers grew, it became ever more difficult for Indians to find work. Increasingly, they were relegated to only the most menial, low-paying jobs. As their incomes declined, most of the Kwakiutl in Victoria came to live in an overcrowded Indian ghetto. The poor living conditions there provided ideal conditions for the rapid spread of disease. Nearly half of the remaining

Indians of coastal British Columbia died in epidemics during the 1860s and 1870s.

City-dwelling Kwakiutl also faced the anger and prejudice of the growing non-Indian population. Whites generally viewed Indians, at best, as their intellectual, moral, and cultural inferiors. At worst, they were seen as dirty, disgusting, and dishonest savages who were barely superior to beasts. Some whites believed that if the Indians were converted to Christianity and educated in white schools, they could become fit to live among non-Indians. However, many racist whites considered them such a blight on humanity and an affront to civilization that, to these whites, the sooner they vanished from the face of the earth the better. Expressions of prejudice against Indians were considered acceptable, and sometimes even honorable, by white society. Newspapers and other writings of settlers and administrators in British Columbia contained countless articles and letters condemning Indians and their ways. Many were written by people who had never talked with or even met an Indian. Such strong prejudice served a useful purpose for whites, for it allowed them to justify treating Indians however they wished, without any concern for decency or justice.

From the start of the Fraser River gold rush, settlers clamored for the removal of Indians from areas of white settlement. They often claimed it was intolerable for moral Christian people to be brought into daily contact with

debauched Indian savages. Violence, alcoholism, theft, and prostitution were in fact common in the crowded Indian ghetto in Victoria, but for the most part, the settlers' cries for removal were completely unfounded. Their claims were little more than thinly disguised rationalizations for confiscating the Indians' valuable land.

Another widely held idea was that land and its resources should belong to whoever could make the greatest profit from it. The colonists therefore saw themselves as the rightful possessors of British Columbia because they planned to become wealthy from exploiting it. In their eyes, it was a moral act to seize Indian territory and harvest its resources. Consequently, some of the most honored families in British Columbia made their fortune from lands that they gave themselves permission to steal.

Not all Indian groups were dispossessed at the same time. For nearly 20 years after the expansion of Victoria, the Kwakiutl were relatively isolated from the wholesale land grabbing that was occurring farther south. Although they were strongly influenced by the economic conditions in the colony, they still had little direct contact with whites. The Kwakiutl were proud that while their Salish, Nootka, Tsimshian, and Haida neighbors seemingly had adopted white ways and lost much of their traditional culture, they remained relatively unaffected. However, through the authorities' experiences with these other groups, the government had dev-

eloped highly effective methods to dispossess the Indians and destroy their culture. When its policies were finally applied to the Kwakiutl in the 1880s, the change in the Indians' fate was devastating and inevitable.

Throughout the 1860s, in opposition to British and Canadian law, the colonial government of British Columbia insisted that the Indians had no claim to their own land, despite the fact that the Northwest Coast Indians had very clear ideas about land ownership and usage rights. However, the national government of the Dominion of Canada, which was formed in 1867, put little pressure on the colony to reform its policies, because it wanted British Columbia to become a province of Canada. Even after it joined the dominion in 1871, British Columbia still simply refused to effect any type of honest or humane treatment of the Indians. When the laws supported Indian claims and rights, provincial and federal officials either ignored the laws or wrote new ones. Their attempts to gain some political standing were consistently rebuffed by the provincial bureaucracy. For decades, commissions set up to settle Indian land disputes ignored the speeches of dispossessed Indians, who eloquently and passionately spoke about the theft of their ancestral lands and livelihood. In theory, these commissions were created to protect Indians from mistreatment, but in practice they rubber-stamped prior land grabbing, reduced the size of reserves, and further restricted Indian rights.

A photograph of the village of Xumtaspi-Nawittl, circa 1884. The signs posted on the houses' facades show the inhabitants' eagerness to attract the attention and dollars of American seamen. One reads, CHEAP. The Home of the Head Chief of All Tribes in This Country. White Man Can [Get] Information. The other reads, BOSTON. . . . He Is True and Honest. He Don't Give No Trouble to No White Man.

In the 1880s, the Canadian government began breaking up Indian reserves into small plots called allotments. Allotments were to be owned as private property. The officials overseeing the allotment of reserves followed the principle that Indians should be given title to only those lands they actually used. The result was the complete fragmentation of Indian territories. For example, if a family owned a house, collected berries along the

bluffs of a nearby river, and fished from a certain rocky point, they might be allotted only the land on which the house stood, the berry patch, and the fishing point. All the land separating these disparate sites would then be granted to non-Indians. Tens of thousands of acres that previously had been allotted to the Indians were confiscated without compensation and sold to settlers.

Although the Kwakiutl continued to hunt and fish for a portion of their food,

The 1918 communion class at a mission established in Nootka territory. Although missionaries were less active among the Kwakiutl than among other Northwest Coast Indian groups, many Kwakiutl became Christians in the late 19th century.

the allotment system made it impossible to survive solely by following traditional food-gathering activities. Most also had to earn wages, usually working as fishermen or as laborers in canneries. However, income from fishing was undependable, especially as overharvesting caused fish populations to diminish. Jobs in canneries were also hard to come by because their non-Indian owners preferred hiring whites over Indians. As more and more immigrants from Japan arrived in British Columbia, the Kwakiutl were faced with even more competition for these jobs. Those Indians who could find employment discovered that despite their hard work, low wages and poor working conditions trapped them in a cycle of deepening poverty.

The government also subjugated Indians by enacting anti-Indian laws and regulations. The Indian Liquor Ordinance of 1867 prohibited the sale of liquor to, and the use of liquor by, Indians. Several laws passed during the 1870s denied Indians the vote, guaranteeing that they would have essentially no representation in the national or provincial governments. The law that today's natives of British Columbia find most emblematic of their mistreatment is the Indian Act of 1876, which provided the foundation for the administration of Indian affairs in Canada. By banning Indian social and religious practices, including the potlatch and Winter Ceremonials, this act made it a misdemeanor to engage in the central rituals of Kwakiutl culture. People who violated the law were subject to fines, confiscation of ceremonial items, and imprisonment. The Indian Act essentially made it illegal to be an Indian in British Columbia.

Responsibility for the enforcement of anti-Indian laws fell primarily to agents, government officials charged with overseeing the implementation of Indian policy. Agents were supposed to represent Indian interests to officials in Victoria, the capital of British Columbia, but their primary job was to watch for Indian uprisings and encourage Indians to abandon their traditions. Agents who were too sympathetic to Indian concerns sometimes were removed from office.

At the same time, missionaries worked to indoctrinate Indians in the beliefs of white Canadians. The Indians had already learned much about western ways from their contact with traders and other whites. In fact, by the last half of the 19th century, Indian culture and white culture in the Northwest Coast were intricately intertwined. However, missionaries generally were not content with this melding of cultures. They sought to put an end to any and all Indian ways and to compel Indians to accept Christian values.

The Indians first had learned about Christianity from sailors, but these ideas initially had had little influence. They only began to take hold after the chaos of the postcontact years threw Indians' religious beliefs into turmoil. Indian religions could not explain the drastic social changes or shattering

rates of death by disease experienced by the natives.

The missionaries who came to the Northwest Coast in the late 19th century were often puritanical, uncompromising, and completely insensitive to Indian culture and concerns. Much of their energy was devoted to ending Indian rituals. The most zealous burned—or convinced potential Indian converts to destroy—masks and other sacred and secular ritual items. They also chopped down or mutilated totem poles, defaced traditional grave markers, and painted over crest designs.

For these missionaries, it was not enough to attack native religious beliefs. They insisted that all native social practices that differed from those of the English—from baby-naming ceremonies to burial rites—had to be rejected as heathen, frivolous, sinful, degenerate, and evil. They struck at every aspect of Indian culture, preaching with special fervor against traditional Indian family organization. The missionaries required Indian converts to live in single-family dwellings instead of large communal houses, discouraged inviting guests for meals, and demanded that Indians live only on their local reserves or where they worked. Economic factors were already destroying the fabric of the Indian family, for different family members went their separate ways each summer to find wage work. Indeed, some of the most successful missionaires were those that provided some form of steady work for the Indians they converted. In local mission industries, the clergymen taught the Indians to be satisfied with low wages by indoctrinating them in the Christian values of humility and poverty.

The missionaries' presence also intensified a growing schism within Indian society. One faction, the conservatives, felt that their people needed to resist change if they were to survive. Another faction, the progressives, argued that they should adapt to their new situation by adopting some non-Indian ways and forsaking some traditions. Often the view a person supported depended on the amount of power he or she had. Hereditary chiefs tended to hold conservative views so that their power base would remain intact. They often tried to keep missionaries out of their villages or undercut their influence. On the other hand, for those Indians who had been on the outskirts of influence in the fur-trade society, holding progressive beliefs and adopting Christianity could put them in the good graces of a missionary and possibly bring them status and power within their village.

Although missionaries were less active among the Kwakiutl than other tribes, many Kwakiutl converted to Christianity during the late 19th century. For some, conversion was merely a means of gaining admittance to mission schools, obtaining medical care, or receiving some other form of aid at a time when the government was providing little or none of the assistance it had promised. Others became involved in the church because missionaries acted

An 1897 photograph of the residents of Quatsino Sound. Their clothing reveals the different degrees to which these Kwakiutl had assimilated into mainstream Canadian culture. Many of the men, who probably were seamen or another type of wage worker, are dressed in non-Indian clothing. Most of the women, who generally had less opportunity to have contact with whites, are wearing traditional garments.

as needed intermediaries between the Indians and the government. Still others discovered a new set of social values and religious beliefs that helped compensate for the cultural losses they had experienced in the whirlwind of change.

Despite the conversion of many Kwakiutl, the Indians' own ceremonies grew in scope and frequency during this period. The development of the potlatch was especially rapid and important. At the beginning of the 19th century, the potlatch was a small ceremony during which a few dozen blankets were exchanged by the participants. By the end of the century, however, the ceremony involved a massive presentation of wealth—often many thousands of dollars' worth of goods— and hundreds of people from different tribes. In this transformation, the potlatch became the ceremonial focus of Kwakiutl society. To whites, it also came to represent all that was Indian and thus had to be eradicated. ▲

Chief Wakgas of Koskimo holding a Copper, circa 1895.

5

THE POTLATCH ERA

The word *potlatch* is used to refer to a variety of Northwest Coast ceremonies associated with social status and inheritance. Central to it is a host's display of symbols of his status and the distribution of gifts to his guests. To the Kwakiutl, giving away material wealth to others, often to the point of extravagance, was an extremely honorable act. They believed that a person's wealth—both material and spiritual—was not to be hoarded. In properly sharing one's wealth with nonfamily members during a potlatch, a person would also be sharing his or her spiritual wealth with relatives.

The origin of the potlatch is unknown. Some scholars argue that similar ceremonies took place centuries ago. A great deal of food was dispensed at potlatches, leading these scholars to believe that the ceremonies came into existence as a means of distributing the food supply throughout the entire population in times of scarcity. Groups that had extra food one year would invite their friends, relatives, and even rivals from other groups who were experiencing a food shortage. People with surplus food would exchange it for other goods and then give these away, a generous act that added to their prestige. Thus, a desire for prestige came to motivate people to perform ceremonies that equalized the distribution of food.

Other scholars believe that these ceremonies came into being only after various Northwest Coast Indian groups began to settle near trade forts. In this view, the potlatches were new rituals created by combining and recombining the different rites of various numayms and tribes, which perhaps allowed them to safely express and resolve conflicts and to reinforce new alliances.

In order to understand the potlatch, it is necessary to know about Kwakiutl social structure. The essential unit of Kwakiutl society was the numaym. A numaym was a group of relatives who

believed they were descended from a shared ancestor, either real or mythical. Each numaym held the rights to specific resources and to the ceremonial privileges that helped them communicate such rights to others. The most important of these privileges were sacred names, dances, and dramatic mythic narratives concerning the group's origins, history, and its acquisition of its special rights. The ceremonial display of crests was also an important, and jealously guarded, right of a numaym's members.

Numayms also possessed a series of ranked positions, which could be held by only one person at a time. Each position was associated with certain economic rights. For example, holding a particular position might entitle a person to fish in a specific river or to gather a certain type of food. These economic rights were very important, as were the ceremonial prerogatives that came with rank. They might have included the right to perform a certain dance or song, wear a particular mask, or reproduce a certain image on a crest.

Ranked positions were passed on from one generation to the next within a family. Thus, just like members of European royal families, the ranked Kwakiutl (often referred to as the Kwakiutl aristocracy) carefully protected their inheritance by arranging marriages only to others of appropriate rank. Likewise, they put a great deal of energy into performing their ceremonial obligations and thereby defending their rights and privileges.

Holding a potlatch was a particularly important means by which aristocrats established and maintained their social status. Hosts tried to distribute wealth to their guests in excess of what they had received at previous potlatches where they had been guests. The procedures for dispensing gifts also reinforced the rank of all those present. The host first gave gifts to the guest who enjoyed the highest rank in the highest-ranking numaym. He then moved on to the highest-ranking person in the second-highest numaym and continued until the lowest-ranking guest in the lowest-ranking numaym had received gifts.

The potlatch served to reserve status, and hence power, within Kwakiutl society for only a few individuals, but at the same time, it also worked to create an overall connection among the various subgroups of the Kwakiutl Nation. Virtually every Kwakiutl was involved in the potlatch system, whose ceremonial exchange of property symbolized the mutual dependency of all Kwakiutl people and groups. By the late 19th century, the potlatch had developed into a grand, unifying social institution and the focus of traditional Kwakiutl activities.

When non-Indian anthropologists first began to study the Kwakiutl at the end of the 19th century, they were fascinated by potlatches. However, most concluded that they were secular (nonreligious) ceremonies, valued only for their pageantry and excitement. In fact, the potlatch had strong religious mean-

A group of Kwakiutl in ceremonial dress. The chief standing in the center wears a button blanket adorned with the image of a crest animal.

ing to the Kwakiutl, which they hid from outsiders. Decades of contact with agents and missionaries had taught the Indians that non-Indians tended to be hostile toward their religious beliefs. In addition, the Kwakiutl thought that religious knowledge could be obtained only through private insight and communion with the spirits, and thus it was improper to discuss such knowledge with nonbelievers or even with other Indians.

Spirituality permeated every aspect of Kwakiutl society. The Indians believed that people could become wealthy only if they maintained the proper relationship with the spirits, who were the benefactors and protectors of humans. A person's spiritual health was thought to be directly related to his or her ability to distribute gifts at potlatches. Material wealth, the physical "body" of Kwakiutl society, was considered far less important than spiritual wealth, Kwakiutl society's "soul." Only when the two were combined in the proper ceremonial context could individuals become spiritually enlightened.

This melding of the material and spiritual symbolically occurred in one object—the Copper. Coppers were keystone-shaped shields made of beaten copper sheets. Thought of as spiritual boxes, they contained the souls of their owners' ancestors while they awaited reincarnation as the owners' descendants. Coppers thus represented both their owners' secular power to control material wealth and spiritual power to control the reincarnation of their ancestors.

Potlatches were held at critical periods in a person's life—birth, death, puberty, adoption, the assumption of a new ceremonial rank, the building of a big house, the raising of a crest or memorial pole, the purchase or sale of a Copper, and, most importantly, marriage. A marriage between high-ranked aristocrats could involve a complex series of potlatches, reciprocal exchanges, and other ceremonial presentations made by the bride's and groom's families that would continue over a period of 40 years, linking generations in a web of economic and ceremonial obligations. Potlatch ceremonies also could be used to reaffirm status and save face after some misfortune or accident. Competitive potlatches, designed to deride or shame a person's rivals for a contested rank, involved giving guests gifts far greater than they could ever reciprocate.

The rituals of the potlatch, especially the masked dances, were vividly dramatic and theatrically powerful.

A women's potlatch held at Fort Rupert in 1898.

Grandiloquent and forceful, the speeches were made in a special form of Kwakwala reserved for ceremonial use. They were filled with poetry and metaphors, often drawing on the imagery of warfare. This has led some scholars to conclude that in the late 19th century the aggressive urges that the Kwakiutl had once acted out in warfare were now being channeled into competitive potlatching. Thus, people who had once fought with weapons were now doing so with property and words.

The potlatch's poetry of war expresses important ideas as to how the Kwakiutl envisioned their world. They imagined it as a place of violence and turmoil and their own lives as a continual struggle. Just as a salmon has to struggle upstream against the torrent in order to fulfill its destiny, they had to struggle to fight the forces that threatened them and their way of life. The Kwakiutl therefore believed a chief, who was responsible for the financial and spiritual well-being of his kin, needed to be a spiritual warrior, capable of taking the power of the world into himself and redirecting it for human benefit.

In Kwakiutl thought, power came from animals and other nonhuman beings, who were believed to be spiritually and even intellectually superior to humans. The power of these spirit beings was the source of all things, good and bad, in the universe. The spirits were benevolent as long as people respected and honored them. Potlatches, combined with a complex series of ceremonies known as the Winter Ceremonials, were the means through which the Kwakiutl showed such respect.

The Winter Ceremonials, like potlatches, were replete with images of death, violence, and rebirth. Through these rituals, a tribe was elevated to a spiritual plane where it was symbolically joined with the spirit of Man-eater, the Cannibal-at-the-North-End-of-the-World, chief of all souls in the universe, who lived at the end of time and the limits of space.

Although only aristocrats could belong to the societies that performed the sacred dances of the Winter Ceremonials, people of different ranks would cooperate during the ritual. Thus, the normal social order in place during the secular summer season would be suspended to a degree in the sacred winter season. Rank order became secondary to the shared responsibility of the group to perform the ceremonials properly. Like other forms of status, membership in a dance society was inherited, and the right had to be validated through potlatching.

The rituals of the Winter Ceremonials borrowed dances, masks, paraphernalia, texts, and rites from a wide variety of other Indian groups. For instance, the most prestigious of all Kwakiutl ceremonial rites, the *hamatsa* dance, came from a Bella Bella ritual. Constant innovation in ceremonial practice was an important feature of Northwest Coast religion and an integral part of how the Kwakiutl reacted

An untamed Cannibal dancer during the Winter Ceremonials at Fort Rupert, circa 1901. Initiates into the Cannibal society were thought to be imbued with the spirit of the Cannibal-at-the-North-End-of-the-World, which made them behave wildly. Before they could be admitted into the society, they had to be "tamed" through the initiation ceremony.

to external cultural forces. By the end of the 19th century, elements of white culture had also been incorporated into native ceremonies. These rituals therefore came to reflect how Indians were adjusting and redefining their culture in the face of change and instability.

Beginning with the fur trade, contact with whites had completely altered the Kwakiutl economy. Traditionally, resources were controlled by a local chief, whose position was inherited. Whites introduced to the Indians a market economy, in which people exchanged their surpluses for other goods and human labor itself became a commodity. In this new society, power and status came to be determined primarily

by the ownership of property. As status and wealth became increasingly linked, the Kwakiutl began to use money to gain positions of rank that had previously been obtained only through inheritance.

An enormous drop in the Kwakiutl population due to disease also contributed to the growth of the potlatch. According to official censuses, the number of Kwakiutl fell from about 2,300 to just more than 1,000 between 1881 and 1921, the years often regarded as the potlatch era. (In the same period, the total population of British Columbia rose from 50,000 to 525,000.) The sharp population decline had an important effect on all aspects of Kwakiutl culture. As entire families disappeared and ancestral villages were abandoned, traditional patterns of group membership, marriage, and inheritance had to be re-

Five Fool dancers, photographed at Fort Rupert in 1894. Fool dancers policed the audience of the Cannibal dance by hurling rocks at or threatening anyone who did not observe proper ceremonial etiquette.

fashioned to fit the new social realities. Some families held as much as possible to old patterns; others, out of choice or necessity, embraced new social forms.

The Kwakiutl population eventually fell so low that there were more ranked positions than there were people to hold them. A person often took on more than one named position, sometimes in more than one numaym. With these developments, the entire character of the numaym changed from a cooperative group of about 75 members residing in one village to a group of 10 to 15 people scattered in different villages with little economic connection to one another. Likewise, the rules for who could occupy a ranked position were altered. Whereas in the first generations after contact the Kwakiutl aristocracy maintained their status by pooling the wealth and labor of their fellow numaym members, by the end of the 19th century individual wage earners, through hard work and good planning, could have a successful potlatching career. Commoners, who once had no access to high rank and status, now had enough money to compete for the many vacated titles. A small group of these newly rich rank holders, known as the Eagles, held positions of importance.

As the Eagles' wealth increased, so did the amount of property involved in potlatches. Although most potlatches

In the early 20th century, Kwakiutl families sometimes pooled their resources to hold huge potlatches. Among the goods distributed to guests at this potlatch, held at Alert Bay in about 1900, were silver bracelets, enameled basins, coffeepots, kettles, and sewing machines.

remained relatively small in scope, between 1910 and 1921 a large potlatch may have cost the host's family as much as $40,000. Family members sometimes worked hard year-round at different seasonal jobs to make these extravagant displays possible. They would pool their earnings for years or even for decades in order to hold a major potlatch. Items distributed at these rituals included food, blankets, fur or goat-wool robes, Coppers, cedar-bark mats, canoes, and slaves. Goods of non-Indian manufacture, such as sewing machines, outboard motors, pool tables, furniture, gramophones, cooking sets, and musical instruments, were also popular.

In the late 19th and early 20th centuries, the Kwakiutl faced an enormous moral and psychological dilemma. Precontact Kwakiutl society emphasized frugality and mutual responsibility, values well adapted to a time when the population was at the maximum the resources of the land and sea could support. However, as the population dropped and individuals' wealth increased, the surviving Kwakiutl were torn between their old respect for restraint and their new capacity for indulgence. The potlatch served as a means of bridging these conflicting impulses by casting a solemn face on what might have been seen as extravagance. Through the ritual, wealth was linked to remembrance of the dead and respect for the spirits. The huge piles of property displayed at major potlatches, therefore, metaphorically served to build a wall around the Kwakiutl, protecting them from the great changes occurring in their world.

Agents generally had little understanding of these aspects of the potlatch. They saw the ritual merely as wasteful and irrational and vowed to put an end to it through enforcing the antipotlatch law. For the coast tribes, who lived in close proximity to the white authorities, the antipotlatch law was immediately devastating. At more remote villages, however, agents had a much more difficult time eradicating the ritual. Although all Northwest Coast Indians were affected, the war against the potlatch was waged most powerfully against the Kwakiutl.

For many years, Fort Rupert was the center of the Kwakiutl potlatch. In the 1860s, the Fort Rupert Kwakiutl had experienced a sudden influx of cash assets through their domination of the trade in slaves and liquor. As Fort Rupert prospered as a regional trading center, the potlatch served the need for a new way to cement relations among tribes. However, toward the end of the 19th century, when the economics of the potlatch had become firmly based on successful wage earning, Fort Rupert was surpassed as the center of power and prestige by Alert Bay, the location of the Kwawkewith Agency and mission. The establishment of the agency in 1881 was accompanied by the building of schools, a cannery, a sawmill, a church, and a post of the Royal Canadian Mounted Police. These structures and institutions helped integrate Alert Bay into the larger Canadian economy,

A photograph of some of the ceremonial paraphernalia confiscated by Canadian officials following the 1921 arrest of 80 Kwakiutls for participating in an illegal potlatch.

which initially proved to be to the community's financial advantage. Socially and economically, however, the Kwakiutl were regarded by whites as second-class citizens in their own village.

In 1889, Alert Bay agent R. H. Pidcock had one Kwakiutl chief arrested for potlatching. The chief was convicted and sentenced to six months in prison. The sentence, however, was overturned by a judge who argued that the law was too imprecise in its definition of a potlatch. Because virtually every public occasion among the Kwakiutl involved some display of crests and distribution of wealth, the antipotlatch law effectively criminalized many different social events. In addition, because the potlatch also functioned as the Indians' banking system, the law essentially told the Kwakiutl that they had no right to engage in trade or incur debt.

Another Alert Bay agent, William Halliday, took a particularly aggressive

stance toward enforcing the antipotlatch laws. Like many of his contemporaries, he sincerely believed that the potlatch was destructive to the Indians and would prevent them from being successfully assimilated into Canadian society. Many Kwakiutl refused to comply with Halliday's demands. Despite the occasional arrests of participants, they continued to conduct both potlatches and the Winter Ceremonials in secret.

In late December of 1921, a large potlatch, attended by more than 300 guests from virtually every Kwakiutl village, was held at Village Island near Alert Bay. Afterward, several Indian and non-Indian informants pressured Halliday to establish his authority and prosecute some of the participants. He responded by having 80 high-ranked Indians from all the tribes of the Kwakiutl Nation arrested. The quick trial was a travesty, if only because its proceedings were conducted in English and could not be understood by many of the Kwakwala-speaking defendants. Thirty were sentenced to prison for periods ranging from two months to a year, and while there they were physically and emotionally degraded. The 50 other defendants received suspended sentences, but only after they surrendered their potlatch regalia—including masks, costumes, and Coppers—and promised never to potlatch again. The confiscated potlatch paraphernalia, a total of about 600 pieces, was sent to the Royal Ontario Museum and the National Museums in Ottawa. Part of it

was later sold to George Heye, founder of the Museum of the American Indian in New York City. The arrest and imprisonment of so many Kwakiutl chiefs and the confiscation of so much important and valuable native ceremonial material would foment resentment and anger in the Kwakiutl people for the next half century.

The events of 1921 effectively paralyzed the potlatching system among the Kwakiutl for decades. A few Kwakiutl still practiced the ritual, but they felt compelled to take more precautions than ever, including moving to more isolated areas and integrating the ritual into the celebration of white holidays to avoid detection. Many other Kwakiutl abandoned the potlatch entirely.

Potlatching might have come to an end at this time even without the interference of Canadian authorities. Beginning in the early 1920s, the Kwakiutl fell into an economic depression that, for most of the Indians, made it impossible to host a major potlatch or repay one's obligations. However, it is also likely that the economic calamities that befell the Kwakiutl would not have been so disastrous had they been allowed to continue to hold potlatches. As in the past, the ritual might have eased the suffering of the most impoverished families and bound the Kwakiutl people together during a difficult period. Instead, the banning of the potlatch disrupted the communal nature of Kwakiutl economics and created enmities between traditionalists and progressives that still exist. ▲

A Kwakiutl man dancing during a band meeting held at Cape Mudge in 1990.

6

INTO
THE FUTURE

Despite the government's battle against the potlatch, the Kwakiutl today look back upon the years between 1900 and 1920 as a relatively prosperous period. The Kwakiutl's commitment to hard work, their fishing abilities, and their traditional pattern of seasonal migration fit well with the labor needs of the then-growing commercial fishing industry. The Kwakiutl also found work in canneries, on logging crews, and on farms as migrant agricultural laborers.

The situation changed at the beginning of the 1920s, when the structure of fisheries in the Northwest Coast went through a transformation. The salmon population was dropping quickly because of pollution in salmon streams and overharvesting. At the same time, large, expensive gas-powered boats were introduced into the region. Few Kwakiutl could afford to buy one. Without access to this superior technology, they could no longer compete with non-Indian fishermen for the dwindling supply of fish. At the same time, many Kwakiutl cannery workers were losing their jobs. Fishery companies closed many of their outlying canneries, keeping open only those in the southernmost part of British Columbia. Indians wanting to work in the remaining canneries therefore had to leave their villages more or less permanently. Some Indians were replaced by Japanese and Chinese immigrants, whom non-Indian cannery owners preferred to hire.

Kwakiutl villages were almost entirely dependent on income from commercial fishing, so as this source dried up, everyone suffered. The worldwide depression that followed the stock market crash of 1929 greatly compounded the problem. Already impoverished, the Kwakiutl were hit particularly hard by the economic slump.

In response to their worsening standard of living, the Indians of coastal British Columbia began to form associations in the 1920s and 1930s to better promote and protect their rights. Such cooperative efforts were not new. As early as the 1860s, Indians in the region had banded together to pressure the authorities to take their concerns seriously, only to be rebuffed repeatedly. Often the government commissions, such as the Joint Royal Commission of 1914–18, formed to hear Indian grievances, actually served to erode Indian rights and land holdings while funneling profits from Indian resources into white pockets. Because the government had little respect for traditional Indian political organization, the natives realized they could not battle the authorities until they learned to present a united front using non-Indian models of political action.

In 1915, the Allied Tribes of British Columbia was formed. This organization included members from the Kwakiutl, Haida, Tsimshian, Bella Coola, and coastal and interior Salish tribes. For 11 years, the Allied Tribes struggled to present Indian claims to the provincial and federal governments. Despite immense legal obstacles, the organization finally succeeded in getting a hearing before a Special Joint Committee of Parliament in 1927. The Joint Committee stated decisively that the Indians had no claims to the title of their ancestral territory and were not to be compensated for the lands they had lost. However, the committee members did agree to a token increase in funds appropriated annually for the social welfare of British Columbia Indians and to support some Indian claims for fishing, hunting, and land-use rights.

Frightened by the Allied Tribe's potential effectiveness, the Canadian government disallowed all Indian claims immediately after the Joint Committee's decision. In addition, it declared that soliciting, contributing, or spending funds to prosecute Indians' cases against the government was a serious crime. Agents also began to refuse to allow Indians to leave reserves if they were suspected of being involved in off-reserve political activities.

Another important intertribal organization was the Native Brotherhood of British Columbia. Established in 1930, it was to serve as a model for later Indian groups founded throughout Canada. The organization's agenda was inspired by the United States's New Deal, a collection of social, political, and economic programs designed to help the country recover from the Great Depression. The Native Brotherhood worked especially hard to persuade the government to revise hunting and fishing laws, set up vocational schools for Indians, and obtain medical care and welfare funds for needy natives. However, the Kwakiutl did not join the Native Brotherhood, instead creating a similar group of their own—the Pacific Coast Native Fishermen's Association—in 1936. The two organizations merged six years later. The newsletter of the Native Brotherhood, the *Native*

This cannery at Rivers Inlet was one of many such operations in which Kwakiutl tried to find wage work in the early 20th century.

Voice, was founded in 1946 and became an important forum for the expression of Indian concerns, especially the issues of land and resource ownership.

In the late 1940s, the Canadian government decided to reevaluate its Indian policy. The result was the revised Indian Act of 1951. In most ways, the revision differed little from the original Indian Act of 1876. There were, however, two important changes affecting the Kwakiutl. The new act rescinded the antipotlatch laws of the 19th century; the Kwakiutl could once again le-

gally practice this important ritual. It also canceled the older law prohibiting Indians from pressing land claims and granted them the right to vote in provincial elections. (Indians would not be permitted to vote in federal elections until 1960.) However, as a condition of their enfranchisement, Indians had to agree to move off the reserve and remove their name from tribal rolls.

Also in the early 1950s, Indian bands—groups of Indians who shared a common interest in a reserve or in monetary assets—were permitted to

elect their own political representatives for the first time. Each band was to elect 1 councillor for every 100 members, with a minimum of 2 councillors per band. The councillors would meet in a band council as often as they thought necessary to discuss local and tribal issues and then report to Indian Affairs officials. Those bands that demonstrated a special ability to manage their own affairs were allowed to elect band managers, who had slightly more power to implement economic programs for their band.

The formation of band councils was an attempt by the Canadian government to involve Indians more in determining their own well-being. Although the system appeared democratic, the council was still under the firm control of non-Indian administrators. This placed the first councillors in an uncomfortable position, as they were caught between the demands of their band members and those of the government. In remote villages, where people still tended to follow their traditional leaders and resent government-imposed rules and regulations, councillors were often ineffective. In communities less wedded to old ways, councillors held more sway and frequently were able to persuade the government to pay more attention to their needs. Relations between hereditary chiefs and councillors sometimes were strained. Chiefs of

Two men preparing salmon for a potlatch feast at Cape Mudge in 1990. Since potlatching was legalized in 1951, many families have held these ceremonies to reaffirm their status.

high rank resented the modern leaders, who had not properly validated their authority through potlatches. The new leaders resented elders, who they felt were holding on to outmoded economic and social ideas and therefore damaging the Kwakiutl's chances in the modern world.

Another government policy of the 1950s that caused dissension among the Kwakiutl involved the band rolls. In accordance with Canadian principles of descent, which emphasized paternal lines, the government believed that if a native woman married a white man, she was no longer a member of her band. Such women were removed from official band rolls and therefore lost their claim to a portion of the land, resources, funds, or other possessions of the band. (This policy was rescinded in 1985, and the bands have been deciding how to readmit these women, their non-Indian husbands, and children.)

The political and economic upheaval of the mid-20th century was accompanied by major changes in Kwakiutl social structure and values. One important factor was a dramatic rise in population. Between the early 1920s and the early 1960s, the number of Kwakiutl grew from its all-time low of 1,100 to about 2,500. As a result, the group came to include a disproportionate number of young people. In 1962, for example, 75 percent of the Kwakiutl were under the age of 32. Many of these young Kwakiutl chose to move from the smaller, more remote communities to one of the four large villages: Alert Bay,

Fort Rupert, Cape Mudge, and Kingcome Inlet. At these villages, situated near non-Indian communities, the population was about half Kwakiutl and half white.

Alert Bay continued to be the Kwakiutl's administrative and commercial center, a situation that affected the balance of power among the Kwakiutl communities, because many outlying villages could not offer their residents the services and opportunities found at Alert Bay. The advantages of living there or in urban centers, such as Victoria and Vancouver, attracted many Kwakiutl despite their strong sense of community and band affiliation.

As their residents emigrated, remote villages began to suffer a host of social problems common in rural communities everywhere: poor health care, substandard education, malnutrition, alcohol abuse, and the personal and family problems that often accompany the stress of trying to survive on an inadequate income. Though generally more prosperous, the larger Kwakiutl villages also fell victim to social strife. Like other urban centers, they had to cope with crime, racism, substance abuse, and apathy.

Despite their poverty, many Kwakiutl emulated white ways, especially their patterns of consumption. Some people hoped their daughters would marry whites to enhance their social status and chance for economic success. Others tried to enhance their prestige by purchasing non-Indian manufactured goods. Inhabitants of villages

without electricity or running water sometimes owned large appliances, fancy cookware, furniture, and plumbing fixtures.

Although potlatching was once again legal and several important potlatches were given in the 1950s and 1960s, the ritual was not widely practiced to establish status until the 1970s. Families usually remembered the ranks and special privileges they had possessed, but few young people in the 1950s and 1960s had potlatch names, and fewer still validated them through the proper ceremonies. However, some Kwakiutl held potlatches to repay standing debts from the 1920s or to reactivate some important chiefly positions.

Along with the dissolution of the rank system had come a change in family structure. Like white Canadians, the Kwakiutl began to live in nuclear households composed of a married couple and their children. Traditional Indian marriage ceremonies gradually were replaced by white marriage ceremonies. A couple's residence came to be determined by economic factors, even when the couple would have preferred to follow tradition and live in the village of the husband's family. At the same time, the extended-family system gradually diminished in economic and ceremonial importance, although kin groups still had informal bonds. For instance, a group of kinsmen might crew on a boat owned by one of them or relatives might share food.

The simultaneous demise of the potlatch system and the decreased cooperation of extended families marked the end of the traditional ways the Kwakiutl had developed for equalizing wealth. Without the economic safety net of potlatch gifts and financial help from their kin group, the poorest Kwakiutl became dependent on welfare. Government assistance, however, was not always made available to the natives of British Columbia even when it was offered to the non-Indian population.

The poor living conditions of the Kwakiutl and other Canadian Indians were revealed in two large-scale studies by sociologist Harry Hawthorn. The first, conducted in 1958, focused on the Indians of British Columbia; the second, done in 1966 under government sponsorship, examined native groups from across the country. Hawthorn's conclusions amounted to an indictment of Canada's Indian policies that shocked the government. Canadian authorities had expected to be praised for their benevolence toward native peoples, but agents and other personnel of the government's Department of Indian Affairs were identified as the main obstacles to Indian self-government.

Hawthorn and his co-researchers reported that Indians lacked adequate political representation, faced widespread discrimination and racism, and were trapped in a cycle of economic dependency. They criticized the policies of fisheries and housing, health, and ed-

ucational programs for Indians. Their findings also deplored the lack of cultural-awareness programs, urged the teaching of native languages, and stressed the need for vastly improved education, including adult education and vocational training. Hawthorn condemned the methods of law enforcement on reserves, the removal of Indian women from tribal rolls, and the insensitive and outmoded policies of Canadian officials. The studies maintained that, instead of forcing Indians to assimilate into mainstream culture, the government needed to allow Indians to control their own affairs and determine their own future.

Indians had made such charges for many years and been ignored, but now that the same criticisms appeared in an official government report, the authorities were at last ready to listen. One solution was to institute major welfare reforms, including extending unemployment benefits to Indians and instituting significant improvements in their health care and education. The reforms enabled some changes to be made in the Kwakiutl economy. With unemployment insurance and relief payments as supplements to their income, the Kwakiutl no longer had to work off the reserve in canneries, mining, logging, and construction. Instead, they

A 1968 photograph of two Kwakiutl fishermen transporting their eulachon catch. Financial assistance provided by the Canadian government in the late 1960s has allowed many Kwakiutl to abandon wage work and seek their livelihood in commercial fishing.

could increase their participation in the riskier employment of commercial fishing.

The Canadian government also adopted some innovative ideas about how to aid impoverished communities to improve their standard of living. It sent knowledgeable outsiders to Indian communities to help the natives define and realize their own goals and priorities. This method of using and respecting the Indians' own initiative later became standard in a wide range of government-funded programs, from house-building projects to education in native crafts.

Other changes in Indian policy at this time were initiated by Indian groups that demanded recognition of natives' rights. Throughout the 1960s, many Canadian Indians participated in protest marches and petitioned for government reforms. These nonviolent political actions contrasted sharply with the violence perpetrated by some militant groups involved in the Red Power movement in the United States. The relatively conservative approach of Canadian Indians probably owed much to the efforts of Canadian officials to undercut militancy and stifle dissent. They directly interfered with Indian efforts to organize, withheld funds from bands whom they considered contentious, and appointed only the most moderate Indian leaders to positions on advisory councils funded by the government. These councils developed into native political associations that, in the gov-

ernment's eyes, were the only appropriate forums for negotiation between Indians and white administrators.

These Indian associations were highly effective in getting native voices heard. They often began as organizations of volunteers but sometimes developed into sophisticated instruments for representing Indian interests. Many of the groups were short-lived. Nevertheless, taken together, they allowed Indians to present their grievances with more vehemence and power than ever before. Among the most important organizations were the National Indian Council, the North American Indian Brotherhood, the Confederation of the Native Indians of British Columbia, the Union of British Columbia Chiefs, and the National Indian Brotherhood.

Unifying many different tribes with different cultures, histories, religions, and ideas about the proper role of Indians in the future proved difficult. For instance, in 1967 the leaders of the major Indian organizations in British Columbia attempted to write and quickly ratify a unified constitution governing Indian land claims. They meant to counter Canadian legislators who were still determined in their refusal to recognize Indian claims to the title of Canada's lands and resources. Although most Indians agreed that new approaches to the legal settlement of Indian claims were needed, the leaders ran into a storm of protest. Many band councils and chiefs were angered that they had not been consulted. Further-

A classroom of Indian and non-Indian students involved in the Campbell River Native Studies Program. Several bands have established school programs that emphasize Kwakiutl culture and are tailored for the special educational needs of their children.

more, they did not feel that the organization's leaders, many of whom were highly assimilated, were necessarily qualified to speak for all the Indian peoples of British Columbia.

The course of Indian political action was dramatically altered in 1969. Delegates of the National Indian Brotherhood, along with those of other Indian organizations, were invited to consult with the federal government on new revisions of the Indian Act. At first, the delegates had some difficulty establishing their priorities. The situation changed, however, when the government released a document entitled "Statement of the Government of Canada on Indian Policy, 1969." Now known as the White Paper, the report was issued as a response to Hawthorn's findings.

The White Paper announced that Canada was considering a five-year plan to terminate the special legal status

of Indians, abolish the Indian Affairs branch of the national government, and turn the administration of Indian affairs over to other federal agencies or provincial governments. Control of reserves would be turned over to Indians, and all further land claims would be invalidated.

The White Paper elicited a storm of protest from Indians throughout Canada. British Columbia's Indians were particularly vocal, owing to their province's unrelentingly dismal record in its treatment of natives. They claimed that with the White Paper the government was declaring its intention to ignore all of its responsibilities to Indians. They maintained that any solution to Indian problems had to be based on the economic development of Indian lands, not on a blanket refusal by the federal government to honor its historical obligations.

Formal native responses to the White Paper came in several briefs, all of which shared the philosophy that Indians should be given far greater control over their lives and that Indian claims should be addressed. The brief authored by the Indians of British Columbia was known as the Brown Paper. It called for attention to their land claims and demands for economic development, self-government, and educational improvements.

The federal and provincial governments did in fact begin to explore reforms in their treatment of British Columbia's Indians. They committed themselves to working with recognized Indian associations and responded favorably to the idea of self-determination. Grants were offered to support moderate political action groups, and these organizations began to propose specific programs. Economic development and the improvement of housing, education, and health care were among their primary concerns. The federal government also grudgingly began to make some limited changes in the way in which Indians were governed that would make bands more self-directing, although these changes were always more elaborate in theory than in practice. Indian agents and other government officials still retained significant overt and covert power over Indian communities.

The social programs initiated in the late 1960s and 1970s were only partially successful. Although Indians' goals were to achieve social, economic, and political independence, increased government welfare and assistance have in many ways made the Indians more dependent than ever. In this sense, the system that in theory was supposed to protect Canada's Indians has in fact entrapped them.

Like many of Canada's native peoples, the Kwakiutl have not been excluded economically and politically from the larger society. Today many see their political separateness as a blessing and believe their isolation has helped them survive as a group. Although they are proud that they are not as assimilated as some other Indian peoples, the Kwakiutl nevertheless do want accep-

tance and equality in the non-Indian world.

For much of this century, schools have been the major arena of social interaction between the Kwakiutl and whites. After 1945, the federal government encouraged most Indian students to attend integrated schools, but their curricula were usually designed to train middle-class whites for professions closed to Indians. Aside from literacy in English and proficiency in basic mathematics, this education therefore offered Indian youths little they could use in their future lives. Frustrated by an educational system that ignored their needs and problems, very few Kwakiutl progressed past the elementary level. Those who did had to cope with loneliness, racism, discrimination, and alien cultural values. The immense difficulties that these students faced produced an extraordinarily high dropout rate of Kwakiutl high school students in the 1960s: Estimates ranged from 60 to 99 percent.

Nella Nelson teaches native studies in Victoria. Like many other Kwakiutl professionals, she has chosen a career through which she can help improve the lot of her people.

Linguist Peter Wilson (above) teaches his class how to correctly pronounce Kwakwala. The words written on the board (from top to bottom) mean "one thousand," "noon," "to know," and "sick." Instructors from the Campbell River Native Studies Program (below) take a class in how to teach the Kwakwala language. Elders J. J. Wallas and Jim Henderson help them with dialect differences, sentence structure, and pronunciation.

The Canadian government's recent educational reforms have improved conditions for native peoples attending integrated schools, but many Kwakiutl still feel that provincial schools serve Indians poorly. Seeing education as their primary road to success in the modern world, several bands have responded by developing their own school programs, training their own teachers, and adopting classroom procedures specifically oriented to the needs of Indian children. These schools supplement the standard subjects with courses that promote Kwakiutl cultural interests in fishing, forestry, carpentry, and traditional art and ceremony. Opportunities for meaningful vocational training through government- and band-supported programs set up by the Indian Affairs branch and the bands have also increased in the last two decades. The courses offered include instruction in boat operations and fishing, office skills, and tribal administration.

The number of Kwakiutl attending college and professional schools has grown steadily in the last 20 years. The increase is largely due to programs at universities and community colleges geared to enrolling and supporting Indian students. With more educational opportunities, Kwakiutl graduates are now able to move into professions formerly not open to them. Hoping to improve the lot of their people, many are interested in careers in education, social work, and law.

One of the main focuses of the Kwakiutl's educational efforts has been promoting a resurgence in the use of the Kwakwala language. At boarding and provincial schools, Kwakiutl students were often instructed by their teachers, who feared they would not learn English if they retained their native tongue, never to speak Kwakwala. To revive Kwakwala, the Kwakiutl today are offering instruction both to adults and children. Several bands have developed standardized orthographies of their own Kwakwala dialect and have produced primers, texts, dictionaries, and workbooks. Despite the vigor and determination of this reeducation program, most Kwakiutl speak English as their primary language, and Kwakwala remains in danger of becoming extinct.

Children are also being initiated into Kwakiutl ceremonial life. Much of the incredibly detailed knowledge of ceremonial practices was lost during the 19th century. However, when the antipotlatch laws were rescinded, there were still some elders who remembered the ancient rituals. Young men and women began to learn the proper ways of dancing, and ceremonies that had long been unperformed have been reborn. For example, in 1984 at Cape Mudge, a First Salmon ceremony—a ritual in which the carcasses of the first 4 salmon caught in a year are returned to the sea as a means of honoring the fish—was held for the first time in more than 70 years. Potlatches and rituals involved with the building of houses and community centers, raising of poles, opening of the fishing season, and other important traditional events—

such as initiation into a secret society or a transfer of titles—have become central to contemporary Kwakiutl life.

Today some of the fundamental practices of 19th-century Kwakiutl ceremony have been altered to fit the changed nature of Kwakiutl life in the late 20th century: Less emphasis is placed on the dancer performing as an individual, many elaborate stage tricks and illusions have disappeared, and much of the religious underpinnings for the dances has dissipated. The complicated rituals of the Winter Ceremonials, which used to last for weeks, if not months, are now condensed into a single lengthy evening during the Christmas season. Although ceremonies still can be performed only by those families that have the hereditary right to do so, the rituals now express the shared heritage of the Kwakiutl and link the entire tribe together. Gradually, Kwakiutl ceremonialism once again is becoming a living, creative tradition in which new rituals that serve the needs of people today are being invented within the context of traditional symbolism and values. In the view of some Kwakiutl, the old ceremonies harken back to what they see as an outmoded past, but for many more the revitalization of their ceremonial life has restored an emotional and moral focus to their life.

The traditional rituals of the Kwakiutl now exist in tandem with those of the Anglican church, of which most Kwakiutl are nominal members. Anglican clergy have incorporated traditional Kwakiutl symbols, such as the cedar bark, the salmon, and the Tree-of-Life, into their services. A mission boat sails on an irregular schedule to those villages without a resident minister, so Anglican services tend to be infrequent in most Kwakiutl communities.

The third area in which the Kwakiutl have concentrated their revitalization efforts is native art. Art has always been central to Kwakiutl culture, but during the last half of the 19th century, the Indians experienced a great creative explosion in which they produced a vast number of unique and powerful objects. However, few pieces of art from this period remain in Kwakiutl hands. Many were confiscated by Canadian and church authorities or were sold or traded to collectors or museums during hard economic times. Tourists and unscrupulous collectors also traveled to deserted villages and plundered poles and statues to keep for themselves or sell.

Long ago, the Kwakiutl supported dozens of fine artists, and nearly everyone engaged in some type of artistic endeavor. By the early 20th century, however, the government's suppression of their ceremonial tradition had greatly diminished the role of artists in their society. The few practicing artists left produced work that best suited the taste of non-Indian clients. In the 1960s, young Kwakiutl began to seek art training from elders. These new artists not only copied the older styles but also generated entirely new graphic forms, providing a visual link between traditional and modern Kwakiutl designs.

In the late 20th-century, the Kwakiutl have revived many of their most important ceremonies.

Some carvers today have shown themselves to be the equals of the greatest artists of the past as they push Northwest Coast art into new directions while reintroducing it into traditional ritual contexts.

Modern Kwakiutl art has become a highly desirable product in non-Indian art markets. As a result, artists can earn as much in a few months of carving as a fisherman might earn in a year. The development of a new, wealthy class of artists has changed the balance of power in Kwakiutl politics. The fame that families of carvers have gained in the white world is often translated into

wealth and prestige in their relations at home.

Many wonderful examples of Kwakiutl art, old and new, can be found in natural-history and art museums around the world. Especially large collections are housed in Vancouver, Victoria, New York, Chicago, Washington, D.C., and London. The Royal British Columbia Museum in Victoria has instituted an innovative program that commissions contemporary artists to produce carvings and other ritual materials. These objects are part of the museum's collections but may be borrowed by natives for use in ceremonies. Through this program, Kwakiutl art is treated as the aesthetic equal of Western art without removing it from its living ceremonial context.

Many of the art masterpieces that were confiscated by agents after the 1921 Village Island potlatch have recently been returned to the Kwakiutl. Both the Royal Ontario Museum and the National Museums in Ottawa agreed to give back the Indian materials in their collections. (Negotiations for the return of pieces held by the Museum of the American Indian in New York City have been less successful.) Two museums—the Kwagiulth Museum in Cape Mudge and the U'Mista Cultural Centre in Alert Bay—were opened in 1979 and in 1980, respectively, to house the potlatch material. These openings occasioned great festivities, which in a sense celebrated the return of the spiritual heart of Kwakiutl life after generations of captivity in white hands.

The museums at Alert Bay and Cape Mudge also serve as social and educational centers. They have played a major role in reenergizing and reestablishing Kwakiutl identity and linking the Kwakiutl to their cultural heritage. In addition to providing art and ceremony training and developing language programs, the museums have established ethnohistory projects, through which they collect oral histories from tribal elders and attempt to document ceremonial activities, myths, songs, and dances that are in danger of being lost. The U'Mista Cultural Centre has also produced two films—one that presents the native point of view of the potlatch era and one that chronicles the survival of Kwakiutl traditions despite the best efforts of Canadian authorities to suppress them.

In the last decade, the Kwakiutl have united with the other tribes of coastal British Columbia to pursue their political objectives more effectively. In Kwakiutl eyes, the most important issues are those involving land and resource rights, such as whether Indian land claims are legitimate and whether Indians should be paid reparations for the land, logging, fishing, and mineral rights that have been taken from them. The problems of aboriginal rights and economic development have become an international issue in which the Northwest Coast will be an important test case.

The Kwakiutl are also asserting themselves politically through their band councils. At present, there are 14 Kwakiutl bands (comprising about 20 tribes), each of which functions as an independent, self-governing political entity. Their councils provide forums for discussion of a wide range of concerns, from fishing to allowing outsiders access to their villages. They also oversee the provision of electricity, water control, sanitation, housing, fire prevention, road maintenance, and other community services and public works. In addition, some councils supervise community programs for health, education, and welfare.

Although bands are partially supported by federal grants and other moneys, many are now seeking to generate their own funds. Some bands act as economic corporations, responsible for community development, job-training, and business operations, such as hatcheries, marinas, coffee shops, hotels, and laundromats. Bands sometimes lease their reserve lands for logging and gravel mining, and some provide members with limited employment in band administration and education. Some bands also have loan programs that enable their members to obtain capital at lower rates of interest than would normally be available.

The majority of Kwakiutl seem committed to a vision of their future that is based on community development and economic equality. Nevertheless, they know that economic development is not a simple process nor will it provide a simple solution to their problems. In addition, a strong current of resistance to government programs, coupled with a sense of the benefits of isolationism, remains a feature of Kwakiutl culture. The Kwakiutl feel that generations of Canadian officials have avoided dealing with the problems they have imposed on the Indians. They wonder if the present generation of officials, or those to come, ever will realize their moral obligation to offer Canada's native peoples even a little of the justice they deserve.

The Kwakiutl, once linked to the outside world only by slow ferries and transistor radios, now own speedboats, floatplanes, and satellite dishes. Their society has been altered by edict, circumstance, and necessity to resemble mainstream Canadian society. Even though they may be dissatisfied with Canadian laws and angered by the obstacles to their success in the Canadian economy, the Kwakiutl are afraid that any end to their special land and resource rights will render them merely another small minority in a world that is dominated by far more powerful groups and interests. They are unwilling to lose the government's wardship unless the survival of their culture and communities is guaranteed. The political, enonomic, and cultural struggle of the Kwakiutl will have to continue for generations to come.

Today the problems facing the Kwakiutl are like those of Indians else-

Kwakiutl elder Agnes Alfred weaving a basket. Through the efforts of both young and old alike, Kwakiutl culture continues to thrive.

where. Will they retain their individual heritage as they become more economically and socially assimilated? In learning to live in a society whose rules are made by non-Indians, can they remember and act upon what it really means to be an Indian? How can they convince the larger white society to respect the unique values and insights of their culture? And how can they convince the larger society to allow them to live with dignity in the ways they choose for themselves?

The deep appreciation of Kwakiutl culture once felt only by anthropologists is growing among the Canadian population. However, it will still be a long time before admiration for Indian art broadens into acceptance of Indians as equals. The Kwakiutl look forward to a time when the people of Canada will truly accept the multicultural diversity they praise in principle and learn to value the unique features of Kwakiutl culture as an essential part of Canadian and human heritage. ▲

BIBLIOGRAPHY

Assu, Harry, and Joy Inglis. *Assu of Cape Mudge.* Vancouver: University of British Columbia Press, 1989.

Bancroft-Hunt, Norman, and Werner Forman. *People of the Totem: The Indians of the Pacific Northwest.* New York: Putnam, 1979.

Boas, Franz. *Kwakiutl Ethnography.* Chicago: University of Chicago Press, 1966.

————. *Religion of the Kwakiutl Indians.* Part 2. 1930. Reprint. New York: AMS Press, 1969.

Bruggmann, Maximilien, and Peter R. Gerber. *Indians of the Northwest Coast.* New York: Facts on File, 1989.

Drucker, Philip. *Cultures of the North Pacific Coast.* New York: HarperCollins, 1965.

————. *Indians of the Northwest Coast.* Garden City, NY: Natural History Press, 1963.

Fladmark, Knut R. *British Columbia Prehistory.* Ottawa, Ontario: National Museum of Man, 1986.

Ford, Clellan S. *Smoke from Their Fires: The Autobiography of a Kwakiutl Chief.* New Haven: Yale University Press, 1941.

Halpin, Marjorie. *Totem Poles: An Illustrated Guide.* Vancouver: University of British Columbia Press, 1981.

Hawthorn, Audrey. *Kwakiutl Art.* Seattle: University of Washington Press, 1979.

Kirk, Ruth. *Tradition & Change on the Northwest Coast.* Seattle: University of Washington Press, 1986.

McNair, Peter L., Alan L. Hoover, and Kevin Neary. *The Legacy: Continuing Traditions of Canadian Northwest Coast Indian Art.* Victoria: British Columbia Provincial Museum, 1980.

Rohner, Ronald P., and Evelyn C. Rohner. *The Kwakiutl: Indians of British Columbia.* New York: Holt, Rinehart & Winston, 1970.

Stewart, Hilary. *Cedar.* Seattle: University of Washington Press, 1984.

Swan, Luke, and David W. Ellis. *Teachings of the Tides.* Penticton, British Columbia: Theytus Books, 1981.

Wallas, J. J., as told to Pamela Whitaker. *Kwakiutl Legends.* Victoria, British Columbia: Hancock House, 1981.

THE KWAKIUTL AT A GLANCE

CULTURE AREA   *Northwest Coast*

GEOGRAPHY   *The northern and eastern coasts of Vancouver Island and the adjacent mainland of British Columbia*

LINGUISTIC FAMILY   *Wakashan*

FIRST CONTACT   *George Vancouver, English, 1792*

CURRENT POPULATION   *Approximately 3,500*

CURRENT STATUS   *Fourteen Kwakiutl bands are now recognized by Canada's Department of Indian Affairs and Northern Development*

GLOSSARY

allotment Policy initiated by the Canadian government in the 1880s, aimed at breaking up communally owned Indian land into small, privately owned plots.

anthropology The study of the physical, social, and historical characteristics of human beings.

archaeology The recovery and study of evidence of human ways of life, especially that of prehistoric peoples but also including that of historic peoples.

assimilation The complete absorption of one group into another group's cultural tradition.

band A group of Indians who share a common interest in a reserve or monetary asset.

barter Trade without the exchange of money.

black market The illegal selling or buying of commodities.

Copper Keystone-shaped shields made of beaten copper sheets; thought to contain the souls of their owners' ancestors while they awaited reincarnation as the owners' descendants.

crest designs Visual images of creatures to whom the Kwakiutl's ancestors are spiritually connected.

culture The learned behavior of humans; nonbiological, socially taught activities; the way of life of a group of people.

ethnohistory The study of the evolution of cultures.

eulachon A herringlike fish whose oil was an important part of the traditional Kwakiutl diet; also known as a candlefish.

extended family Several generations of people connected by kinship and marriage who live with or near each other; includes parents, children, grandparents, aunts and uncles, and other relatives.

First Salmon ceremony A Kwakiutl ritual in which the carcasses of the first four salmon caught in a year are returned to the sea as a means of honoring the fish.

headflattening The painless practice of strapping an infant's head between a pair of padded boards in order to flatten the front of his or her skull. Flattened heads were considered a mark of great beauty among the Kwakiutl.

Indian Acts A series of acts passed by the Canadian government during the 19th century. The Indian acts determined the nature of the political institutions that would represent Canadian Indians. These acts also made the Indians wards of the state, thus limiting their legal rights.

Kwakwala The native language of the Kwakiutl.

lineage A group of individuals related through descent from a common ancestor; a descent group whose members recognize as relatives people on the mother's side only or the father's side only.

mission A religious center founded by advocates of a particular demonination who are trying to convert nonbelievers to their faith.

missionaries Advocates of a particular religion who travel to convert nonbelievers to their faith.

monopoly The exclusive control of a commodity or service by one group and/or control of the region in which the commodity or service is distributed.

myth A story of an event of the prehistoric past. Myths often explain a practice, belief, or natural phenomenon.

nuclear family A family unit consisting of a mother, father, and one or more of their children.

numaym The basic unit of Kwakiutl society. These large groups of relatives shared the ownership of resources, living sites, and myths.

potlatch A special feast during which the host gives gifts and food to many guests in order to establish or increase his status. A potlatch might be held to inaugurate a new house, commemorate the death of a village member, or celebrate a marriage or the naming of a chief's heir.

reserve A tract of land retained by Indians for their own occupation and use.

totem The emblem or symbol of a clan or family, usually an animal or plant that the family claims as its mythical ancestor. These images were carved into totem poles and house posts.

totem pole A cedar pole decorated with elaborate carvings that either was erected outside a house or formed part of a house's frame. The carvings signified the residents' status by depicting important incidents in their family's mythic history.

treaty A contract negotiated between representatives of a national government and one or more Indian tribes. Treaties dealt with the cessation of military action, the surrender of political independence, the establishment of boundaries, terms of land sales, and related matters.

weir A fence made of wooden slats, which was constructed in a riverbed to trap fish where they could be caught easily.

Winter Ceremonials A complex series of rituals held by the Kwakiutl in the sacred winter season. The Ceremonials were performed in order to show the Kwakiutl's respect for powerful spirit beings.

INDEX

INDEX

Rocky Mountains, 19, 67
Royal British Columbia
Museum, 106
Royal Canadian Mounted
Police, 87
Royal Ontario Museum, 89,
106
Russia, 39, 40

Salalberries, 25
Salish, 43, 60, 67, 70, 72, 92
Salish (language), 14
Salmon, 24, 25, 68, 91, 103
Salmonberries, 25
San Francisco, California, 40
Santiago, 40
Scarlet fever, 61
Sea gulls, 24
Sea lions, 24
Seals, 24
Sea otters, 24, 40–42, 57, 59,
60
Sea urchins, 24
Seymour Narrows, 45
Shells, 35
Siberia, 19
Skunk cabbage, 24
Slavery, 60

Smallpox, 61, 63
Smelt, 24
Soapberries, 25
Southern Kwakiutl, 13. *See
also* Kwakiutl
Spain, 40, 41, 42, 43, 46
Special Joint Committee of
Parliament, 92
Squid, 24
Squirrels, 24
"Statement of the
Government of Canada
on Indian Policy, 1969"
(White Paper), 99, 100
Stone traps, 25
Strawberries, 25
Sturgeon, 24
Sugar, 46
Syphilis, 61

Tahiti, 61
Tea, 46
Thompson River, 67
Tlingit, 14, 40, 60, 63
Tobacco, 46
Totem poles, 30–32
Tsimshian, 14, 72, 92
Tuberculosis, 61

U'Mista Cultural Centre, 106
Union of British Columbia
Chiefs, 98

Vancouver, George, 43–46
Vancouver Island, 13, 14,
41, 42–43, 65, 67, 95, 107;
Kwakiutl settlement,
70–71
Victoria, British Columbia,
13, 67, 70, 71, 72, 75, 95
Village Island, 89, 107

Washington, 48, 65
Washington, D.C., 106
Weasels, 24
Weirs, 25–26
Whales, 24
Winter Ceremonials, 75, 83,
89, 104
Wolves, 24
Wood, 26–27

Yakutat Bay, 19
Yellow cedar, 32, 33
Yew, 32

118

PICTURE CREDITS

STANLEY WALENS is a psychological anthropologist and ethnohistorian who works as a consultant and researcher based in San Diego, California. He received his B.A. from Haverford College and his Ph.D. in anthropology from Northwestern University and has been on the faculties of the University of Virginia and the University of California. He is the author of numerous articles and two other books on the Indians of the Northwest Coast, *Feasting with Cannibals: An Essay on Kwakiutl Cosmology* (1982) and the forthcoming two-volume *Smoke and Mirrors: New Perspectives on the Critical Discourse of NorthWest Coast Indian History and Art.*

———————————

FRANK W. PORTER III, general editor of INDIANS OF NORTH AMERICA, is director of the Chelsea House Foundation for American Indian Studies. He holds a B.A., M.A., and Ph.D. from the University of Maryland. He has done extensive research concerning the Indians of Maryland and Delaware and is the author of numerous articles on their history, archaeology, geography, and ethnography. He was formerly director of the Maryland Commission on Indian Affairs and American Indian Research and Resource Institute, Gettysburg, Pennsylvania, and he has received grants from the Delaware Humanities Forum, the Maryland Committee for the Humanities, the Ford Foundation, and the National Endowment for the Humanities, among others. Dr. Porter is the author of *The Bureau of Indian Affairs* in the Chelsea House KNOW YOUR GOVERNMENT series.

Date Due

moved 8/12			

BRODART, CO.   Cat. No. 23-233   Printed in U.S.A.

| Books are produced in the United States using U.S.-based materials | Books are printed using a revolutionary new process called THINKtech™ that lowers energy usage by 70% and increases overall quality | Books are durable and flexible because of Smyth-sewing | Paper is sourced using environmentally responsible foresting methods and the paper is acid-free |

Center Point Large Print

600 Brooks Road / PO Box 1
Thorndike, ME 04986-0001 USA

(207) 568-3717

US & Canada:
1 800 929-9108
www.centerpointlargeprint.com